Logistics and
Supply Chain
Management

FT Prentice Hall
FINANCIAL TIMES

In an increasingly competitive world, we believe it's quality of thinking that gives you the edge – an idea that opens new doors, a technique that solves a problem, or an insight that simply makes sense of it all. The more you know, the smarter and faster you can go.

That's why we work with the best minds in business and finance to bring cutting-edge thinking and best learning practice to a global market.

Under a range of leading imprints, including *Financial Times Prentice Hall*, we create world-class print publications and electronic products bringing our readers knowledge, skills and understanding, which can be applied whether studying or at work.

To find out more about Pearson Education publications, or tell us about the books you'd like to find, you can visit us at **www.pearsoned.co.uk**

PEARSON
Education

Logistics and Supply Chain Management

Creating Value-Adding Networks

Third edition

MARTIN CHRISTOPHER

FT Prentice Hall
FINANCIAL TIMES

An imprint of **Pearson Education**

Harlow, England • London • New York • Boston • San Francisco • Toronto
Sydney • Tokyo • Singapore • Hong Kong • Seoul • Taipei • New Delhi
Cape Town • Madrid • Mexico City • Amsterdam • Munich • Paris • Milan

PEARSON EDUCATION LIMITED

Edinburgh Gate
Harlow CM20 2JE
Tel: +44 (0)1279 623623
Fax: +44 (0)1279 431059
Website: www.pearsoned.co.uk

First published 1992
Second edition 1998
Third edition published in Great Britain 2005

© Pearson Education Limited 2005

The right of Martin Christopher to be identified as
author of this work has been asserted by him in accordance
with the Copyright, Designs and Patents Act 1988.

ISBN 0 273 68176 1

British Library Cataloguing-in-Publication Data
A catalogue record for this book is available
from the British Library.

Library of Congress Cataloging-in-Publication Data
A catalog record for this book is available
from the Library of Congress

10 9 8 7 6 5 4 3 2 1
09 08 07 06 05

Typeset by 30
Printed and bound in Great Britain by
Biddles Ltd, King's Lynn

*The publisher's policy is to use paper manufactured
from sustainable forests.*

About the Author

Martin Christopher is Professor of Marketing and Logistics at Cranfield School of Management, one of Europe's leading business schools, which is itself a part of Cranfield University. His work in the field of logistics and supply chain management has gained international recognition. He has published widely and is recognized as a leading authority on how supply chains can be managed to provide sustainable advantage. Martin Christopher is also co-editor of the *International Journal of Logistics Management* and is a regular contributor to conferences and workshops around the world.

At Cranfield, Martin Christopher directs the Centre for Logistics and Supply Chain Management, the largest activity of its type in Europe. The work of the centre covers all aspects of logistics and supply chain management and offers both full-time and part-time Masters degree courses as well as extensive management development programmes. Research plays a key role in the work of the centre and contributes to its international standing.

Martin Christopher is an Emeritus Fellow of the Chartered Institute of Logistics and Transport on whose Council he sits. In 1988 he was awarded the Sir Robert Lawrence Gold Medal for his contribution to logistics education.

Contents

Preface

It is only relatively recently that logistics and supply chain management have emerged as key business concerns. When the first edition of this book appeared in 1992 there were only a few other texts addressing these subjects, today there are many.

However, even though awareness of the importance of logistics and the supply chain is now much greater, there are still many companies where these ideas have yet to be fully implemented. The good news though is that, generally, logistics and supply chain management have moved much higher up the agenda in organizations in every industry and sector.

Another significant development since the first edition has been the growing recognition that supply chains are, in reality, networks. These networks are complex webs of independent – but interdependent – organizations. As a result of increased out-sourcing of tasks that were once performed in-house, the complexity of these webs has grown and, hence, with it the need for active co-ordination of the network. For this reason alone the importance of supply chain management is heightened considerably.

This new edition of *Logistics and Supply Chain Management* builds on the ideas and concepts of the earlier versions but as new thinking emerges and best practice gets even better, the need for revision and up-dating becomes inevitable. For example, in this third edition there is an even greater emphasis on responsiveness, reflecting the increased volatility of demand in many markets. Another addition is a new chapter on supply chain risk, recognizing that as networks become more complex so does their vulnerability to disruption increase.

In preparing this book I have drawn greatly on the idea and thoughts of others. I have been fortunate to work in the stimulating environment of the Centre for Logistics and Supply Chain Management at Cranfield University and have benefited greatly from interaction with colleagues, post-graduate students and practising managers.

Outside Cranfield I have gained much through a number of fruitful collaborations, particularly with Alan Braithwaite, Chairman of LCP

Worldwide, Professor John Gattorna of the Sydney Business School, Australia, Professor Douglas Lambert of Ohio State University, USA, and Professor Denis Towill of Cardiff University, UK.

Finally, I would like to thank Dr Helen Peck who has researched and written most of the case studies in the book and Tracy Stickells who has skilfully masterminded the production of the manuscript – their efforts are greatly appreciated.

Martin Christopher
Professor of Marketing and Logistics
Centre for Logistics and Supply Chain Management
Cranfield University, UK

Logistics, the supply chain and competitive strategy

This chapter:

Introduces the concept of logistics with a brief review of its origins in military strategy and its subsequent adoption within industry.

●

Highlights the principles of competitive strategy and the pursuit of differentiation through the development of productivity and value advantage.

●

Explains the concept of the value chain and the integrative role of logistics within the organization.

●

Describes the emerging discipline of supply chain management, defining it and explaining how and why it takes the principles of logistics forward.

●

Discusses the impact upon logistics and supply chain management of the significant changes in the wider competitive environment.

ogistics and supply chain management are not new ideas. From the building of the pyramids to the relief of hunger in Africa, the principles underpinning the effective flow of materials and information to meet the requirements of customers have altered little.

Throughout the history of mankind wars have been won and lost through logistics strengths and capabilities – or the lack of them. It has been argued that the defeat of the British in the American War of Independence can largely be attributed to logistics failure. The British Army in America depended almost entirely upon Britain for supplies. At the height of the war there were 12,000 troops overseas and for the most part they had not only to be equipped, but fed from Britain. For the first six years of the war the administration of these vital supplies was totally inadequate, affecting the course of operations and the morale of the troops. An organization capable of supplying the army was not developed until 1781 and by then it was too late.[1]

In the Second World War logistics also played a major role. The Allied Forces' invasion of Europe was a highly skilled exercise in logistics, as was the defeat of Rommel in the desert. Rommel himself once said that '… before the fighting proper, the battle is won or lost by quartermasters'.

However, whilst the Generals and Field Marshals from the earliest times have understood the critical role of logistics, strangely it is only in the recent past that business organizations have come to recognize the vital impact that logistics management can have in the achievement of competitive advantage. Partly this lack of recognition springs from the relatively low level of understanding of the benefits of integrated logistics. As early as 1915, Arch Shaw pointed out that:

> It is only in the recent past that business organizations have come to recognize the vital impact that logistics management can have in the achievement of competitive advantage.

The relations between the activities of demand creation and physical supply ... illustrate the existence of the two principles of interdependence and balance. Failure to co-ordinate any one of these activities with its group-fellows and also with those in the other group, or undue emphasis or outlay put upon any one of these activities, is certain to upset the equilibrium of forces which means efficient distribution.

... The physical distribution of the goods is a problem distinct from the creation of demand ... Not a few worthy failures in distribution campaigns have been due to such a lack of co-ordination between demand creation and physical supply ...

Instead of being a subsequent problem, this question of supply must be met and answered before the work of distribution begins.[2]

It is paradoxical that it has taken almost 100 years for these basic principles of logistics management to be widely accepted.

What is logistics management in the sense that it is understood today? There are many ways of defining logistics but the underlying concept might be defined as:

Logistics is the process of strategically managing the procurement, movement and storage of materials, parts and finished inventory (and the related information flows) through the organization and its marketing channels in such a way that current and future profitability are maximized through the cost-effective fulfilment of orders.

This basic definition will be extended and developed as the book progresses, but it makes an adequate starting point.

Supply chain management is a wider concept than logistics

Logistics is essentially a planning orientation and framework that seeks to create a single plan for the flow of product and information through a business. Supply chain management builds upon this framework and seeks to achieve linkage and co-ordination between the *processes* of other entities in the pipeline, i.e. suppliers and customers, and the organization itself. Thus, for example, one goal of supply chain management might be to reduce or eliminate the buffers of inventory that exist between organizations in a chain through the sharing of information on demand and current stock levels. This is the concept of 'Co-Managed Inventory' (CMI) that will be discussed in more detail later in the book.

It will be apparent that supply chain management involves a significant change from the traditional arm's-length, even adversarial, relationships that so often typified buyer/supplier relationships in the past. The focus of supply chain management is on co-operation and trust and the recognition that, properly managed, the 'whole can be greater than the sum of its parts'.

The definition of supply chain management that is adopted in this book is:

> *The management of upstream and downstream relationships with suppliers and customers to deliver superior customer value at less cost to the supply chain as a whole.*

Thus the focus of supply chain management is upon the management of *relationships* in order to achieve a more profitable outcome for all parties in the chain. This brings with it some significant challenges since there may be occasions when the narrow self interest of one party has to be subsumed for the benefit of the chain as a whole.

Whilst the phrase 'supply chain management' is now widely used, it could be argued that it should really be termed '*demand chain management*' to reflect the fact that the chain should be driven by the market, not by suppliers. Equally the word 'chain' should be replaced by '*network*' since there will normally be multiple suppliers and, indeed, suppliers to suppliers as well as multiple customers and customers' customers to be included in the total system.

Figure 1.1 illustrates this idea of the firm being at the centre of a network of suppliers and customers.

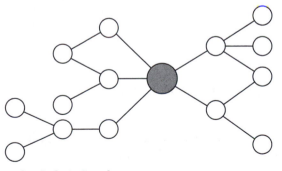

Fig. 1.1 The supply chain network

Extending this idea it has been suggested that a supply chain could more accurately be defined as:

> *A network of connected and interdependent organisations mutually and co-operatively working together to control, manage and improve the flow of materials and information from suppliers to end users.*

Source: J Aitken[3]

Competitive advantage

A central theme of this book is that effective logistics and supply chain management can provide a major source of competitive advantage – in other words a position of enduring superiority over competitors in terms of customer preference may be achieved through better management of logistics and the supply chain.

The foundations for success in the marketplace are numerous, but a simple model is based around the triangular linkage of the company, its customers and its competitors – the 'Three Cs'. Figure 1.2 illustrates the three-way relationship.

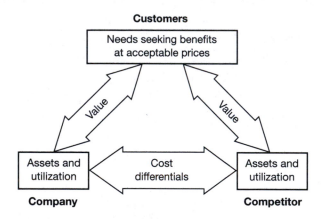

Fig. 1.2 Competitive advantage and the 'Three Cs'

Source: Ohmae, K., *The Mind of the Strategist*, Penguin Books, 1983.

The source of competitive advantage is found firstly in the ability of the organization to differentiate itself, in the eyes of the customer, from its competition and secondly by operating at a lower cost and hence at greater profit.

Seeking a sustainable and defensible competitive advantage has become the concern of every manager who is alert to the realities of the marketplace. It is no longer acceptable to assume that good products will sell themselves, neither is it advisable to imagine that success today will carry forward into tomorrow.

Let us consider the bases of success in any competitive context. At its most elemental, commercial success derives from either a cost advantage or a value advantage or, ideally, both. It is as simple as that – the most profitable competitor in any industry sector tends to be the lowest cost producer or the supplier providing a product with the greatest perceived differentiated values.

Put very simply, successful companies either have a cost advantage or they have a value advantage, or a combination of the two. Cost advantage gives a lower cost profile and the value advantage gives the product or offering a differential 'plus' over competitive offerings.

Let us briefly examine these two vectors of strategic direction.

1 Cost advantage

In many industries there will typically be one competitor who will be the low-cost producer and often that competitor will have the greatest sales volume in the sector. There is substantial evidence to suggest that 'big is beautiful' when it comes to cost advantage. This is partly due to economies of scale, which enable fixed costs to be spread over a greater volume, but more particularly to the impact of the 'experience curve'.

The experience curve is a phenomenon with its roots in the earlier notion of the 'learning curve'. Researchers in the Second World War discovered that it was possible to identify and predict improvements in the rate of output of workers as they became more skilled in the processes and tasks on which they were working. Subsequent work by Bruce Henderson, founder of the Boston Consulting Group, extended this concept by demonstrating that all costs, not just production costs, would decline at a given rate as volume increased (see Figure 1.3). In fact, to be precise, the relationship that the experience curve describes is between real unit costs and cumulative volume.

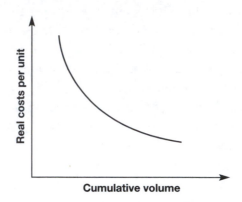

Fig. 1.3 The experience curve

Traditionally it has been suggested that the main route to cost reduction was by gaining greater sales volume and there can be no doubt about the close linkage between relative market share and relative costs. However, it must also be recognized that logistics and supply chain management can provide a multitude of ways to increase efficiency and productivity and hence contribute significantly to reduced unit costs. How this can be achieved will be one of the key themes of this book.

> Logistics and supply chain management can provide a multitude of ways to increase efficiency and productivity and hence contribute significantly to reduced unit costs.

2 Value advantage

It has long been an axiom in marketing that 'customers don't buy products, they buy benefits'. Put another way, the product is purchased not for itself but for the promise of what it will 'deliver'. These benefits may be intangible, i.e. they relate not to specific product features but rather to such things as image or service. Alternatively the delivered offering may be seen to outperform its rivals in some functional aspect.

Unless the product or service we offer can be distinguished in some way from its competitors there is a strong likelihood that the marketplace will view it as a 'commodity' and so the sale will tend to go to the cheapest supplier. Hence the importance of seeking to add additional values to our offering to mark it out from the competition.

What are the means by which such value differentiation may be gained? Essentially the development of a strategy based upon added values will normally require a more segmented approach to the market. When a company scrutinizes markets closely it frequently finds that there are distinct 'value segments'. In other words, different groups of customers within the total market attach different importance to different benefits. The importance of such benefit segmentation lies in the fact that often there are substantial opportunities for creating differentiated appeals for specific segments. Take the motor car as an example. A model such as the Ford Mondeo is not only positioned in the middle range of European cars but within that broad category specific versions are aimed at defined segments. Thus we find the basic, small engine, two-door model at one end of the spectrum and the four-door, high performance version at the other extreme. In between are a whole variety of options each of which seeks to satisfy the needs of quite different 'benefit segments'. Adding value through differentiation is a powerful means of achieving a defensible advantage in the market.

Equally powerful as a means of adding value is service. Increasingly it is the case that markets are becoming more service sensitive and this of course poses particular challenges for logistics management. There is a trend in many markets towards a decline in the strength of the 'brand' and a consequent move towards 'commodity' market status. Quite simply this means that it is becoming progressively more difficult to compete purely on the basis of brand or corporate image. Additionally, there is increasingly a convergence of technology within product categories, which means that it is often no longer possible to compete effectively on the basis of product differences. Thus the need to seek differentiation through means other than technology. Many companies have responded to this by focusing upon service as a means of gaining a competitive edge. Service in this context relates to the process of developing relationships with customers through the provision of an augmented offer. This augmentation can take many forms including delivery service, after-sales services, financial packages, technical support and so forth.

In practice what we find is that the successful companies will often seek to achieve a position based upon both a cost advantage and a value advantage. A useful way of examining the available options is to present them as a simple matrix. Let us consider these options in turn.

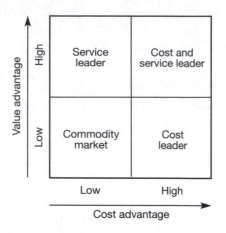

Fig. 1.4 Logistics and competitive advantage

For companies who find themselves in the bottom left hand corner of our matrix (Figure 1.4) the world is an uncomfortable place. Their products are indistinguishable from their competitors' offerings and they have no cost advantage. These are typical commodity market situations and ultimately the only strategy is either to move to the right of the matrix, i.e. to cost leadership, or upwards towards service leadership. Often the cost leadership route is simply not available. This particularly will be the case in a mature market where substantial market share gains are difficult to achieve. New technology may sometimes provide a window of opportunity for cost reduction but in such situations the same technology is often available to competitors.

Cost leadership strategies have traditionally been based upon the economies of scale, gained through sales volume. This is why market share is considered to be so important in many industries. However, if volume is to be the basis for cost leadership then it is preferable for that volume to be gained early in the market life cycle. The 'experience curve' concept, briefly described earlier, demonstrates the value of early market share gains – the higher your share relative to your competitors the lower your costs should be. This cost advantage can be used strategically to assume a position of price leader and, if appropriate, to make it impossible for higher-cost competitors to survive. Alternatively, price may be maintained, enabling above-average profit to be earned, which potentially is available to further develop the position of the product in the market.

However, an increasingly powerful route to achieving a cost advantage comes not necessarily through volume and the economies of scale but instead through logistics and supply chain management. In many industries, logistics costs represent such a significant proportion of total costs that it is possible to make major cost reductions through fundamentally re-engineering logistics processes. The means whereby this can be achieved will be returned to later in this book.

The other way out of the 'commodity' quadrant of the matrix is to seek a strategy of differentiation through service excellence. We have already commented on the fact that markets have become more 'service-sensitive'. Customers in all industries are seeking greater responsiveness and reliability from suppliers; they are looking for reduced lead times, just-in-time delivery and value-added services that enable them to do a better job of serving their customers. In Chapter 2 we will examine the specific ways in which superior service strategies, based upon enhanced logistics management, can be developed.

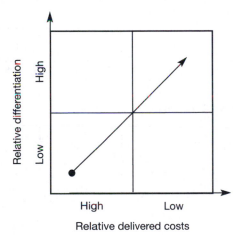

Fig. 1.5 The challenge to logistics and supply chain management

One thing is certain: there is no middle ground between cost leadership and service excellence. Indeed the challenge to management is to identify appropriate logistics and supply chain strategies to take the organization to the top right hand corner of the matrix. Companies who occupy that position have offers that are distinctive in the value they deliver and are also cost competitive. Clearly it is a position of some strength, occupying 'high ground' that is extremely difficult for competitors to attack. Figure 1.5 clearly presents the challenge: it is to seek out strategies that will take the business away from the 'commodity' end of the market towards a securer position of strength based upon differentiation and cost advantage.

Logistics management, it can be argued, has the potential to assist the organization in the achievement of both a cost advantage and a value advantage. As Figure 1.6 suggests, in the first instance there are a number of important ways in which productivity can be enhanced through logistics and supply chain management. Whilst these possibilities for leverage will be discussed in detail later in the book, suffice it to say that the opportunities for better capacity utilization, inventory reduction and closer integration with suppliers at a planning level are considerable. Equally the prospects for gaining a value advantage in the marketplace through superior customer service should not be underestimated. It will be argued later that the way we service the customer has become a vital means of differentiation.

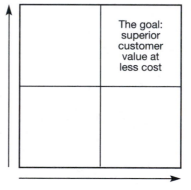

Value advantage

Logistics leverage opportunities:

• Tailored services
• Reliability
• Responsiveness

The goal: superior customer value at less cost

Cost advantage
Logistics leverage opportunities:

• Capacity utilization
• Asset turn
• Synchronous supply

Fig. 1.6 Gaining competitive advantage

To summarize, those organizations that will be the leaders in the markets of the future will be those that have sought and achieved the twin peaks of excellence: they have gained both cost leadership and service leadership.

The underlying philosophy behind the logistics and supply chain concept is that of planning and co-ordinating the materials flow from source to user as an integrated system rather than, as was so often the case in the past, managing the goods flow as a series of independent activities. Thus under this approach the goal is to link the marketplace, the distribution network, the manufacturing process and the procurement activity in such a way that customers are serviced at higher levels and yet at lower cost. In other words the goal is to achieve competitive advantage through both cost reduction and service enhancement.

The supply chain becomes the value chain

Of the many changes that have taken place in management thinking over the last 20 years or so perhaps the most significant has been the emphasis placed upon the search for strategies that will provide superior value in the eyes of the customer. To a large extent the credit for this must go to Michael Porter, the Harvard Business School professor, who through his research and writing[4] has alerted managers and strategists to the central importance of competitive relativities in achieving success in the marketplace.

One concept in particular that Michael Porter has brought to a wider audience is the 'value chain':

> Competitive advantage cannot be understood by looking at a firm as a whole. It stems from the many discrete activities a firm performs in designing, producing, marketing, delivering, and supporting its product. Each of these activities can contribute to a firm's relative cost position and create a basis for differentiation ... The value chain disaggregates a firm into its strategically relevant activities in order to understand the behaviour of costs and the existing and potential sources of differentiation. A firm gains competitive advantage by performing these strategically important activities more cheaply or better than its competitors.[5]

Value chain activities (shown in Figure 1.7) can be categorized into two types – primary activities (inbound logistics, operations, outbound logistics, marketing and sales, and service) and support activities (infrastructure, human resource management, technology development and procurement). These activities are integrating functions that cut across the traditional functions of the firm. Competitive advantage is derived from the way in which firms organize and perform these activities within the value chain. To gain competitive advantage over its rivals, a firm must deliver value to its customers by performing these activities more efficiently than its competitors or by performing the activities in a unique way that creates greater differentiation.

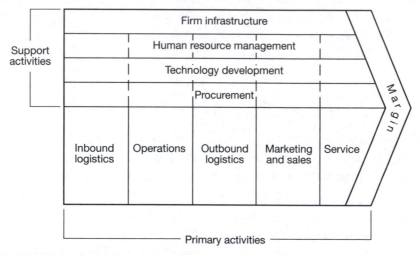

Fig. 1.7 The value chain

Source: Porter, M.E., *Competitive Advantage*, The Free Press, 1985.

The implication of Michael Porter's thesis is that organizations should look at each activity in their value chain and assess whether they have a real competitive advantage in the activity. If they do not, the argument goes, then perhaps they should consider outsourcing that activity to a partner who can provide that cost or value advantage. This logic is now widely accepted and has led to the dramatic upsurge in outsourcing activity that can be witnessed in almost every industry.

The effect of outsourcing is to extend the value chain beyond the boundaries of the business. In other words, the supply chain becomes the value chain. Value (and cost) is created not just by the focal firm in a network, but by all the entities that connect to each other.

Outsourcing has made supply chains more complex and hence has made the need for effective supply chain management even more pressing.

The mission of logistics management

It will be apparent from the previous comments that the mission of logistics management is to plan and co-ordinate all those activities necessary to achieve desired levels of delivered service and quality at lowest possible cost. Logistics must therefore be seen as the link between the marketplace and the supply base. The scope of logistics spans the organization, from the management of raw materials through to the delivery of the final product. Figure 1.8 illustrates this total systems concept.

> The scope of logistics spans the organization, from the management of raw materials through to the delivery of the final product.

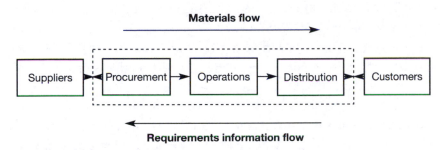

Fig. 1.8 Logistics management process

Logistics management, from this total systems viewpoint, is the means whereby the needs of customers are satisfied through the co-ordination of the materials and information flows that extend from the marketplace, through the firm and its operations and beyond that to suppliers. To achieve this company-wide integration clearly requires a quite different orientation than that typically encountered in the conventional organization.

For example, for many years marketing and manufacturing have been seen as largely separate activities within the organization. At best they have coexisted, at worst there has been open warfare. Manufacturing priorities and objectives have typically been focused on operating efficiency, achieved through long production runs, minimized set-ups and change-overs and product standardization. On the other hand, marketing has sought to achieve competitive advantage through variety, high service levels and frequent product changes.

15

In today's more turbulent environment there is no longer any possibility of manufacturing and marketing acting independently of each other. The internecine disputes between the 'barons' of production and marketing are clearly counter-productive to the achievement of overall corporate goals.

It is no coincidence that in recent years both marketing and manufacturing have become the focus of renewed attention. Marketing as a concept and a philosophy of customer orientation now enjoys a wider acceptance than ever. It is now generally accepted that the need to understand and meet customer requirements is a prerequisite for survival. At the same time, in the search for improved cost competitiveness, manufacturing management has been the subject of a massive revolution. The last decade has seen the rapid introduction of flexible manufacturing systems (FMS), of new approaches to inventory based on materials requirements planning (MRP) and just-in-time (JIT) methods and, perhaps most important of all, a sustained emphasis on total quality management (TQM).

Equally there has been a growing recognition of the critical role that procurement plays in creating and sustaining competitive advantage as part of an integrated logistics process. Leading-edge organizations now routinely include supply-side issues in the development of their strategic plans. Not only is the cost of purchased materials and supplies a significant part of total costs in most organizations, but there is a major opportunity for leveraging the capabilities and competencies of suppliers through closer integration of the buyers' and suppliers' logistics processes.

In this scheme of things, logistics is therefore essentially an integrative concept that seeks to develop a system-wide view of the firm. It is fundamentally a *planning* concept that seeks to create a framework through which the needs of the marketplace can be translated into a manufacturing strategy and plan, which in turn links into a strategy and plan for procurement. Ideally there should be a 'one-plan' mentality within the business which seeks to replace the conventional stand-alone and separate plans of marketing, distribution, production and procurement. This, quite simply, is the mission of logistics management.

The supply chain and competitive performance

Traditionally most organizations have viewed themselves as entities that exist independently from others and indeed need to compete with them in order to survive. There is almost a Darwinian ethic of the 'survival of the fittest' driving much of corporate strategy. However, such a philosophy can be self-defeating if it leads to an unwillingness to co-operate in order to compete. Behind this seemingly paradoxical concept is the idea of supply chain integration.

The supply chain is the network of organizations that are involved, through upstream and downstream linkages, in the different processes and activities that produce value in the form of products and services in the hands of the ultimate consumer. Thus, for example, a shirt manufacturer is a part of a supply chain that extends upstream through the weavers of fabrics to the manufacturers of fibres, and downstream through distributors and retailers to the final consumer. Each of these organizations in the chain are dependent upon each other by definition and yet, paradoxically, by tradition do not closely co-operate with each other.

Supply chain management is not the same as 'vertical integration'. Vertical integration normally implies ownership of upstream suppliers and downstream customers. This was once thought to be a desirable strategy but increasingly organizations are now focusing on their 'core business' – in other words the things they do really well and where they have a differential advantage. Everything else is 'outsourced' – in other words it is procured outside the firm. So, for example, companies that perhaps once made their own components now only assemble the finished product, e.g. automobile manufacturers. Other companies may also subcontract the manufacturing as well, e.g. Nike in footwear and sportswear. These companies have sometimes been termed 'virtual' or 'network' organizations.

Clearly this trend has many implications for supply chain management, not the least being the challenge of integrating and co-ordinating the flow of materials from a multitude of suppliers, often offshore, and similarly managing the distribution of the finished product by way of multiple intermediaries.

In the past it was often the case that relationships with suppliers and downstream customers (such as distributors or retailers) were adversarial rather than co-operative. It is still the case today that some companies will seek to achieve cost reductions or profit improvement at the expense of their supply chain partners. Companies such as these do not realize that simply transferring costs upstream or downstream does not make them any more competitive. The reason for this is that ultimately all costs will make their way to the final marketplace to be reflected in the price paid by the end user. The leading-edge companies recognize the fallacy of this conventional approach and instead seek to make the supply chain as a whole more competitive through the value it adds and the costs that it reduces overall. They have realized that the real competition is not company against company but rather supply chain against supply chain.

It must be recognized that the concept of supply chain management, whilst relatively new, is in fact no more than an extension of the logic of logistics. Logistics management is primarily concerned with optimizing flows within the organization, whilst supply chain management recognizes that internal integration by itself is not sufficient. Figure 1.9 suggests that there is in effect an evolution of integration from the stage 1 position of complete functional independence where each business function such as production or purchasing does their own thing in complete isolation from the other business functions. An example would be where production seeks to optimize its unit costs of manufacture by long production runs without regard for the build-up of finished goods inventory and heedless of the impact it will have on the need for warehousing space and the impact on working capital.

Stage 2 companies have recognized the need for at least a limited degree of integration between adjacent functions, e.g. distribution and inventory management or purchasing and materials control. The natural next step to stage 3 requires the establishment and implementation of an 'end-to-end' planning framework that will be fully described later in this book.

Stage 4 represents true supply chain integration in that the concept of linkage and co-ordination that is achieved in stage 3 is now extended upstream to suppliers and downstream to customers. There is thus a crucial and important distinction to be made between *logistics* and *supply chain management*.

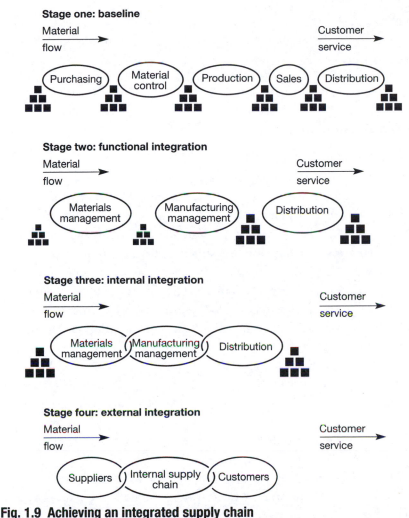

Fig. 1.9 Achieving an integrated supply chain
Source : Stevens, G.C., 'Integrating the Supply Chain', *International Journal of Physical Distribution and Materials Management*, Vol. 19, No. 8, 1989.

Dell Inc.: using the supply chain to compete

The personal computer (PC) sector was still in its infancy when, in 1983, medical student Michael Dell began buying up remainder stocks of outdated IBM PCs from local retailers. Dell upgraded the machines in his college dorm, then sold them on at bargain prices to eager customers. Dell abandoned his studies soon afterwards to concentrate on his growing computer business. By 1985 Dell Computer had switched from upgrading old IBMs to building its own machines. Even then,

Dell was different from other computer manufacturers of its day. The machines themselves were technologically unremarkable, but it was the way in which they were sold – directly to the customer – that gave the upstart company a unique advantage over established PC makers.

Dell's business model

While the industry leaders vied to introduce PCs with ever faster and more impressive technology, they gave little consideration to the mundane business of supply chain management. The computers they produced were invariably made-to-forecast and because of the way they were sold – through shops, resellers and systems integrators – were then destined to languish for an average of two months in warehouses or on shop shelves before being purchased by a customer. In doing so they exposed their makers to the inherent double jeopardy created by the dynamics and economics of the industry. Firstly, component costs have been falling since the industry's inception, particularly the all-important processors that had fallen in price by an average of 30 per cent per year.[1] The longer these components wait to be sold, the worse value they become. Historically, component costs accounted for around 80 per cent of the total cost of a PC. Secondly, there is the risk that a step-change in technology may make millions of dollars' worth of finished product obsolete overnight, forcing manufacturers to compensate resellers for unloading stocks at a loss.

By selling directly to the customer Dell was able to configure and assemble every PC to order, which in turn enabled it to maintain its cost advantage over conventional rivals. Dell's low-priced machines with their bespoke configuration were an attractive option for customers who were confident enough to buy direct. Nevertheless, for many years received wisdom in the industry considered Dell to be nothing more than a successful niche player. It was widely believed that the majority of business-to-business customers, and indeed consumers buying PCs for the home, would always prefer to purchase their equipment through traditional channels. Distributors and retailers would reassure the customer that help would be at hand should something go wrong. Moreover, consumers could see and touch the products before purchase.

In the early 1990s Dell embarked on a brief flirtation with conventional retail distribution channels in a bid to break out of its perceived niche. The move was a mistake. Retail sales plummeted as soon as Dell offered a new PC through its direct channel. Dell was obliged to compensate the retailers for their losses. As a result, the company posted its first ever loss ($36m) in 1993.[2] The ill-judged foray was a salutary lesson in the perils of attempting to operate through conflicting distribution channels and a vindication of its original low-cost direct sales strategy. Dell pulled out of the retail market in 1994 and retrenched with a vengeance, rebounding immediately with profits of $149m. From this point on Dell concentrated on finding ways to leverage the strengths of its original direct sales strategy.

The arrival of the Internet offered Dell the opportunity to develop an even more cost-effective version of its direct-sales approach. The company was not the first PC retailer to venture into cyberspace, though no other manufacturer was better placed to make such a move. Within six months of opening for business through its website, Dell was clocking up Internet sales of $1m per day, with sales through the channel growing by 20 per cent per month.[3] Far from remaining a small niche option, direct buyers soon accounted for a third of all PC sales in the US, up from only 15 per cent in 1991. Not more than 36 hours after placing an Internet order, customers' bespoke PCs trundled off the production lines and onto delivery trucks. In fact more than 80 per cent of Dell's orders were built, customized and shipped within eight hours. More time was spent testing the machines and loading software than actually assembling them. For most direct-to-customer sales Dell could expect to see payment within 24 hours of order placement, while Compaq (global market leader at the time) had to wait around 35 days for payment through primary dealers. Even other direct sellers were apt to take over a fortnight to convert an order in cash.

Dell's own operations continue to be constantly re-examined to squeeze every possible moment of non-value-adding time out of procurement and assembly processes. As a result, the total number of interventions or 'touches' involved in the manufacture of a Dell PC has been reduced to 60, against an industry average of around 130. The simplification is facilitated in part by Dell's focus on common components and, from the late 1990s, the formation of long-term relationships with suppliers, including competitors such as IBM and Toshiba.

▶

▶

On the inbound side too Dell works to minimize inventory and increase return on capital employed. Many components are not ordered from a supplier before Dell receives a customer order. To achieve such levels of co-operation and integration, Dell progressively reduced its number of suppliers from 204 companies in 1992 to just 47 by 1997. Numbers would eventually rise to above 1992 levels as product ranges expanded, but by 2003 around 30 suppliers provided 75 per cent of Dell's direct material purchase.

Most of the company's suppliers maintain eight to ten days of inventory in vendor warehouses located not more than 15 minutes away from Dell's own factories in Texas, Ireland and Malaysia. The company decided that it was preferable to source from suppliers close to its plants, rather than from more distant offshore locations, even though local manufacturing costs may be higher. IT links with key suppliers allow Dell to schedule production lines in its factories every two hours.

> We have no inventory and no warehouses in any of our factories. Instead, we're able to pull material into our factories based on actual orders ... We literally push a button and two things happen. We lock in the schedule by actual order and order number into the factory. At the same time we send a message over the Internet to our third-party logistics providers, suppliers logistics centres or hubs.
>
> Dick Hunter, Dell VP Americas Manufacturing Operations[4]

Suppliers have 90 minutes to pull material off the rack and deliver it to Dell's factory door. Suppliers have access to hub-level inventory holdings and are responsible for restocking the hubs and delivering to the factories on a consignment stock basis. Bulky finished subassemblies, such as monitors and speakers, are treated differently. Instead of shipping them to Dell's factories, they are sent directly to the customer from the supplier's hub (located close to the market rather than close to Dell's factory), saving Dell approximately $30 per item in freight costs. Dell is billed for the components only when they leave the supplier's warehouse in response to a customer order. The supplier receives payment approximately 45 days later.

Dell endeavours to dual source most of its components, but single sources some items, such as chips from Intel. Where essential components (such as disk drives) cannot be sourced or assembled as quickly as the computers could be bolted together, Dell works with suppliers to shorten their own lead times or improve forecasting. Dell's own

forecasts are posted on its extranet. Fortunately, demand for components is much more predictable than demand for finished goods,
though shortages of some critical components (most notably microprocessors) can be a problem across the industry. Here again, the
direct sales method placed Dell at an advantage over those makers
who used traditional routes to market. Because Dell communicates
directly with its customers, it is able to shape demand by steering customers towards configurations using readily available components.
The model enables Dell to carry only four days' inventory, while many
of its competitors continue to hold between 20–30 days worth.[5]

Twenty-first century price wars

Dell's mastery of its own business model allowed it to grow at a rate
that was more than three times the industry average throughout the
1990s. By the end of the decade it was challenging global market leader
Compaq to become the world's biggest PC maker (by unit sales).
Importantly, Dell's operating margins had been maintained regardless
of relentless downward pressure on prices. However, things seemed to
take a dramatic downturn in February 2001 when Dell revealed its
fourth quarter results. The announcement was accompanied by the
news of the first ever redundancies in its 16-year history: 1700 jobs,
accounting for 4 per cent of its workforce, were to go immediately.
Some analysts had seen it coming, others scurried to investigate.

   In the US, still home to more than 70 per cent of its business,
demand for Dell's core product – the mid-range office desktop – was
weakening. Michael Dell maintained his stance that reports of the
death of the PC were exaggerated. Nevertheless, it was clear that
demand for PCs had fallen sharply after a pre-Y2K boom in sales.
Across the industry manufacturers were suffering a post-millennium
hangover and everyone was feeling the pinch. To the alarm of its competitors Dell resorted to slashing PC prices in a bid to increase its share
of the US market, a region where its rivals were already struggling to
turn a profit. Dell went on to announce a further 4000 redundancies in
May 2001 as the industry descended into a full-blooded price war.
There was speculation that Dell might be prepared to lower its margins as far as 3.5 per cent, pushing most of its rivals well into the red.

▶ IBM's PC unit was already making a loss but, being focused on the corporate market, it was managing to claw back margin on its service packages. For the smaller players, the future looked bleak. Some, such as Micron Electronics, had already bailed out of the PC sector, while others were to do the same before the year was over. Meanwhile news of an impending merger with Hewlett Packard damaged Compaq's sales, apparently allowing Dell to capitalize on confusion in the marketplace. It gained a 31 per cent share of the US market at the expense of its nearest rivals. Despite the aggressive price-cutting, analysts believed that Dell had managed to maintain margins of around 7 per cent,[6] but in the post-Enron and post-9/11 malaise Wall Street was nervous. There were whisperings that Dell might be too aggressive in its accounting practices and rumours that it made suppliers hold back inventory at the end of a quarter to improve its figures.[7]

> I'm not going to suggest that there couldn't be incidents where we did things that could appear like that ... but on a broad scale, no, that does not reflect our activities at all.
>
> Michael Dell[8]

The merger between Hewlett Packard and Compaq had been designed to protect their evaporating margins, but post-merger integration did not go smoothly. Outside the US efforts to cut costs through rationalization across the two companies repeatedly fell foul of labour and tax laws or systems requirements in other national markets, while in the US the newly combined group found that Best Buy, the largest retailer of Hewlett Packard PCs, was keen to restrict shelf space for the new giant, fearing that the enlarged company could wield too much power. Hewlett Packard and other established industry players had repeatedly tried to improve their own cost structures by emulating Dell's direct sales formula, but many retreated after running into the same channel conflicts as Dell had encountered with its foray into retail sales.

New territories

By November 2001, Dell was undisputed leader of the still contracting global PC market, but analysts were anxious about Dell's dependence on its depressed domestic market. The company had been expanding overseas for some years but had struggled in Europe, particularly in Germany where it had experienced great difficulty in establishing a management team schooled in and capable of delivering the Dell model. In terms of market share, it had latterly managed to improve its position, but continental Europeans did not embrace the direct sales model as readily as their US and British counterparts. By 2001, more than 50 per cent of UK companies were buying hardware online, in Germany only 27 per cent did so, while in Italy online buying was as low as 17 per cent.[9]

A report by independent technology analysts Gartner Dataquest, in the third quarter of 2001, showed that demand for PCs across continental Europe was down 11 per cent on the previous year. Amongst the top five vendors, only Dell had achieved growth, up 5.6 per cent. Compaq (still European market leader) had recorded a fall of 18.8 per cent.[10]

> We are number one in the world, but have only 13% of the market after year-on-year of aggressive growth ... Michael Dell has stated he wants 40% market share worldwide, so we are not going to ease off ... At a minimum we are aiming for 25%. It will take several years to get there.
>
> Paul Bell, Dell's European Operations Manager[11]

> Without changing the business model, Dell's target is unrealistic. The rate of growth is dependent on the rate of change in the business buying culture. Dell has already cornered around half of the direct sales business in Europe, so the propensity to grow is limited by the overall size of the direct market ... Dell's Anglo-Saxon model has mapped most readily to the UK and Australia. But Dell could find it can't colonise the world without taking on the cultural peculiarities of those continental European countries.
>
> Brian Gammage, Analyst, Gartner Dataquest.[12]

Internet sales had risen in Europe and in Asia as the 1990s drew to a close, but analysts still wondered whether Dell was being over-ambitious. To achieve such total worldwide domination of the PC market and *keep* it Dell could not ignore China. Dell first established an assembly operation making 'Smart PCs' in China through a Taiwanese contractor. In 2002 it began making them itself in its own factory in Xiamen in southern China, but once again Dell would have to risk a departure from its proven business model. China lacked the direct marketing infrastructure, high levels of Internet usage and automated payment systems that made Dell's direct sales model workable

▶

▶ elsewhere. Instead Dell produces low-cost standardized products in Xiamen. The Smart PCs are shown to would-be customers by sales teams in shopping malls in the wealthier Chinese cities. Customers can touch and see the product before ordering by phone, with payment on delivery or by arrangement through local banks.[13]

Beyond PCs

By 2001 Dell was not only the leading PC maker worldwide, but it had risen to become the leading supplier of servers in the US. Nevertheless, 83 per cent of Dell's revenues still came from desktops and portables. In the harsh economic climate of the day observers continued to question whether Dell had the vision, products and skills to remain competitive in the twenty-first century. Could it survive in an age when attention was turning towards innovative non-PC devices? Could the root of Dell's success – its ability to customize and deliver otherwise standardized desktop computers – now be its downfall?

> People are more concerned with what it takes, for instance, to download MP3 music files and burn their own CDs than they are with what kind of computer they use to do it. Meanwhile many corporations now provide workers with a new PC every four years – up from every three years, which had been standard practice.
>
> Mark Tebbe, Internet Consultant, Lante[14]

> The PC business has been about products, feeds and speeds. Now customers don't give a rat's ass about how fast the processor is. The issue is, 'How do I get stuff done with my computer?'
>
> Aaron Goldberg, Analyst, Ziff-Davis Media[15]

Much of the real action in the industry appeared to be in the markets for wireless networks and hand-held computing, but Dell appeared to steer clear of these new exciting opportunities. Instead it started to diversify into low-cost storage and networking support where it had high hopes of growth in the European, Middle Eastern and African (EMEA) markets.

> We need to keep the financial health strong by diversifying ... Our job is not to stake our future on the big grey desktop ... We are looking to double storage revenues across EMEA next year.
>
> Paul Bell, European Operations Manager, Dell[16]

In March 2002 Dell announced an alliance with Philips, Europe's biggest supplier of consumer electronics. Philips would supply cathode ray and flat screens or semiconductors to some Dell suppliers. It would also provide rewritable disk drives and wireless technology. In exchange, Dell would supply servers and workstations for internal use by Philips. It would also carry some Philips products on its website, giving the Dutch brand visibility in the US, a market where it had long struggled to establish a profitable presence.[17]

Elsewhere, despite the calls for diversification, Dell's plans to build its networking business provoked the same old responses from its critics. Once again there was speculation that without intermediaries Dell would be unable to meet the service requirements of the sector. Yet again Dell went on to confound its critics, developing its service offer through partnerships with leading service suppliers such as EDS. Consulting services were becoming a critical factor in many large corporate account bids, but Dell signalled that it would not be putting significant resources into building its own services capability as IBM had done. It was far more interested in the less glamourous peripheral hardware products, such as the switches that connect small- and medium-sized computer networks, and storage to support low- to medium-powered servers. Margins were high in both sectors, up to 50 per cent in switches.

Other niches were also attracting Dell's attention. In 2003 Dell unveiled its first range of printers. Its share price rose by 1 per cent on the day, while Hewlett Packard's dropped by the same amount. Soon afterwards, the launch of its first hand-held computer was received with news that market leader Palm would be merging with its rival Handspring. By now a distinct pattern was emerging. Dell was picking off high-volume, high-margin categories of PC-related hardware. It was doing so once industry standards had emerged, which in turn signalled to customers that the item was becoming a commodity. Commodities are fair game for price competition, the very thing Dell's competitors fear most!

References
1. *The Economist*, 'Dell Computer: Selling PCs like Bananas', 5 October 1996, p. 99.
2. Serwer, Andrew E., 'Michael Dell Turns the PC World Inside Out', *Fortune*, 8 September 1997, pp. 38–44.
3. McWilliams, Gary, 'Whirlwind on the Web', *Business Week*, 7 April 1997, pp. 132, 134, 136.

▶

4. Jacobs, Daniel G., 'Anatomy of a Supply Chain', *Transportation & Distribution*, June 2003, pp. 60–62.

5. *Ibid.*

6. *Financial Times*, 'The Dell Curve', Lex Column, 5 October 2001.

7. Serwer, A., 'Dell Does Domination', *Fortune*, 21 January 2002, pp. 43–47.

8. *Ibid.*

9. Ashwood, Ashley, 'Dell Moves up a Gear as PC Industry Declines', *Financial Times*, 9 November 2001.

10. *Ibid.*

11. *Ibid.*

12. *Ibid.*

13. Einhorn, B. 'Dell Takes a Different Tack in China', *Business Week Online*, 3 December 2001.

14. Kirkpatrick, David, 'Please Don't call us PC', *Fortune*, 16 October 2000, pp. 81–84.

15. *Ibid.*

16. Ashwood, Ashley, 'Dell Moves up a Gear as PC Industry Declines', *Financial Times*, 9 November 2001.

17. Crambe, Gordon, 'Philips and Dell Agree on Global Alliance', *Financial Times*, 28 March 2002.

The changing competitive environment

As the competitive context of business continues to change, bringing with it new complexities and concerns for management generally, it also has to be recognized that the impact on logistics and supply chain management of these changes can be considerable. Indeed, of the many strategic issues that confront the business organization today, perhaps the most challenging are in the area of logistics.

Much of this book will be devoted to addressing these challenges in detail but it is useful at this stage to highlight what are perhaps the most pressing currently. These are:

● The new rules of competition
● Globalization of industry
● Downward pressure on price
● Customers taking control

The new rules of competition

We are now entering the era of 'supply chain competition'. The fundamental difference from the previous model of competition is that an organization can no longer act as an isolated and independent entity in competition with other similarly 'stand-alone' organizations. Instead, the need to create value delivery systems that are more responsive to fast-changing markets and are much more consistent and reliable in the delivery of that value requires that the supply chain as a whole be focused on the achievement of these goals.

In the past the ground rules for marketing success were obvious: strong brands backed up by large advertising budgets and aggressive selling. This formula now appears to have lost its power. Instead, the argument is heard, companies must recognize that increasingly it is through their *capabilities* and *competencies* that they compete.[6]

Essentially, this means that organizations create superior value for customers and consumers by managing their *core processes* better than competitors manage theirs. These core processes encompass such activities as new product development, supplier development, order fulfilment and customer management. By performing these fundamental activities in a more cost-effective way than competitors, it is argued, organizations will gain the advantage in the marketplace. This principle is powerfully expressed in the words of Jorma Ollila, the Chairman and CEO of Nokia:

> Our experienced and unique way of operating is what we see as increasingly putting us ahead of the competition. As we move forward in this complex industry, winning will be less about what we do and more about the way we do it.

One capability that is now regarded by many companies as fundamental to success in the marketplace is the management of in-bound and out-bound logistics. As product life cycles shorten, as customers adopt just-in-time practices and as sellers' markets become buyers' markets then the ability of the organization to respond rapidly and flexibly to demand can provide a powerful competitive edge.

A major contributing factor influencing the changed competitive environment has been the trend towards 'commoditization' in many markets. A commodity market is characterized by perceived product equality in the eyes of customers resulting in a high preparedness to substitute one make of product for another. Research increasingly suggests that consumers are less loyal to specific brands but instead will have a portfolio of brands within a category from which they make their choice. In situations such as this actual product availability becomes a major determinant of demand. There is evidence that more and more decisions are being taken at the point of purchase and if there is a gap on the shelf where Brand X should be, but Brand Y is there instead, then there is a strong probability that Brand Y will win the sale.

It is not only in consumer markets that the importance of logistics process excellence is apparent. In business-to-business and industrial markets it seems that product or technical features are of less importance in winning orders than issues such as delivery lead times and flexibility. This is not to suggest that product or technical features are unimportant – rather it is that they are taken as a 'given' by the customer. Quite simply, in today's marketplace the order-winning criteria are more likely to be service-based than product-based.

> In today's marketplace the order-winning criteria are more likely to be service-based than product-based.

A parallel development in many markets is the trend towards a consolidation of demand. In other words customers – as against consumers – are tending to grow in size whilst becoming fewer in number. The retail grocery industry is a good example in that in most northern European countries a handful of large retailers account for over 50 per cent of all sales in any one country. This tendency to the concentration of buying power is being accelerated as a result of global mergers and acquisitions. The impact of these trends is that these more powerful customers are becoming more demanding in terms of their service requirements from suppliers.

At the same time as the power in the distribution channel continues to shift from supplier to buyer, there is also a trend for customers to reduce their supplier base. In other words they want to do business with fewer suppliers and often on a longer-term basis. The successful companies in the coming years will be those that recognize these trends and seek to establish strategies based upon establishing closer relationships with key accounts. Such strategies will focus upon seeking innovative ways to create more value for these customers. These strategies will be 'vertical' rather than 'horizontal' in that the organization will seek to do more for fewer customers rather than looking for more customers to whom to sell the same product. The car industry provides a good example of this phenomenon with 'lead' suppliers taking on much greater responsibility for the delivery of entire systems or modules to the assembly line.

Such a transition from volume-based growth to value-based growth will require a much greater focus on managing the core processes that we referred to earlier. Whereas the competitive model of the past relied heavily on *product* innovation this will have to be increasingly supple-mented by *process* innovation. The basis for competing in this new era will be:

Competitive advantage = Product excellence × Process excellence

Figure 1.10 suggests that traditionally for many companies the investment has mainly been on product excellence and less on process excellence.

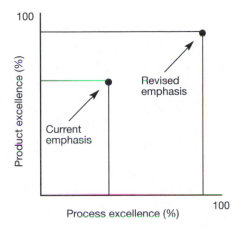

Fig. 1.10 Investing in process excellence yields greater benefits

This is not to suggest that product innovation should be given less emphasis – far from it – but rather that more emphasis needs to be placed on developing and managing processes that deliver greater value for key customers.

We have already commented that product life cycles are getting shorter. What we have witnessed in many markets is the effect of changes in technology and consumer demand combining to produce more volatile markets where a product can be obsolete almost as soon as it reaches the market. There are many current examples of shorten-ing life cycles but perhaps the personal computer symbolizes them all. In this particular case we have seen rapid developments in technology that have first created markets where none existed before and then almost as quickly have rendered themselves obsolete as the next gener-ation of product is announced.

Such shortening of life cycles creates substantial problems for logistics management. In particular, shorter life cycles demand shorter lead times – indeed our definition of lead time may well need to change. Lead times are traditionally defined as the elapsed period from receipt of customer order to delivery. However, in today's environment there is a wider perspective that needs to be taken. The real lead time is the time taken from the drawing board, through procurement, manufacture and assembly to the end market. This is the concept of strategic lead time and the management of this time span is the key to success in managing logistics operations.

There are already situations arising where the life cycle is shorter than the strategic lead time. In other words the life of a product on the market is less than the time it takes to design, procure, manufacture and distribute that same product! The implications of this are considerable both for planning and operations. In a global context the problem is exacerbated by the longer transportation times involved.

Ultimately, therefore, the means of achieving success in such markets is to accelerate movement through the supply chain and to make the entire logistics system far more flexible and thus responsive to these fast-changing markets.

Globalization of industry

A further strategic issue that provides a challenge for logistics management is the continued trend towards globalization.

A global company is more than a multinational company. In the global business materials and components are sourced worldwide and products may be manufactured offshore and sold in many different countries, perhaps with local customization.

Such is the trend towards globalization that it is probably safe to forecast that before long most markets will be dominated by global companies. The only role left for national companies will be to cater for specific and unique local demands, for example in the food industry.

For global companies like Hewlett Packard, Philips and Caterpillar, the management of the logistics process has become an issue of central concern. The difference between profit and loss for an individual product can hinge upon the extent to which the global pipeline can be optimized, because the costs involved are so great. The global company seeks to achieve competitive advantage by identifying world markets for its products and then to develop a manufacturing and logistics strategy to support its marketing strategy. So a company like Caterpillar, for example, has dispersed assembly operations to key overseas markets and uses global logistics channels to supply parts to offshore assembly plants and after-markets. Where appropriate, Caterpillar will use third-party companies to manage distribution and even final finishing. So, for example, in the US a third-party company in addition to providing parts inspection and warehousing attaches options to fork lift trucks. Wheels, counterweights, forks and masts are installed as specified by Caterpillar. Thus local market needs can be catered for from a standardized production process.

Globalization also tends to lengthen supply chains as companies increasingly move production offshore or source from more distant locations. The impetus for this trend, which in recent years has accelerated dramatically, is the search for lower labour costs. However, one implication of these decisions is that 'end-to-end' pipeline times may increase significantly. In time-sensitive markets, longer lead times can be fatal.

'Time-based competition' is an idea that will be returned to many times in later chapters. Time compression has become a critical management issue. Product life cycles are shorter than ever, customers and distributors require just-in-time deliveries and end users are ever more willing to accept a substitute product if their first choice is not instantly available.

The globalization of industry, and hence supply chains, is inevitable. However, to enable the potential benefits of global networks to be fully realized, a wider supply chain perspective must be adopted. It can be argued that for the global corporation competitive advantage will increasingly derive from excellence in managing the complex web of relationships and flows that characterize their supply chains.

Downward pressure on price

Whilst the trend might not be universal there can be no doubting that most markets are more price competitive today than they were a decade ago. Prices in the high streets and the shopping malls continue to fall in many countries and upstream of the retail store the prices of

components, raw materials and industrial products with some excep-
tions follow the same downward pattern.

Whilst some of this price deflation can be explained as the result of
normal cost reduction through learning and experience effects, the
rapid fall in the price of many consumer goods has other causes. Figure
1.11 shows the comparative rate at which VCR and DVD player prices
fell in the UK market. The striking feature is that whilst it took 20
years for a VCR to fall in price from £400 to just over £40, it took only
five years for a DVD player to fall by the same amount. The same phenomenon is apparent in markets as diverse as clothing, home
furnishings and air travel.

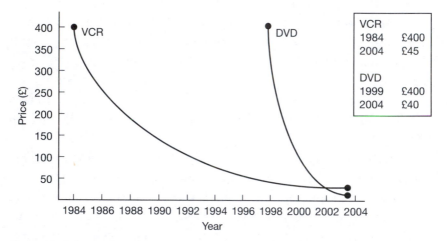

Fig. 1.11 Price deflation in consumer electronics (UK high street prices)

A fundamental change in the global competitive landscape is driving prices
to levels that in real terms are as low as they have ever been. A number of
causal factors have contributed to this new market environment.

First, there are new global competitors who have entered the marketplace supported by low-cost manufacturing bases. The dramatic rise of
China as a major producer of quality consumer products is evidence
of this. Secondly, the removal of barriers to trade and the deregulation of
many markets has accelerated this trend, enabling new players to rapidly
gain ground. One result of this has been overcapacity in many industries.
Overcapacity implies an excess of supply against demand and hence leads
to further downward pressure on price.

A further cause of price deflation, it has been suggested, is the Internet, which makes price comparison so much easier. The Internet has also enabled auctions and exchanges to be established at industry-wide levels, which have also tended to drive down prices.

In addition, there is evidence that customers and consumers are more value conscious than has hitherto been the case. Brands and suppliers that could once command a price premium because of their perceived superiority can no longer do so as the market recognizes that equally attractive offers are available at significantly lower prices. The success of many retailers' own-label products or the inroads made by low-cost airlines proves this point.

Against the backdrop of a continued downward pressure on price, it is self-evident that, in order to maintain profitability, companies must find a way to bring down costs to match the fall in price.

The challenge to the business is to find new opportunities for cost reduction when, in all likelihood, the company has been through many previous cost-reduction programmes. It can be argued that the last remaining opportunity of any significance for major cost reduction lies in the wider supply chain rather than in the firm's own operations.

This idea is not new. Back in 1929 Ralph Borsodi[7] expressed it in the following words:

> In 50 years between 1870 and 1920 the cost of distributing necessities and luxuries has nearly trebled, while production costs have gone down by one-fifth … What we are saving in production we are losing in distribution.

The situation that Borsodi describes can still be witnessed in many industries today. For example, companies who thought they could achieve a leaner operation by moving to just-in-time (JIT) practices often only shifted costs elsewhere in the supply chain by forcing suppliers or customers to carry that inventory. The car industry, which to many is the home of lean thinking and JIT practices, has certainly exhibited some of those characteristics. A recent analysis of the western European automobile industry[8] showed that whilst car assembly operations were indeed very lean with minimal inventory, the same was not true upstream and downstream of those operations. Figure 1.12 shows the profile of inventory through the supply chain from the tier 1 suppliers down to the car dealerships.

35

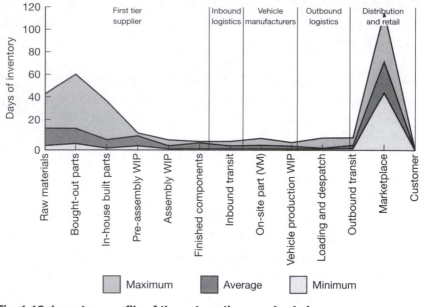

Fig. 1.12 Inventory profile of the automotive supply chain
Source: Holweg & Pil.[9]

In this particular case the paradox is that most inventory is being held when it is at its most expensive, i.e. as a finished product. The true cost of this inventory to the industry is considerable. Whilst inventory costs will vary by industry and by company, it will be suggested in Chapter 3 that the true cost of carrying inventory is rarely less that 25 per cent per year of its value. In the conditions in which the automobile industry currently finds itself, this alone is enough to make the difference between profit and loss.

This example illustrates the frequently encountered failure to take a wider view of cost. For many companies their definition of cost is limited only to those costs that are contained within the four walls of their business entity. However, as has been suggested earlier, since today's competition takes place not between companies but between supply chains the proper view of costs has to be 'end-to-end' since all costs will ultimately be reflected in the price of the finished product in the final marketplace.

The need to take a supply chain view of cost is further underscored by the major trend that is observable across industries worldwide towards outsourcing. For many companies today, most of their costs lie outside their legal boundaries; activities that used to be performed in-house are now outsourced to specialist service providers. The amazing growth of contract manufacturing in electronics bears witness to this trend. If the majority of an organization's costs lie outside the business then it follows that the biggest opportunities for improvement in their cost position will also be found in that wider supply chain.

The customers take control

So much has been written and talked about service, quality and excellence that there is no escaping the fact that the customer in today's marketplace is more demanding, not just of product quality, but also of service.

> The customer in today's market-place is more demanding, not just of product quality, but also of service.

As more and more markets become in effect 'commodity' markets, where the customer perceives little technical difference between competing offers, the need is for the creation of differential advantage through added value. Increasingly a prime source of this added value is through customer service.

Customer service may be defined as the consistent provision of time and place utility. In other words, products don't have value until they are in the hands of the customer at the time and place required. There are clearly many facets of customer service, ranging from on-time delivery through to after-sales support. Essentially the role of customer service should be to enhance 'value-in-use', meaning that the product becomes worth more in the eyes of the customer because service has added value to the core product. In this way significant differentiation of the total offer (that is the core product plus the service package) can be achieved.

Those companies that have achieved recognition for service excellence, and thus have been able to establish a differential advantage over their competition, are typically those companies where logistics management is a high priority. Companies like Xerox, Toyota, Benetton and Dell are typical of such organizations. The achievement of competitive advantage through service comes not from slogans or expensive so-called customer care programmes, but rather from a combination of a carefully thought-out strategy for service, the development of appropriate delivery systems and commitment from people, from the chief executive down.

The attainment of service excellence in this broad sense can only be achieved through a closely integrated logistics strategy. In reality, the ability to become a world-class supplier depends as much upon the effectiveness of one's operating systems as it does upon the presentation of the product, the creation of images and the influencing of consumer perceptions. In other words, the success of McDonald's, WalMart or any of the other frequently cited paragons of service excellence is due not to their choice of advertising agency, but rather to their recognition that managing the logistics of service delivery on a consistent basis is the crucial source of differential advantage.

Managing the '4Rs'

As we move rapidly into the era of supply chain competition a number of principles emerge to guide the supply chain manager. These can be conveniently summarized as the '4Rs' of responsiveness, reliability, resilience and relationships.

1 Responsiveness

In today's just-in-time world the ability to respond to customers' requirements in ever-shorter time-frames has become critical. Not only do customers want shorter lead times, they are also looking for flexibility and increasingly customized solutions. In other words the supplier has to be able to meet the precise needs of customers in less time than ever before. The key word in this changed environment is *agility*. Agility implies the ability to move quickly and to meet customer demand sooner. In a fast-changing marketplace agility is actually more important than long-term strategy in a traditional business planning sense. Because future demand patterns are uncertain, by definition this makes planning more difficult and, in a sense, hazardous.

In the future, organizations must be much more *demand-driven* than *forecast-driven*. The means of making this transition will be through the achievement of agility, not just within the company but across the supply chain.

2 Reliability

One of the main reasons why any company carries safety stock is because of uncertainty. It may be uncertainty about future demand or uncertainty about a supplier's ability to meet a delivery promise, or about the quality of materials or components. Significant improvements in reliability can only be achieved through re-engineering the processes that impact performance. Manufacturing managers long ago discovered that the best way to improve product quality was not by quality control through inspection but rather to focus on process control. The same is true for logistics reliability.

A key to improving reliability in logistics processes is enhanced *pipeline visibility*. It is often the case that there is limited visibility of downstream demand at the end of the pipeline. This problem is exacerbated the further removed from final demand the organization or supply chain entity is. Thus the manufacturer of synthetic fibres may have little awareness of current demand for the garments that incorporate those fibres in the material from which they are made.

If a means can be found of opening up the pipeline so that there is clear end-to-end visibility then reliability of response will inevitably improve.

3 Resilience

Today's marketplace is characterized by higher levels of turbulence and volatility. The wider business, economic and political environments are increasingly subjected to unexpected shocks and discontinuities. As a result, supply chains are vulnerable to disruption and, in consequence, the risk to business continuity is increased.

Whereas in the past the prime objective in supply chain design was probably cost minimization or possibly service optimization, the emphasis today has to be upon resilience. Resilience refers to the ability of the supply chain to cope with unexpected disturbances. There is evidence that the tendencies of many companies to seek out low-cost solutions because of pressure on margins may have led to leaner, but more vulnerable, supply chains.

Resilient supply chains may not be the lowest-cost supply chains but they are more capable of coping with the uncertain business environment. Resilient supply chains have a number of characteristics, of which the most important is a business-wide recognition of where the supply chain is at its most vulnerable. Managing the critical nodes and links of a supply chain, to be discussed further in Chapter 8, becomes a key priority. Sometimes these 'critical paths' may be where there is dependence on a single supplier, or a supplier with long replenishment lead times, or a bottleneck in a process.

Other characteristics of resilient supply chains are their recognition of the importance of strategic inventory and the selective use of spare capacity to cope with 'surge' effects.

4 Relationships

The trend towards customers seeking to reduce their supplier base has already been commented upon. In many industries the practice of 'single sourcing' is widespread. It is usually suggested that the benefits of such practices include improved quality, innovation sharing, reduced costs and integrated scheduling of production and deliveries. Underlying all of this is the idea that buyer/supplier relationships should be based upon partnership. Increasingly companies are discovering the advantages that can be gained by seeking mutually beneficial, long-term relationships with suppliers. From the suppliers' point of view, such partnerships can prove formidable barriers to entry for competitors. The more processes are linked between the supplier and the customer the more the mutual dependencies increase and hence the more difficult it is for competitors to break in.

Supply chain management by definition is about the management of relationships across complex networks of companies that, whilst legally independent, are in reality interdependent. Successful supply chains will be those that are governed by a constant search for win-win solutions based upon mutuality and trust. This is not a model of relationships that has typically prevailed in the past. It is one that will have to prevail in the future as supply chain competition becomes the norm.

These four themes of responsiveness, reliability, resilience and relationships provide the basis for successful logistics and supply chain management. They are themes that will be explored in greater detail later in this book.

Summary

This chapter familiarizes the reader with the tenets of competitive strategy and within them the vectors of strategic direction: cost and value advantage. Managers are urged to look beyond the traditional touchstones of the experience curve and the link between relative costs and market share. They are encouraged to seek out and develop logistics and supply chain strategies that exploit numerous latent opportunities to increase efficiency and productivity to deliver significant advances in customer service. They may include efforts to realize better capacity utilization, inventory reduction and/or service improvements through closer co-operation with suppliers. Behind every enduring example of differentiation through service excellence there is evidence of a well thought through strategy for managing the logistics of service delivery.

Vertically integrated businesses continue to be dismembered, refocused and transformed into virtual ones held together not by ownership but by closely integrated core business processes and financial engineering. Instead of rivalry and mistrust within the supply chain, new competitive pressures are demanding speed and flexibility, which themselves require greater openness and trust. In fact the ability to manage process innovation and integration are becoming as important capabilities as product innovation.

References

1. Bowler, R.A., *Logistics and the Failure of the British Army in America 1775–1783*, Princeton University Press, 1975.
2. Shaw, A.W., *Some Problems in Market Distribution*, Harvard University Press, 1915.
3. Aitken, J., *Supply Chain Integration within the Context of a Supplier Association*, Cranfield University, Ph.D. Thesis, 1998.
4. Porter, M.E., *Competitive Strategy*, The Free Press, 1980; *Competitive Advantage*, The Free Press, 1985.
5. See note 4 above.
6. Stalk, G., Evans, P. and Shulman, L.E., 'Competing on Capabilities: The New Rule of Corporate Strategy', *Harvard Business Review*, March–April 1992; Prahalad, C. and Hamel, G., 'The Core Competence of the Corporation', *Harvard Business Review*, May–June 1990.
7. Borsodi, R., *The Distribution Age*, D. Appleton & Co, 1929.
8. Holweg, M. and Pil, F.K., *The Second Century*, MIT Press, 2004.
9. *Ibid.*

Logistics and customer value

This chapter:

Highlights the importance of managing the marketing and logistics interface on an integrated basis.

●

Emphasizes the need to understand the multiple elements of service from the customers' perspective.

●

Explains the importance of customer retention and the lifetime value of a customer.

●

Outlines the idea of a service-driven logistics system based upon identified service priorities and a customer base segmented according to service requirements.

●

Introduces the idea of the 'perfect order' as the basis for measuring service performance.

Earlier in Chapter 1 the mission of logistics management was defined simply in terms of providing the means whereby customers' service requirements are met at lowest cost. In other words the ultimate purpose of any logistics system is to satisfy customers. It is a simple idea that is not always easy to recognize if you are a manager involved in activities such as production scheduling or inventory control which may seem to be some distance away from the marketplace. The fact is of course that everybody in the organization has a stake in customer service. Indeed many successful companies have started to examine their internal service standards in order that everyone who works in the business understands that they must service someone – if they don't, why are they on the payroll?

The objective should be to establish a chain of customers that links people at all levels in the organization directly or indirectly to the marketplace.[1] Xerox is a company that has worked hard to implement the idea of the internal customer. They have even extended the idea to the point of linking bonuses to an index of customer satisfaction. In organizations like Xerox, managing the customer service chain through the business and onwards is the central concern of logistics management.

The marketing and logistics interface

Even though the textbooks describe marketing as the management of the 'Four Ps' – product, price, promotion and place – it is probably true to say that, in practice, most of the emphasis has always been placed on the first three. 'Place', which might better be described in the words of the old cliché, 'the right product, in the right place at the right time', was rarely considered part of mainstream marketing.

There are signs that this view is rapidly changing, however, as the power of customer service as a potential means of differentiation is increasingly recognized. In more and more markets the power of the brand has declined and customers are more willing to accept substitutes; even technology differences between products have been reduced so that it is harder to maintain a competitive edge through the product itself. In situations like this it is customer service that can provide the distinctive difference between one company's offer and that of its competitors.

Two factors have perhaps contributed more than anything else to the growing importance of customer service as a competitive weapon. One is the continual increase in customer expectations; in almost every market the customer is now more demanding, more 'sophisticated' than he or she was, say, 30 years ago. Likewise, in industrial purchasing situations we find that buyers expect higher levels of service from vendors, particularly as more companies convert to just-in-time logistics systems.

The second factor is the slow but inexorable transition towards 'commodity' type markets. By this is meant that increasingly the power of the 'brand' is diminishing as the technologies of competing products converge, thus making product differences difficult to perceive – at least to the average buyer. Take, for example, the current state of the personal computer market. There are many competing models which in reality are substitutable as far as most would-be purchasers are concerned.

Faced with a situation such as this the customer may be influenced by price or by 'image' perceptions but overriding these aspects may well be 'availability' – in other words, is the product in stock, can I have it now? Since availability is clearly an aspect of customer service, we are in effect saying that the power of customer service is paramount in a situation such as this. Nor is it only in consumer markets that we are encountering the force of customer service as a determinant of purchase; there is much evidence from industrial markets of the same phenomenon.

Delivering customer value

Ultimately the success or failure of any business will be determined by the level of customer value that it delivers in its chosen markets. Customer value can be defined quite simply as the difference between the perceived benefits that flow from a purchase or a relationship and the total costs incurred. Another way of expressing the idea is:

$$\text{Customer value} = \frac{\text{Perceptions of benefits}}{\text{Total cost of ownership}}$$

It is better to refer to the 'total cost of ownership' rather than price since so often a purchase or a relationship will involve significant costs other than price. Equally the benefits that are perceived to flow from the purchase or a relationship will often be greater than the tangible product features or functionality. For example, there may be little difference between two competitive products in terms of technical performance, but one may be superior in terms of the customer support that is provided.

One way to define 'competitive advantage' is simply that the successful companies will generally be those that deliver more customer value than their competitors. In other words, their ratio of benefits to costs is superior to other players in that market or segment.

Logistics management is almost unique in its ability to impact both the numerator and the denominator of the customer value ratio. This point becomes clearer if we expand the ratio as follows:

$$\text{Customer value} = \frac{\text{Quality} \times \text{Service}}{\text{Cost} \times \text{Time}}$$

Each of the four constituent elements can briefly be defined as follows:

Quality: The functionality, performance and technical specification of the offer.

Service: The availability, support and commitment provided to the customer.

Cost: The customer's transaction costs including price and life cycle costs.

Time: The time taken to respond to customer requirements, e.g. delivery lead times.

Each of these four elements requires a continuous programme of improvement, innovation and investment to ensure continued competitive advantage.

One company that has built a global leadership position in its markets is Caterpillar, marketing machines and diesel engines for the construction and mining industries. Caterpillar has for many years focused on developing not just its manufacturing capabilities and innovative products but also its customer support and responsiveness. Underpinning these initiatives has been a continuing emphasis on creating superior logistics and supply chain management capabilities. Caterpillar has developed a world-class reputation for customer support, in particular its guarantee to provide 48-hour availability on parts no matter how remote the location. In the industries where Caterpillar's equipment is used, the cost of 'down-time' can be significant, hence the importance of responsive service. Through close partnership with its worldwide network of dealers and distributors and through advanced inventory and information management systems, Caterpillar offers levels of customer support – and thus customer value – that few companies in any industry can match.

What is customer service?

It has been suggested that the role of customer service is to provide 'time and place utility' in the transfer of goods and services between buyer and seller. Put another way, there is no value in the product or service until it is in the hands of the customer or consumer. It follows that making the product or service 'available' is what, in essence, the distribution function of the business is all about. 'Availability' is in itself a complex concept, impacted upon by a galaxy of factors which together constitute customer service. These factors might include delivery frequency and reliability, stock levels and order cycle time, for example. Indeed it could be said that ultimately customer service is determined by the interaction of all those factors that affect the process of making products and services available to the buyer.

In practice, we see that many companies have varying views of customer service. LaLonde and Zinszer[2] in a major study of customer service practices suggested that customer service could be examined under three headings:

1. Pre-transaction elements
2. Transaction elements
3. Post-transaction elements

The pre-transaction elements of customer service relate to corporate policies or programmes, e.g. written statements of service policy, adequacy of organizational structure and system flexibility. The transaction elements are those customer service variables directly involved in per-

Table 2.1 The components of customer service

Pre-transaction elements

For example:

● *Written customer service policy*
(Is it communicated internally and externally? Is it understood? Is it specific and quantified where possible?)

● *Accessibility*
(Are we easy to contact/do business with? Is there a single point of contact?)

● *Organization structure*
(Is there a customer service management structure in place? What level of control do they have over their service process?)

● *System flexibility*
(Can we adapt our service delivery systems to meet particular customer needs?)

Transaction elements

For example:

● *Order cycle time*
(What is the elapsed time from order to delivery? What is the reliability/variation?)

● *Inventory availability*
(What percentage of demand for each item can be met from stock?)

● *Order fill rate*
(What proportion of orders are completely filled within the stated lead time?)

● *Order status information*
(How long does it take us to respond to a query with the required information? Do we inform the customer of problems or do they contact us?)

Post-transaction elements

For example:

● *Availability of spares*
(What are the in-stock levels of service parts?)

● *Call-out time*
(How long does it take for the engineer to arrive and what is the 'first call fix rate'?)

● *Product tracing/warranty*
(Can we identify the location of individual products once purchased? Can we maintain/extend the warranty to customers' expected levels?)

● *Customer complaints, claims, etc.*
(How promptly do we deal with complaints and returns? Do we measure customer satisfaction with our response?)

forming the physical distribution function, e.g. product and delivery reliability. The post-transaction elements of customer service are generally supportive of the product while in use, for instance, product warranty, parts and repair service, procedures for customer complaints and product replacement.

Table 2.1 indicates some of the many elements of customer service under these three headings.

In any particular product/market situation, some of these elements will be more important than others and there may be factors other than those listed above which have a significance in a specific market. Indeed the argument that will be developed later is that it is essential to understand customer service in terms of the differing requirements of different market segments and that no universally appropriate list of elements exists; each market that the company services will attach different importance to different service elements.

It is because of the multivariate nature of customer service and because of the widely differing requirements of specific markets that it is essential for any business to have a clearly identified policy towards customer service. It is surprising perhaps that so few companies have defined policies on customer service, let alone an organization flexible enough to manage and control that service, when it is considered that service can be the most important element in the company's marketing mix. A considerable body of evidence exists that supports the view that if the product or service is not available at the time the customer requires it and a close substitute is available then the sale will be lost to the competition. Even in markets where brand loyalty is strong a stock-out might be sufficient to trigger brand switching.

> It is because of the multivariate nature of customer service and because of the widely differing requirements of specific markets that it is essential for any business to have a clearly identified policy towards customer service.

The impact of out-of-stock

A recent study[3] identified that a significant cost penalty is incurred by both manufacturers and retailers when a stock-out occurs on the shelf. The research found that on a typical day a shopper in the average supermarket will face stock-outs on 8 per cent of items in the categories studied. The reaction of customers when faced with a stock-out was highlighted by the same study. As Figure 2.1 illustrates, over a quarter of shoppers bought a different brand and 37 per cent said they would shop elsewhere for that product. This represents bad news for both the manufacturer and the retailer. Even worse, other research[4] has suggested that over two-thirds of shopping decisions are made at the point of purchase, i.e. the purchase is triggered by seeing the product on the shelf. If the product is not on the shelf then the purchase will not be triggered. Persistent stock-outs can also drive customers away from the brand and/or the store permanently. The potential loss of business for both manufacturers and retailers caused by out-of-stock situations is clearly significant.

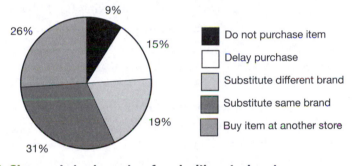

Fig. 2.1 Shopper behaviour when faced with a stock-out
Source: Corsten, D. and Gruen, T., 'Stock-outs cause walkouts', *Harvard Business Review*, May 2004.

In industrial markets, too, the same pressures on purchasing source loyalty seem to be at work. It is perhaps not surprising that as more and more companies adopt 'just-in-time' strategies, with minimal inventories, they require even higher levels of response from suppliers. The demand is for ever shorter delivery lead times and reliable delivery. The pressure on suppliers is further increased as these same customers seek to rationalize their supplier base and to do business with fewer suppliers. Becoming a preferred supplier in any industry today inevitably means that a high priority must be placed on delivering superior customer service.

Many companies have suffered in this new competitive environment because in the past they have focused on the traditional aspects of marketing – product development, promotional activities and price competition.

However, whilst these are still necessary dimensions of a successful marketing strategy they are not sufficient. Equally damaging has been the focus on cost reduction that has driven many companies' operational and logistics strategy – particularly as a result of recession. Cost reduction is a worthy goal as long as it is not achieved at the expense of value creation. Low-cost strategies may lead to *efficient* logistics but not to *effective* logistics. More often than not today the order winning criteria are those elements of the offer that have a clearly identifiable positive impact upon the customers' own value-creating processes.

One powerful way of highlighting the impact that customer service and logistics management can have on marketing effectiveness is outlined in Figure 2.2. The suggestion here is that customer service impacts not only on the ultimate end user but also on intermediate customers such as distributors. Traditionally marketing has focused on the end customer – or consumer – seeking to promote brand values and to generate a 'demand pull' in the marketplace for the company's products. More recently we have come to recognize that this by itself is not sufficient. Because of the swing in power in many marketing channels away from manufacturers and towards the distributor (e.g. the large concentrated retailers) it is now vital to develop the strongest possible relations with such intermediaries – in other words to create a customer franchise as well as a consumer franchise.

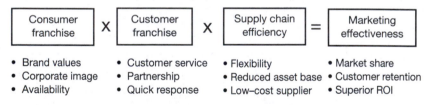

Fig. 2.2 The impact of logistics and customer service on marketing

The impact of both a strong consumer franchise and a customer franchise can be enhanced or diminished by the efficiency of the supplier's logistics system. It is only when all three components are working optimally that marketing effectiveness is maximized. To stress the interdependence of these three components of competitive performance it is suggested that the relationship is multiplicative. In other words the combined impact depends upon the product of all three.

Customer service and customer retention

It will be apparent from what has been said that organizations that compete only on the product's features will find themselves at a severe disadvantage to those companies that augment the basic product with added-value services. It was one of the leading thinkers in marketing, Theodore Levitt, who first said that 'people don't buy products, they buy benefits'. The idea behind this statement is that it is the totality of the 'offer' that delivers customer value. A simple example would be that a finished product in a warehouse is the same as a finished product in the hands of the customer in terms of its tangible features. Clearly, however, the product in the hands of the customer has far more value than the product in the warehouse. Distribution service in this case has been the source of added value. Figure 2.3 develops this idea with the concept of the 'service surround'.

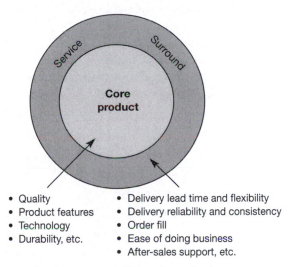

- Quality
- Product features
- Technology
- Durability, etc.

- Delivery lead time and flexibility
- Delivery reliability and consistency
- Order fill
- Ease of doing business
- After-sales support, etc.

Fig. 2.3 Using service to augment the core product

At the centre is the core product, which is the basic product as it leaves the factory. The outer 'halo' represents all the added value that customer service and logistics provide. Clearly it is not only customer service and logistics activity that add value; in many cases advertising, branding and the packaging can all enhance the perceived value of the product to the customer. However, it is increasingly evident, as we have seen, that it takes more than branding to differentiate the product.

What impact does the service surround have on the customer?

One of the classic definitions of marketing is that it is concerned with 'getting and keeping customers'. In practice, if we look at where most organizations' marketing efforts focus, it is on the 'getting' of customers, rather than on the 'keeping' of them. Thus an examination of the typical marketing plan will show a bias towards increasing market share rather than towards customer retention. Whilst new customers are always welcome in any business it has to be realized that an existing customer can provide a higher profit contribution and has the potential to grow in terms of the value and frequency of purchases.

The importance of customer retention is underlined by the concept of the 'lifetime value' of a customer. The lifetime value of a customer is calculated as follows:

Lifetime value = Average transaction value × Yearly frequency of purchase × Customer 'life expectancy'

Clearly if customers can be persuaded to remain loyal to a supplier, their lifetime value can be significantly increased. A further benefit comes from the fact that the longer the customer stays with us the more profitable they become. A study by consulting company Bain and Co[5] found higher customer retention rates correlated strongly with profitability. The reasons for this are that a retained customer typically costs less to sell to and to service. Also as the relationship develops there is a greater likelihood that they will give a greater part of their business to a supplier whom they are prepared to treat as a partner. This is the idea of 'share of wallet' whereby the goal is to increase the total spend that is captured by the company. Furthermore, satisfied customers tell others and thus the chance increases that further business from new customers will be generated through this source.

A simple measure of customer retention is to ask the question: 'How many of the customers that we had 12 months ago do we still have today?' This measure is the real test of customer retention. It can be extended to include the value of purchases made by the retained customer base to assess how successful the company has been in increasing the level of purchasing from these accounts (see Figure 2.4).

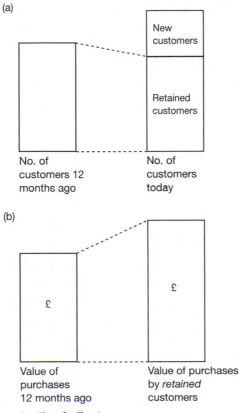

(a)

New customers

Retained customers

No. of customers 12 months ago

No. of customers today

(b)

£

£

Value of purchases 12 months ago

Value of purchases by *retained* customers

Fig. 2.4 Customer retention indicators

A prime objective of any customer service strategy should be to enhance customer retention. Whilst customer service obviously also plays a role in winning new customers it is perhaps the most potent weapon in the marketing armoury for the keeping of customers.

There is rapidly emerging a new focus in marketing and logistics on the creation of 'relationships' with customers. The idea is that we should seek to create such a level of satisfaction with customers that they do not feel it necessary even to consider alternative offers or suppliers. Many markets are characterized by a high level of 'churn' or 'promiscuity' amongst the customer base. In these markets customers will buy one brand on one occasion and then are just as likely to buy another on the next occasion.

The principle behind 'relationship marketing' is that the organization should consciously strive to develop marketing strategies to maintain and strengthen customer loyalty.[6] So, for example, an airline might develop a frequent-flyer programme, or a credit card company might award points based upon the value of purchases made with the card that can then be redeemed for cash or awards. At the other extreme a company like IBM will consciously seek to develop long-term relationships with its customers through training programmes, client seminars, frequent customer communication and so on.

Market-driven supply chains

Most traditional supply chains were designed to optimize the internal operations of the supplying company. Thus a manufacturer might be motivated to establish supply and distribution arrangements that would enable production efficiencies to be maximized. Typically this would entail manufacturing in large batches, shipping in large quantities and buffering the factory, both upstream and downstream, with inventory. In this way the goal of becoming a 'low-cost producer' could be achieved.

Whilst this approach was fine from the perspective of the manufacturing organization, it clearly did not come anywhere close to being 'customer-centric' in the sense of designing the supply chain around the needs of the customer. With the continuing transfer of power in the distribution channel from the producer to the consumer, this conventional philosophy has become less and less appropriate. Now, instead of designing supply chains from the 'factory outwards' the challenge is to design them from the 'customer backwards'.

This new perspective sees the consumer not at the end of the supply chain but at its start. In effect this is the philosophical difference between supply chain management and what more properly might be called 'demand chain management'.

As one author has suggested:

> Managing demand chains is ... fundamentally different to managing supply chains. It requires turning the supply chain on its head, and taking the end user as the organization's point of departure and not its final destination.

Baker[7]

Figure 2.5 suggests an appropriate sequence of actions to create a market-driven supply chain.

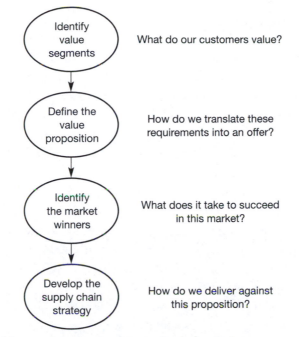

Identify value segments	What do our customers value?
Define the value proposition	How do we translate these requirements into an offer?
Identify the market winners	What does it take to succeed in this market?
Develop the supply chain strategy	How do we deliver against this proposition?

Fig. 2.5 Linking customer value to supply chain strategy

This sequence begins with an understanding of the value that customers seek in the market in which the company competes. This customer insight will enable the identification of the real market segmentation, i.e. the clusters of customers who share the same value preferences. The Spanish fashion chain Zara provides an excellent example of how market understanding and supply chain excellence can create real value for its target customers.

ZARA

Zara is one of world's most successful and dynamic apparel businesses. It is the flagship of Inditex, a vertically integrated retail and manufacturing group based in Galicia in north-west Spain. The first Zara store opened in the city of La Coruña in 1975, the brain child of Amanico Ortega, owner of a small clothing factory. Ortega was looking for a better way to run his business, one which would avoid the inefficiency of making clothes that might not sell. In the intervening decades more

▶

▶ than 600 Zara stores – most owned directly by the company – have opened throughout Spain and 43 other countries worldwide.

Zara produces and sells highly fashionable apparel for men, women and children, but its core customers are fashion conscious 18–35-year-old women. It offers them the very latest design trends at affordable mass-market prices. Physical product quality is good enough to see out the season, but not necessarily longer. By then the same customers will have moved onto the next 'hot' look. The customers are loyal, frequent shoppers who visit a Zara store on average 17 times per year.[1] To retain their interest, stock is constantly varied and updated. New deliveries arrive on a twice weekly basis. Few products are available in store for more than a month, adding a sense of exclusivity and urgency to buy. The stores themselves are sited in fashionable prestige locations, their interiors are smart, fresh, modern and regularly refurbished to retain their contemporary appeal.

Zara is a design-sensitive, but not designer-led operation. The company does not seek to set new trends itself, just to be a very fast and flexible follower. It employs a large cadre of design staff who interpret the latest in international fashion trends, often identified by 'cool hunters' who glean inspiration through visits to fashion shows, competitors' stores, university campuses, pubs, cafes and clubs, plus any other venues or events deemed to be relevant to the lifestyles of the target customers. The team's understanding of directional fashion trends is further guided by regular inflows of sales data and other information from all of the company's stores and sites around the world.

Zara's positioning puts it in direct competition with some of the best known operators in the apparel industry, including US-based The Limited and Gap, as well as the highly successful vertically integrated European retailers, Mango, Mexx and the Italian giant Benetton. All are exponents of quick response logistics. However, Zara's rapid growth and ongoing success in such a fiercely competitive environment is testament to its ability to implement an operating strategy – based on the dual objectives of minimizing stock and responding quickly to market needs[2] – even more effectively than its internationally acclaimed rivals.

The process of supplying goods to the stores begins with the cross-functional teams – comprising fashion, commercial and retail specialists –

working within Zara's Design Department at the company's headquarters in La Coruña. Fashion specialists within the Design Department are responsible for the initial designs, fabric selection and choice of prints and colours. It is then up to the team's commercial management specialists to ascertain the likely commercial viability of the items proposed. If the design is accepted – two-thirds are not – the commercial specialists proceed to negotiate with suppliers, agree purchase prices, analyze costs and margins, and fix a standard cross-currency price position for the garment. Store prices reflect the price position agreed for goods sold in Spain, plus the cost of distribution. Hence a shopper in the UK will pay 50 per cent more for the same item as a shopper in Spain. For customers in the US and Japan the price is more than double.

The size of the production run – i.e. the number of garments required – and launch dates (the latter vary between countries in accordance with custom and climate) are also determined at this point.

Approximately 20 per cent of merchandise – items with the broadest and least transient appeal – is imported as finished goods from low-cost manufacturing centres, mostly in Asia. The rest is produced by quick response. Around 50 per cent of all Zara's merchandise is manufactured in-house using the company's own highly automated factories and a network of smaller contractors clustered around La Coruña. The remainder is produced elsewhere in Spain or in other European countires.

Raw materials are procured through the company's buying offices in Europe and Asia, with material coming in from Mauritius, New Zealand, Australia, Morocco, China, Korea, India, Turkey, Italy and Germany. The global sourcing policy, using a broad supplier base, provides the widest possible selection of fashion fabrics, while reducing the risk of dependence on any source or supplier. Approximately half of the material is purchased in 'gray', to be dyed or printed and finished by one of Inditex's other Galician subsidiaries. The turnaround time for this process is only one week, illustrating how high production costs in Europe are offset by the benefits of proximity and control.

Zara's manufacturing systems are similar in many ways to those developed and employed so successfully by Benetton in northern Italy, but refined using ideas developed in conjunction with Toyota. Only those operations which enhance cost-efficiency through economies of

▶

▶ scale are conducted in-house (such as dying, cutting, labelling and packaging). All other manufacturing activities, including the labour-intensive finishing stages, are completed by networks of hundreds of small subcontractors, each specializing in one particular part of the production process or garment type. These subcontractors work exclusively for Zara's parent, Inditex SA. In return they receive the necessary technological, financial and logistical support required to achieve stringent time and quality targets. Inventory costs are kept to a minimum because Zara pays only for the completed garments.

Finished goods are forwarded to the company's two distribution centres in La Coruña and Zaragoza where they are labelled, price-tagged (all items carry international price tags showing the price in relevant currencies) and packed. From there they are carried by third-party contractors by road and/or air to their penultimate destinations. Road is used for journeys of 24 hours or less, while airfreight is used for longer distances. All deliveries are completed within 48 hours.

In an industry where lead times of many months are common, Zara has reduced its lead time for more than half of the garments it sells to a level unmatched by any of its European or North American competitors. The whole design, production and delivery cycle takes only four to five weeks. Design modifications and restocking of existing products, if required, is completed within 14 days. The system is flexible enough to cope with sudden changes in demand and shop-by-shop stock allocations are calculated centrally, rather than in-store, because production is always kept at a level slightly below expected sales to keep stock moving. True to its original objectives, the company has consciously opted for undersupply, viewing it as a lesser evil than holding slow-moving or obsolete stock.

References
1. Bonace, Jaime and Cervino, Julio, 'Global Integration Without Expatriates', *Human Resource Management Journal*, Vol. 7, No. 3, 1997, pp. 89–100.
2. Ghemawat, P. and Nueno, J.L., *Zara: Fast fashion*, Harvard Business School Publishing, Boston, MA, 2002, p. 15

Identifying customers' service needs

It is important to remember that no two customers will ever be exactly the same in terms of their service requirements. However, it will often be the case that customers will fall into groups or 'segments' that are characterized by a broad similarity of service needs. These groupings might be thought of as 'service segments'. The logistics planner needs therefore to know just what the service issues are that differentiate customers. Market research can be of great assistance in understanding this service segmentation and it is often surprising to see how little formal research is conducted in this crucial area.

How might such a research programme be implemented?

The first point to emphasize is that customer service is perceptual. Whatever our own 'hard' internal measures of service might say our service performance is, perceptions are the reality. We might use measures which, whilst providing useful measures of productivity, do not actually reflect the things the customer values. For example, whilst 'stock availability' is a widespread internal measure of performance, a more appropriate external measure from the customer's viewpoint could be 'on-time delivery'. Hence it is critical that we develop a set of service criteria that are meaningful to customers.

The approach to service segmentation suggested here follows a three-stage process:

1 Identify the key components of customer service as seen by customers themselves.
2 Establish the relative importance of those service components to customers.
3 Identify 'clusters' of customers according to similarity of service preferences.

1 Identifying the key components of customer service

A common failing in business is to assume that 'we know what our customers want'. However, the truth is that it is so easy to become divorced from the reality of the marketplace when management is consumed with the day-to-day pressures of running a business. How should we know which aspects of service are most highly rated by the customer? Given the complexity of the market that the typical company serves how might it better understand the segmentation of those markets in terms of service requirements? What does it take for a company to become the supplier of choice?

Clearly it is important to develop an understanding of the service needs of customers through detailed research.

The first step in research of this type is to identify the key sources of influence upon the purchase decision. If, for example, we are selling components to a manufacturer, who will make the decision on the choice of supplier? This is not always an easy question to answer as in many cases there will be several people involved. The purchasing manager of the company to which we are selling may only be acting as an agent for others within the firm. In other cases his influence will be much greater. Alternatively if we are manufacturing products for sale through retail outlets, is the decision to stock made centrally or by individual store managers? The answers can often be supplied by the sales force. The sales representative should know from experience who are the decision makers.

Given that a clear indication of the source of decision-making power can be gained the customer service researcher at least knows who to research. The question remains as to which elements of the vendor's total marketing offering have what effect upon the purchase decision.

Ideally once the decision-making unit in a specific market has been identified, an initial, small-scale research programme should be initiated based upon personal interviews with a representative sample of buyers. The purpose of these interviews is to elicit, in the language of the customers, firstly, the importance they attach to customer service vis-à-vis the other marketing mix elements such as price, product quality, promotion, etc., and secondly, the specific importance they attach to the individual components of customer service.

The importance of this initial step in measuring customer service is that relevant and meaningful measures of customer service are generated by the customers themselves. Once these dimensions are defined we can identify the relative importance of each one and the extent to which different types of customer are prepared to trade off one aspect of service for another.

2 Establishing the relative importance of customer service components

One of the simplest ways of discovering the importance a customer attaches to each element of customer service is to take the components generated by means of the process described in step 1 and to ask a representative sample of customers to rank order them from the 'most important' to the 'least important'. In practice this is difficult, particularly with a large number of components, and would not give any insight into the relative importance of each element. Alternatively a form of rating scale could be used. For example, the respondents could be asked to place a weight from 1 to 10 against each component according to how much importance they attached to each element. The problem here is that respondents will tend to rate most of the components as highly important, especially since those components were generated on the grounds of importance to customers in the first place. A partial solution is to ask the respondent to allocate a total of 100 points amongst all the elements listed, according to perceived importance. However, this is a fairly daunting task for the respondent and can often result in an arbitrary allocation.

Fortunately a relatively recent innovation in consumer research technology now enables us to evaluate very simply the implicit importance that a customer attaches to the separate elements of customer service. The technique is based around the concept of trade-off and can best be illustrated by an example from everyday life. In considering, say, the purchase of a new car we might desire specific attributes, e.g. performance in terms of speed and acceleration, economy in terms of petrol consumption, size in terms of passenger and luggage capacity and, of course, low price. However, it is unlikely that any one car will meet all of these requirements so we are forced to trade off one or more of these attributes against the others.

The same is true of the customer faced with alternative options of distribution service. The buyer might be prepared to sacrifice a day or two on lead time in order to gain delivery reliability, or to trade-off order completeness against improvements in order entry, etc. Essentially the trade-off technique works by presenting the respondent with feasible combinations of customer service elements and asking for a rank order of preference for those combinations. Computer analysis then determines the implicit importance attached by the respondent to each service element.[8]

3 Identifying customer service segments

Now that we have determined the importance attached by different respondents to each of the service attributes previously identified, the final step is to see if any similarities of preference emerge. If one group of respondents, for example, has a clearly distinct set of priorities from another then it would be reasonable to think of them both as different service segments.

How can these customer service segments be identified? One technique that has been successfully used in this connection is cluster analysis. Cluster analysis is a computer-based method for looking across a set of data and seeking to 'match' respondents across as many dimensions as possible. Thus if two respondents completed the step 2 trade-off analysis in a similar way their importance scores on the various service dimensions would be similar and hence the cluster analysis would assign them to the same group.

One study in an industrial market suggested that the traditional way of segmenting customers according to 'Standard Industrial Classification' (SIC) had little relevance to purchasing behaviour. The classic categorization of customers according to industry sector did not correlate with the attributes they sought from suppliers. Instead it seemed that some companies were very time-sensitive in terms of delivery reliability – a 'just-in-time' segment – regardless of the industry they were in. In the same way there was a very clear 'price' segment, which also cut across conventional industrial classifications. A further segment was much more responsive to a 'relationship' approach, valuing technical support and close supplier liaison much more highly. As a result of this research the supplier was better able to focus its marketing efforts and to re-engineer its supply chain strategy to achieve a better match with customer requirements.

The challenge to logistics management is to create appropriate supply chain solutions to meet the needs of these different value segments. More than likely there will be the need for multiple supply chain solutions since 'one size will not fit all'. This issue will be dealt with in detail in Chapter 4 where the concept of supply chain agility is discussed.

Defining customer service objectives

The whole purpose of supply chain management and logistics is to provide customers with the level and quality of service that they require and to do so at less cost to the total supply chain. In developing a market-driven logistics strategy the aim is to achieve 'service excellence' in a consistent and cost-effective way.

> The whole purpose of supply chain management and logistics is to provide customers with the level and quality of service that they require and to do so at less cost to the total supply chain.

The definition of appropriate service objectives is made easier if we adopt the concept of the *perfect order*. The perfect order is achieved when the customer's service requirements are met in full. Clearly such a definition is specific to individual customers, but it is usually possible to group customers into segments and then to identify, along the lines described earlier, the key service needs of those segments. The perfect order is achieved only when each of those service needs is met to the customer's satisfaction.

The measure of service is therefore defined as the percentage of occasions on which the customer's requirements are met in full. Normally this percentage would be measured across all customers over a period of time. However, it can also be used to measure service performance at the individual customer level and indeed at any level, e.g. segment, country or by distribution centre.

One frequently encountered measure of the perfect order is 'on-time, in-full' (OTIF). An extension of this is on-time, in-full and error-free. This latter element relates to documentation, labelling and damage to the product or its packaging. To calculate the actual service level using the perfect order concept requires performance on each element to be monitored and then the percentage achievement on each element to be multiplied together.

For example, if the actual performance across all orders for the last 12 months was as follows:

On-time : 90%
In-full   : 80%
Error-free : 70%

the actual perfect order achievement would be:

$$90\% \times 80\% \times 70\% = 50.4\%$$

In other words the likelihood that a perfect order was achieved during the period under review was only 50.4 per cent!

The cost benefit of customer service

All companies have to face a basic fact: there will be significant differences in profitability between customers. Not only do different customers buy different quantities of different products, but the cost to service these customers will typically vary considerably. This issue will be explored more fully in Chapter 3.

The 80/20 rule will often be found to hold: 80 per cent of the profits of the business come from 20 per cent of the customers. Furthermore, 80 per cent of the total costs to serve will be generated from 20 per cent of the customers (but probably not the same 20 per cent!). Whilst the proportion may not be exactly 80/20 it will generally be in that region. This is the so-called Pareto Law, named after a nineteenth century Italian economist.

The challenge to customer service management therefore is, firstly, to identify the real profitability of customers and then, secondly, to develop strategies for service that will improve the profitability of all customers. What has to be recognized is that there are costs as well as benefits in providing customer service and that therefore the appropriate level and mix of service will need to vary by customer type.

The basic relationship between the level of service and the cost is often depicted as a steeply rising curve (Figure 2.6).

The curve assumes that demand for the item is 'normally' distributed, i.e. it takes on the classic bell-shape. A feature of the normal distribution is that once its two key parameters, the mean ($\bar{x}$) and standard deviation (σ), are known, the probability of a given value occurring can be easily calculated. Thus, as Figure 2.7 shows, if the distribution depicted describes daily sales for a particular product, it can be calculated that on approximately 68 per cent of occasions total demand would be within plus or minus one standard deviation either side of the mean; on approximately 95 per cent of occasions total demand would lie within plus or minus two standard deviations either side of the mean and on 99 per cent of occasions three standard deviations either side of the mean.

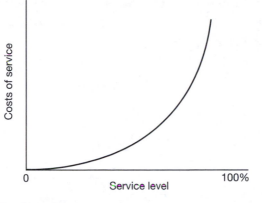

Fig. 2.6 The costs of service

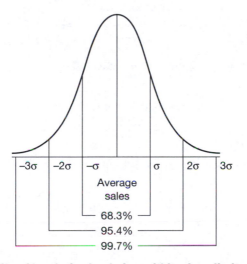

Fig. 2.7 Probability of level of sales being within given limits

In calculating how much safety stock is required the inventory manager is only concerned with those occasions when demand is greater than average. If sales are approximately normally distributed, demand will be lower than average approximately 50 per cent of the time, and thus a 50 per cent service level would be maintained with no safety stock. It is on those occasions when demand exceeds the average that safety stock is required. In other words we must focus attention on the area of the curve to the right of the mean. Thus, by setting a stock level one standard deviation greater than the mean, the manager can achieve a service level of approximately 84 per cent. By setting the level two

67

standard deviations greater than the mean the service level would be approximately 98 per cent and with three standard deviations it would be 99.9 per cent (Figure 2.8).

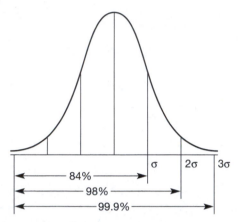

Fig. 2.8 Service levels and the normal distribution

What this highlights is that as the desired service level rises, it takes a disproportionate investment in inventory to achieve small incremental improvements in availability.

The table below illustrates this effect:

Inventory level	Service level
$\bar{x}$	50%
$\bar{x} + \sigma$	84%
$\bar{x} + 2\sigma$	98%
$\bar{x} + 3\sigma$	99.9%

- If inventory equivalent to average expected daily demand ($\bar{x}$) is held then the service level would be 50 per cent.
- If safety stock equivalent to one standard deviation of demand (σ) is held then the service level would be 84 per cent, etc.

However, if it is possible to find alternative service strategies for servicing customers, say, for example, by speeding up the flow of information about customer requirements and by using faster modes of transport, then the same level of service can be achieved with less inventory – in effect pushing the curve to the right (Figure 2.9). This is the idea of substituting information and responsiveness for inventory. In other words if we can gain earlier warning of customer requirements and our lead times are short, then we can reduce our reliance on inventory.

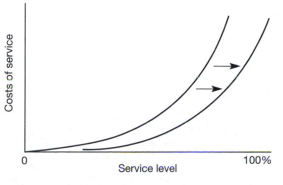

Fig. 2.9 Shifting the costs of service

Setting customer service priorities

Whilst it should be the objective of any logistics system to provide all customers with the level of service that has been agreed or negotiated, it must be recognized that there will inevitably need to be service priorities. In this connection the Pareto Law, or 80/20 rule, can provide us with the basis for developing a more cost-effective service strategy. Fundamentally, the service issue is that since not all our customers are equally profitable nor are our products equally profitable, should not the highest service be given to key customers and key products? Since we can assume that money spent on service is a scarce resource then we should look upon the service decision as a resource allocation issue.

Figure 2.10 shows how a typical company might find its profits varying by customer and by product.

The curve is traditionally divided into three categories: the top 20 per cent of products and customers by profitability are the 'A' category; the next 50 per cent or so are labelled 'B'; and the final 30 per cent are category 'C'. The precise split between the categories is arbitrary as the shape of the distribution will vary from business to business and from market to market.

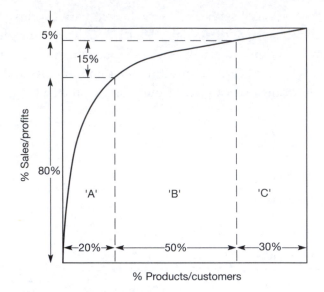

Fig. 2.10 The 'Pareto' or 80/20 rule

The appropriate measure should be profit rather than sales revenue or volume. The reason for this is that revenue and volume measures might disguise considerable variation in costs. In the case of customers this cost is the 'cost to serve' and we will later suggest an approach to measuring customer profitability. In the case of product profitability we must also be careful that we are identifying the appropriate service-related costs as they differ by product. One of the problems here is that conventional accounting methods do not help in the identification of these costs.

What we should be concerned to do at this stage in the analysis is to identify the contribution to profit that each product (at the individual stock keeping unit (SKU) level) makes. By contribution we mean the difference between total revenue accruing and the directly attributable costs that attach as the product moves through the logistics system.

Looking first at differences in product profitability, what use might be made of the A,B,C categorization? Firstly it can be used as the basis for classic inventory control whereby the highest level of service (as represented by safety stock) is provided for the 'A' products, a slightly lower level for the 'B' products and lower still for the 'Cs'. Thus we might seek to follow the stock holding policy shown below:

Product category	Stock availability
A	99%
B	97%
C	90%

Alternatively, and probably to be preferred, we might differentiate the stock holding by holding the 'A' items as close as possible to the customer and the 'B' and 'C' items further up the supply chain. The savings in stock holding costs achieved by consolidating the 'B' and 'C' items as a result of holding them at fewer locations would normally cover the additional cost of despatching them to the customer by a faster means of transportation (e.g. overnight delivery).

Perhaps the best way to manage product service levels is to take into account both the profit contribution and the individual product demand.

We can bring both these measures together in the form of a simple matrix in Figure 2.11. The matrix can be explained as follows.

Quadrant 1: Seek cost reductions

Because these products have high volume it would suggest that they are in frequent demand. However, they are also low in profit contribution and the priority should be to re-examine product and logistics costs to see if there is any scope for enhancing profit.

Quadrant 2: Provide high availability

These products are frequently demanded and they are more profitable. We should offer the highest level of service on these items by holding them as close to the customer as possible and with high availability. Because there will be relatively few of these items we can afford to follow such a strategy.

Quadrant 3: Review

Products in this category should be regularly appraised with a view to deletion from the range. They do not contribute to profits (or at least only marginally) and they are slow movers from a sales point of view. Unless they play a strategic role in the product portfolio of the firm then there is probably a strong case for dropping them.

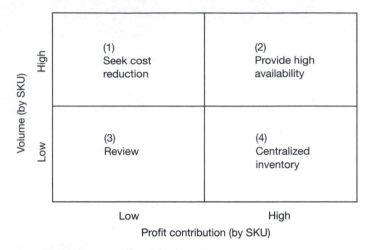

Fig. 2.11 Managing product service levels

Quadrant 4: Centralized inventory

Because these products are highly profitable but only sell at a relatively slow rate they are candidates for centralized management. In other words, they should be kept in some central location, as far back up the supply chain as possible in order to reduce the total inventory investment, and then shipped by express transport direct to customers.

This concept of service prioritization by product can be extended to include customer priorities. Because the same 80/20 rule applies to customers as it does to products, it makes sense to focus resources on key accounts as well as key products.

Figure 2.12 shows that if the 80/20 rule applies both to products and customers then all businesses are actually very dependent upon a very few customers buying a few high profit lines. Indeed the arithmetic is easy:

> 20% of customers buying 20% of the products
> = 4% of all customer/product transactions

Which provides:

> 80% of 80% of total profit = 64%

In other words, just 4 per cent of transactions (measured order line by order line) gives us 64 per cent of all our profit!

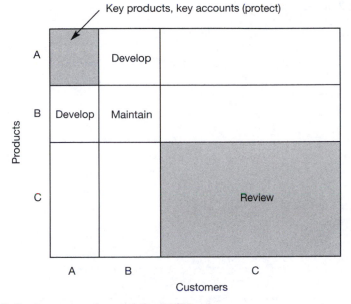

Fig. 2.12 Customer service and the 80/20 rule

How can we make use of this important fact? The first thing is obviously to offer the highest levels of service and availability to key customers ordering key products. At the other end of the spectrum we should constantly review the less profitable customers and the less profitable products. In between there is scope for a degree of pragmatism, perhaps based upon the 'critical value' of an item to the customer. This is particularly relevant when developing a service strategy for spare parts. The idea is that if certain items are essential for, say, the operation of a machine where the downtime costs are high then those parts would be accorded a high critical value. If appropriate a 'weight' could be assigned on the basis of criticality and the 80/20 ranking based on profit could be adjusted accordingly. Table 2.2 provides an example.

Table 2.2 Critical value analysis

Products	Profitability rank order	Critical value to customers			Rank × Critical value	Order of priority for service
		1	2	3		
C	1			x	3	1
P	2		x		4	2 =
R	3		x		6	5
B	4	x			4	2 =
X	5	x			5	4
Y	6			x	18	8
Z	7		x		14	7
H	8	x			8	6
J	9			x	27	10
K	10		x		20	9

Critical values: 1 = Sale lost
2 = Slight delay acceptable
3 = Longer delay acceptable

Setting service standards

Obviously if service performance is to be controlled then it must be against predetermined standards.

Ultimately the only standard to be achieved is 100 per cent conformity to customer expectations. This requires a clear and objective understanding of the customers' requirements and at the same time places an obligation upon the supplier to shape those expectations. In other words there must be a complete match between what the customer expects and what we are willing and able to provide. This may require negotiation of service standards since clearly it is in neither party's interest to provide service levels that would lead to a long-term deterioration in profitability – either for the supplier or the customer.

What are the customer service elements for which standards should be set?

To be effective these standards must be defined by the customers themselves. This requires customer research and competitive benchmarking studies to be conducted so that an objective definition of customer service for each market segment may be identified.

However, for the moment we can indicate some of the key areas where standards are essential:

- Order cycle time
- Stock availability
- Order-size constraints
- Ordering convenience
- Frequency of delivery
- Delivery reliability
- Documentation quality
- Claims procedure
- Order completeness
- Technical support
- Order status information

Let us examine each of these in turn.

Order cycle time

This is the elapsed time from customer order to delivery. Standards should be defined against the customer's stated requirements.

Stock availability

This relates to the percentage of demand for a given line item (stock keeping unit, or SKU) that can be met from available inventory.

Order-size constraints

More and more customers seek just-in-time deliveries of small quantities. Do we have the flexibility to cope with the range of customer demands likely to be placed upon us?

Ordering convenience

Are we accessible and easy to do business with? How are we seen from the customers' viewpoint? Do our systems talk to their systems?

Frequency of delivery

A further manifestation of the move to just-in-time is that customers require more frequent deliveries within closely specified time windows. Again it is flexibility of response that should be the basis for the performance standard.

Delivery reliability

What proportion of total orders are delivered on time? It is a reflection not just of delivery performance but also of stock availability and order processing performance.

Documentation quality

What is the error rate on invoices, delivery notes and other customer communications? Is the documentation 'user friendly'? A surprisingly large number of service failures are from this source.

Claims procedure

What is the trend in claims? What are their causes? How quickly do we deal with complaints and claims? Do we have procedures for 'service recovery'?

Order completeness

What proportion of orders do we deliver complete, i.e. no back orders or part shipments?

Technical support

What support do we provide customers with after the sale? If appropriate do we have standards for call-out time and first-time fix rate on repairs?

Order status information

Can we inform customers at any time on the status of their order? Do we have 'hotlines' or their equivalent? Do we have procedures for informing customers of potential problems on stock availability or delivery?

All of these issues are capable of quantification and measurement against customer requirements. Similarly they are all capable of comparison against competitive performance.

It must be recognized that from the customer's perspective there are only two levels of service – either 100 per cent or 0 per cent. In other words either the customer gets exactly what they ordered at the time and place required or they don't. It must also be remembered that 100 per cent order fill rates are extremely difficult to achieve – the laws of probability see to that! If there are ten items on a particular order and each item is carried in stock at the 95 per cent level of availability then the probability that the complete order can be filled is $(0.95)^{10}$, which is 0.599. In other words, just over a 50/50 chance that we can satisfy the complete order.

Table 2.3 shows how the probability of order fill diminishes as the number of items on the customer order increases.

Table 2.3 Probability of a complete order

Number of lines in order	Line item availability			
	90%	92%	94%	95%
1	.900	.920	.940	.950
2	.810	.846	.884	.903
3	.729	.779	.831	.857
4	.656	.716	.781	.815
5	.590	.659	.734	.774
6	.531	.606.	.690	.735
7	.478	.558	.648	.698
8	.430	.513	.610	.663
9	.387	.472	.573	.630
10	.348	.434	.538	.599
11	.314	.399	.506	.569
12	.282	.368	.476	.540
14	.225	.311	.400	.488
15	.206	.286	.395	.463
16	.195	.263	.372	.440
17	.167	.243	.349	.418
18	.150	.223	.328	.397
19	.135	.205	.309	.377
20	.122	.185	.290	.358

Ideally organizations should establish standards and monitor performance across a range of customer service measures. For example, using the pre-transaction, transaction and post-transaction framework, the following measures provide valuable indicators of performance:

Pre-transaction
- Stock availability
- Target delivery dates
- Response times to queries

Transaction
- Order fill rate
- On-time delivery

- Back orders by age
- Shipment delays
- Product substitutions

Post-transaction
- First call fix rate
- Customer complaints
- Returns/claims
- Invoice errors
- Service parts availability

It is possible to produce a composite index based upon multiple service measures and this can be a useful management tool, particularly for communicating service performance internally. Such an index is shown in Table 2.4 where the weight attached to each service element reflects the importance that the customers attach to those elements.

Table 2.4 Composite service index

Service element	Importance weight (i)	Performance level (ii)	Weighted score (i) × (ii)
Order fill rate	30%	70%	.21
On-time delivery	25%	60%	.15
Order accuracy	25%	80%	.20
Invoice accuracy	10%	90%	.09
Returns	10%	95%	.095
		Index =	0.745

Customer service is one of the most powerful elements available to the organization in its search for competitive advantage and yet it is often the least well managed. The key message of this chapter has been that the quality of customer service performance depends in the main upon the skill with which the logistics system is designed and managed. Put very simply, the output of all logistics activity is customer service.

Summary

Ultimately all businesses compete through seeking to deliver superior customer value and logistics processes provide the means by which customer service is delivered.

Customer service is a multi-faceted concept. It is increasingly important as a means of gaining and maintaining differentiation in the marketplace. Equally, since no two customers are alike it must be recognized that service must be tailored to meet the needs of different customers.

Logistics management can play a key role in enhancing customer lifetime value through increasing customer satisfaction and enhanced customer retention. To achieve this will require the development of a market-driven logistics strategy and the redefinition of service objectives based upon customers' specific requirements. 'Perfect order' achievement should form the basis for the measurement of service performance and the creation of service standard.

References

1. Schonberger, R.J., *Building a Chain of Customers*, The Free Press, 1990.
2. LaLonde, B.J. and Zinszer, P.H., *Customer Service: Meaning and Measurement*, National Council of Physical Distribution Management, Chicago, 1976.
3. Corsten, D. and Gruen, T., 'Stock-Outs Cause Walkouts', *Harvard Business Review*, May 2004.
4. Bayle, M., 'Brand Killers', *Fortune*, 11 August 2003, pp. 51–56.
5. Reichheld, F.A., 'Loyalty and the Renaissance of Marketing', *Marketing Management*, Vol. 2, No. 4, 1994, pp. 10–21.
6. Christopher, M., Payne, A. and Ballantyne, D., *Relationship Marketing: Creating Stakeholder Value*, Butterworth-Heinemann, 2002.
7. Baker, S., *New Consumer Marketing*, John Wiley & Sons, 2003.
8. Christopher, M.C. and Peck, H., *Marketing Logistics*, 2nd Edition, Butterworth-Heinemann, 2003.

Measuring logistics costs and performance

This chapter:

Outlines the many ways in which logistics management can impact on overall return on investment and, ultimately, shareholder value.

●

Explains the rationale behind total cost analysis, a systematic logistics-oriented cost accounting system and the principal requirements for an effective logistics costing system.

●

Emphasizes the importance of customer profitability analysis based upon an understanding of the 'cost-to-serve'.

●

Introduces the concept of direct product profitability and underlines the need to understand the customers' logistics costs.

●

Highlights the need to identify the cost drivers in the logistics pipeline and to replace traditional forms of cost allocation with more appropriate methods.

The costs of satisfying customer demand can be significant and yet, surprisingly, they are not always fully understood by organizations. One reason for this is that traditional accounting systems tend to be focused around understanding *product* costs rather than *customer* costs. Whilst logistics costs will vary by company and by industry, across the economy as a whole that total cost of logistics as a percentage of gross domestic product is estimated to be close to 10 per cent in the US[1] and in other countries costs of similar magnitudes will be encountered.

However, logistics activity does not just generate cost, it also generates revenue through the provision of availability – thus it is important to understand the profit impact of logistics and supply chain decisions. At the same time logistics activity requires resources in the form of fixed capital and working capital and so there are financial issues to be considered when supply chain strategies are devised.

Logistics and the bottom line

Today's turbulent business environment has produced an ever greater awareness amongst managers of the financial dimension of decision making. 'The bottom line' has become the driving force which, perhaps erroneously, determines the direction of the company. In some cases this has led to a limiting, and potentially dangerous, focus on the short term. Hence we find that investment in brands, in R&D and in capacity may well be curtailed if there is no prospect of an immediate payback.

Just as powerful an influence on decision making and management horizons is cash flow. Strong positive cash flow has become as much a desired goal of management as profit.

The third financial dimension to decision making is resource utilization and specifically the use of fixed and working capital. The pressure in most organizations is to improve the productivity of capital – 'to make the assets sweat'. In this regard it is usual to utilize the concept of return on investment (ROI). Return on investment is the ratio between the net profit and the capital that was employed to produce that profit, thus:

$$ROI = \frac{\text{Profit}}{\text{Capital employed}}$$

This ratio can be further expanded:

$$ROI = \frac{\text{Profit}}{\text{Sales}} \times \frac{\text{Sales}}{\text{Capital employed}}$$

It will be seen that ROI is the product of two ratios: the first, profit/sales, being commonly referred to as the margin and the second, sales/capital employed, termed capital turnover or asset turn. Thus to gain improvement on ROI one or other, or both, of these ratios must increase. Typically many companies will focus their main attention on the margin in their attempt to drive up ROI, yet it can often be more effective to use the leverage of improved capital turnover to boost ROI. For example, many successful retailers have long since recognized that very small net margins can lead to excellent ROI if the productivity of capital is high, e.g. limited inventory, high sales per square foot, premises that are leased rather than owned and so on.

Figure 3.1 illustrates the opportunities that exist for boosting ROI through either achieving better margins or higher assets turns or both. Each 'iso-curve' reflects the different ways the same ROI can be achieved through specific margin/asset turn combination. The challenge to logistics management is to find ways of moving the iso-curve to the right.

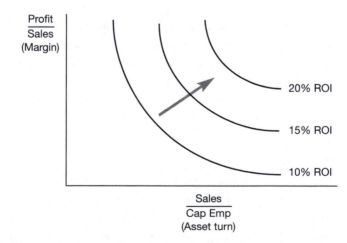

Fig. 3.1 The impact of margin and asset turn on ROI

The ways in which logistics management can impact on ROI are many and varied. Figure 3.2 highlights the major elements determining ROI and the potential for improvement through more effective logistics management.

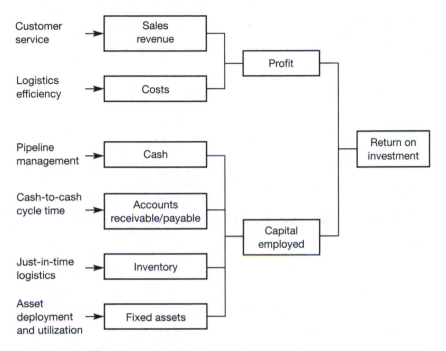

Fig. 3.2 Logistics impact on ROI

Logistics and the balance sheet

As well as its impact on operating income (revenue less costs) logistics can affect the balance sheet of the business in a number of ways. In today's financially-oriented business environment improving the shape of the balance sheet through better use of resources has become a priority.

Once again better logistics management has the power to transform performance in this crucial area. Figure 3.3 summarizes the major elements of the balance sheet and links to each of the relevant logistics management components.

By examining each element of the balance sheet in turn it will be seen how logistics variables can influence its final shape.

Balance sheet	Logistics variable
Assets	
Cash ─────┐ ┌─────	Order cycle time
├───┤	Order completion rate
Receivables ─────┘ └─────	Invoice accuracy
Inventories ─────────────────	Inventory
Property, plant ┌─────	Distribution facilities and equipment
and equipment ───────┤	
└─────	Plant and equipment
Liabilities	
Current liabilities ───────────────	Purchase order quantities
Debt ─────┐	Financing options for inventory,
Equity ─────┘	plant and equipment

Fig. 3.3 Logistics management and the balance sheet

Cash and receivables

This component of current assets is crucial to the liquidity of the business. In recent years its importance has been recognized as more companies become squeezed for cash. It is not always recognized however that logistics variables have a direct impact on this part of the balance sheet. For example, the shorter the order cycle time, from when the customer places the order to when the goods are delivered, the sooner the invoice can be issued. Likewise the order completion rate can affect the cash flow if the invoice is not issued until after the goods are despatched. One of the less obvious logistics variables affecting cash and receivables is invoice accuracy. If the customer finds that his invoice is inaccurate he is unlikely to pay and the payment lead time will be extended until the problem is rectified.

Inventories

Fifty per cent or more of a company's current assets will often be tied up in inventory. Logistics is concerned with all inventory within the business from raw materials, subassembly or bought-in components, through work-in-progress to finished goods. The company's policies on inventory levels and stock locations will clearly influence the size of total inventory. Also influential will be the extent to which inventory levels are monitored and managed, and beyond that the extent to which strategies are in operation that minimize the need for inventory.

Property, plant and equipment

The logistics system of any business will usually be a heavy user of fixed assets. The plant, depots and warehouses that form the logistics network, if valued realistically on a replacement basis, will represent a substantial part of total capacity employed (assuming that they are owned rather than rented or leased). Materials handling equipment, vehicles and other equipment involved in storage and transport can also add considerably to the total sum of fixed assets. Many companies have outsourced the physical distribution of their products partly to move assets off their balance sheet. Warehouses, for example, with their associated storage and handling equipment represent a sizeable investment and the question should be asked: 'Is this the most effective way to deploy our assets?'

Current liabilities

The current liabilities of the business are debts that must be paid in cash within a specified period of time. From the logistics point of view the key elements are accounts payable for bought-in materials, components, etc. This is an area where a greater integration of purchasing with operations management can yield dividends. The traditional concepts of economic order quantities can often lead to excessive levels of raw materials inventory as those quantities may not reflect actual manufacturing or distribution requirements. The phasing of supplies to match the total logistics requirements of the system can be achieved through the twin techniques of materials requirement planning (MRP) and distribution requirements planning (DRP). If premature commitment of materials can be minimized this should lead to an improved position on current liabilities.

Debt/equity

Whilst the balance between debt and equity has many ramifications for the financial management of the total business it is worth reflecting on the impact of alternative logistics strategies. More companies are leasing plant facilities and equipment and thus converting a fixed asset into a continuing expense. The growing use of 'third-party' suppliers for warehousing and transport instead of owning and managing these facilities in-house is a parallel development. These changes obviously affect the funding requirements of the business. They may also affect the means whereby that funding is achieved, i.e. through debt rather than equity. The ratio of debt to equity, usually referred to as 'gearing' or 'leverage', will influence the return on equity and will also have implications for cash flow in terms of interest payments and debt repayment.

Logistics and shareholder value

One of the key measures of corporate performance today is shareholder value. In other words, what is the company worth to its owners? Increasingly senior management within the business is being driven by the goal of enhancing shareholder value. There are a number of complex issues involved in actually calculating shareholder value but at its simplest it is determined by the net present value of future cash flows. These cash flows may themselves be defined as:

Net operating income
less
Taxes
less
Working capital investment
less
Fixed capital investment
=
After-tax free cash flow

More recently there has been a further development in that the concept of economic value added (EVA) has become widely used and linked to the creation of shareholder value. The term EVA originated with the consulting firm Stern Stewart,[2] although its origins go back to the economist Alfred Marshall who, over 100 years ago, developed the concept of 'economic income'.

Essentially EVA is the difference between operating income after taxes less the true cost of capital employed to generate those profits. Thus:

Economic value added (EVA)
= Profit after tax – True cost of capital employed

It will be apparent that it is possible for a company to generate a negative EVA. In other words, the cost of capital employed is greater than the profit after tax. The impact of a negative EVA, particularly if sustained over a period of time, is to erode shareholder value. Equally improvements in EVA will lead to an enhancement of shareholder value. If the net present value of expected future EVAs were to be calculated this would generate a measure of wealth known as market value added (MVA), which is a true measure of what the business is worth to its shareholders. A simple definition of MVA is:

Stock price × Issued shares

less

Book value of total capital invested

=

Market value added

and, as we have already noted,

MVA = Net present value of expected future EVA

Clearly, it will be recognized that there are a number of significant connections between logistics performance and shareholder value. Not only the impact that logistics service can have upon net operating income (profit) but also the impact on capital efficiency (asset turn). Many companies have come to realize the effect that lengthy pipelines and highly capital-intensive logistics facilities can have on EVA and hence shareholder value. As a result they have focused on finding ways in which pipelines can be shortened and, consequently, working capital requirements reduced. At the same time they have looked again at their fixed capital deployment of distribution facilities and vehicle fleets and in many cases have moved these assets off the balance sheet through the use of third-party logistics service providers.

The drivers of shareholder value

The five basic drivers of enhanced shareholder value are shown in Figure 3.4. They are revenue growth, operating cost reduction, fixed capital efficiency, working capital efficiency and tax minimization. All five of these drivers are directly and indirectly affected by logistics management and supply chain strategy.

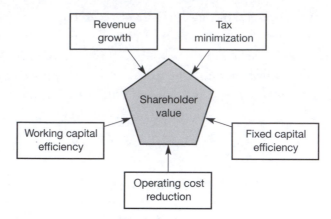

Fig. 3.4 The drivers of shareholder value

Revenue growth

The critical linkage here is the impact that logistics service can have on sales volume and customer retention. Whilst it is not generally possible to calculate the exact correlation between service and sales there have been many studies that have indicated a positive causality.

It can also be argued that superior logistics service (in terms of reliability and responsiveness) can strengthen the likelihood that customers will remain loyal to a supplier. In Chapter 2 it was suggested that higher levels of customer retention lead to greater sales. Typically this occurs because satisfied customers are more likely to place a greater proportion of their purchases with that supplier.

Operating cost reduction

The potential for operating cost reduction through logistics and supply chain management is considerable. Because a large proportion of costs in a typical business are driven by logistics decisions and the quality of supply chain relationships, it is not surprising that in the search for enhanced margins many companies are taking a new look at the way they manage the supply chain.

It is not just the transportation, storage, handling and order processing costs within the business that need to be considered. Rather a total pipeline view of costs on a true 'end-to-end' basis should be taken. Often the upstream logistics costs can represent a significant proportion of total supply chain costs embedded in the final product.

There is also a growing recognition that time compression in the supply chain not only enhances customer service but can also reduce costs through the reduction of non-value-adding activities. This is an issue that we shall return to in Chapter 5.

Fixed capital efficiency

Logistics by its very nature tends to be fixed asset 'intensive'. Trucks, distribution centres and automated handling systems involve considerable investment and, consequently, will often depress return on investment. In conventional multi-echelon distribution systems, it is not unusual to find factory warehouses, regional distribution centres and local depots, all of which represent significant fixed investment.

One of the main drivers behind the growth of the third-party logistics service sector has been the desire to reduce fixed asset investment. At the same time the trend to lease rather than buy has accelerated. Decisions to rationalize distribution networks and production facilities are increasingly being driven by the realization that the true cost of financing that capital investment is sometimes greater than the return it generates.

Working capital efficiency

Supply chain strategy and logistics management are fundamentally linked to the working capital requirement within the business. Long pipelines by definition generate more inventory; order fill and invoice accuracy directly impact accounts receivable and procurement policies also affect cash flow. Working capital requirements can be dramatically reduced through time compression in the pipeline and subsequently reduced order-to-cash cycle times.

Surprisingly few companies know the true length of the pipeline for the products they sell. The 'cash-to-cash' cycle time (i.e. the elapsed time from procurement of materials/components through to sale of the finished product) can be six months or longer in many manufacturing industries. By focusing on eliminating non-value-adding time in the supply chain, dramatic reduction in working capital can be achieved. So many companies have lived with low inventory turns for so long that they assume that it is a feature of their industry and that nothing can be done. They are also possibly not motivated to give working capital reduction a higher priority because an unrealistically low cost of capital is being employed.

Tax minimization

In today's increasingly global economy organizations have choices as to where they can locate their assets and activities. Because tax regimes are different country by country, location decisions can have an important impact on after-tax free cash flow. It is not just corporate taxes on profits that are affected, but also property tax and excise duty on fuel. Customs regulations, tariffs and quotas become further considerations, as do rules and regulation on transfer pricing. For large global companies with production facilities in many different countries and with dispersed distribution centres and multiple markets, supply chain decisions can significantly affect the total tax bill and hence shareholder value.

The role of cash flow in creating shareholder value

There is general agreement with the view of Warren Buffet[3] that ultimately the value of a business to its owners is determined by the net present value of the free cash flow occurring from its operations over its lifetime. Thus the challenge to managers seeking to enhance shareholder value is to identify strategies that can directly or indirectly affect free cash flow. Srivastava *et al.*[4] have suggested that the value of any strategy is inherently driven by:

1. An acceleration of cash flows because risk and time adjustments reduce the value of later cash flows;
2. An increase in the level of cash flows (e.g. higher revenues and/or lower costs, working capital and fixed investment);
3. A reduction in risk associated with cash flows (e.g. through reduction in both volatility and vulnerability of future cash flows) and hence, indirectly, the firm's cost of capital; and
4. The residual value of the business (long-term value can be enhanced, for example, by increasing the size of the customer base).

In effect, what Srivastava *et al.* are suggesting is that strategies should be evaluated in terms of how they either *enhance* or *accelerate* cash flow. Those strategic objectives can be graphically expressed as a cumulative distribution of free cash flow over time (see Figure 3.5) with the objective of building a greater cumulative cash flow, sooner. Obviously the sooner cash is received and the greater the amount then the greater will be the net present value of those cash flows.

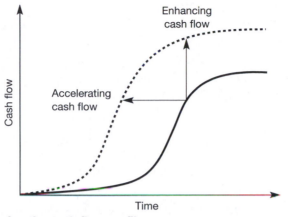

Fig. 3.5 Changing the cash flow profile
Source: Srivastava *et al.*[5]

An example of the impact that logistics issues can have on the financial performance of a company is provided by the comparison of two North American retailers, Wal-Mart and Kmart.

Wal-Mart and Kmart

In 2002 five general merchandise retailers – Wal-Mart, Kmart, Target, Costco and Sears – accounted for 60 per cent of US sales in that sector.[1] Wal-Mart was the undisputed market and cost leader and the main innovator in North American retailing. It was the first to introduce the 'big box' retail format and flexible cross-trained employees who could work in more than one department. Historically Wal-Mart also led the way with aggressive investment in IT. Back in the 1960s it was one of the first to use computers to track inventory and was an early adopter of bar-codes technology in the 1980s. In 1983 it was reported that Wal-Mart was spending only 2 cents in the sales dollar on getting goods into the stores, while its long-established competitor Kmart was spending 5 cents per dollar on the same activities.[2]

Wal-Mart subsequently became a classic case study for supply chain management programmes, due to its use of Electronic Data Interchange (EDI) to improve co-ordination with suppliers. Technological innovations were coupled with a strategy that exploited economies of scale in purchasing and logistics, and gradually expanded operations around central distribution centres. By 1987 it enjoyed a 9 per cent market

▶

share, but was 40 per cent more productive than its competitors as measured by sales per employee.

The introduction soon afterwards of wireless scanning guns and the Retail Link Program, which captures sales data giving real-time visibility of stock holding and sales patterns, were just two more technological innovations that boosted capital and labour productivity. They facilitated more effective micro-merchandising campaigns as well as improved inventory management, allowing a better overall value proposition for customers, not least from significant cost savings, which were passed on to customers in the form of 'every day low prices'.

By 1995 Wal-Mart had increased its market share to 27 per cent and widened the gap on productivity to 48 per cent. Other retailers adopted many of the same practices and technological solutions to improve their own performance. Nevertheless, Wal-Mart maintained a commanding lead, improving its own performance by an additional 22 per cent in the four years to 1999. Wal-Mart's sales per employee leapt from $148,000 to $181,000 between 1995 and 1999. Kmart, for decades the dominant force in general merchandise retailing, only managed to improve its own performance from $109,000 to $133,000 over the same period.

In sharp contrast to Wal-Mart, Kmart had been losing favour with US shoppers for years. Poor in-store presentation and unhelpful staff had eroded customer satisfaction, as had promotional flyers advertising cut-price products that were often missing from the shelves. Sometimes the stock was simply unavailable, while other times it was on site but had been left to linger in the back of the stores before being unpacked and logged on the central tracking system.

Kmart had tried to challenge Wal-Mart on ever more competitive promotional pricing, but its supply chain lacked the co-ordination to respond to the demand volatility the promotions induced. Its on-shelf availability had dropped to 86 per cent, while massively bloated stocks of seasonal items filled its warehouses long after the appropriate sales period had passed. The result was that while Wal-Mart enjoyed a stock-turn of 7.3 in 2000, Kmart could only manage 3.6 turns.

In September 2001 Kmart's Chief Executive issued a statement admitting that: 'I believe the supply chain is really the Achilles heel of Kmart. Just fixing the supply chain could really turbo-charge Kmart.'[3]

Efforts to 'just fix' the supply chain involved the introduction of point-of-sale systems a month earlier and followed a two-year $1.7bn IT upgrade, plus $70m spent on the introduction of hand-held scanners in 2000. The investment was too little too late.

Wal-Mart had spent $4bn on its supply chain system and then forced suppliers to invest a further $40bn in their supply chain operations. The suppliers had no choice other than to adopt the tools required to drive their own costs down further. Kmart had no chance of matching that level of performance. Its sales per square foot were by then only $227, almost half of Wal-Mart's $446.

The impact of the difference in performance of the two companies' supply chains has been dramatic. In January 2002 Kmart became the largest company, ever to file for Chapter 11 bankruptcy. Wal-Mart, the world's largest company, continues to prosper.

References

1. Johnson, B.C. 'Retail: The Wal-Mart effect', *McKinsey Quarterly*, No. 1, 2002.
2. Simpson, L. 'No so Special K', *Supply Management*, 2 March 2002, pp. 22–25.
3. *Ibid.*

Logistics cost analysis

After a century or more of reliance upon traditional cost accounting procedures to provide an often unreliable insight into profitability, managers are now starting to question the relevance of these methods.[6] The accounting frameworks still in use by the majority of companies today rely upon arbitrary methods for the allocation of shared and indirect costs and hence frequently distort the true profitability of both products and customers. Indeed, as we shall see, these traditional accounting methods are often quite unsuited for analyzing the profitability of customers and markets since they were originally devised to measure product costs.

Because logistics management is a flow-oriented concept with the objective of integrating resources across a pipeline which extends from suppliers to final customers, it is desirable to have a means whereby costs and performance of that pipeline flow can be assessed.

Because logistics management is a flow-oriented concept with the objective of integrating resources across a pipeline which extends from suppliers to final customers, it is desirable to have a means whereby costs and performance of that pipeline flow can be assessed.

Probably one of the main reasons why the adoption of an integrated approach to logistics and distribution management has proved so difficult for many companies is the lack of appropriate cost information. The need to manage the total distribution activity as a complete system, having regard for the effects of decisions taken in one cost area upon other cost areas, has implications for the cost accounting systems of the organization. Typically, conventional accounting systems group costs into broad, aggregated categories which do not then allow the more detailed analysis necessary to identify the true costs of servicing customers buying particular product mixes. Without this facility to analyze aggregated cost data, it becomes impossible to reveal the potential for cost trade-offs that may exist within the logistics system.

Generally the effects of trade-offs are assessed in two ways: from the point of view of their impact on total costs and their impact on sales revenue. For example, it may be possible to trade-off costs in such a way that total costs increase, yet because of the better service now being offered, sales revenue also increases. If the difference between revenue and costs is greater than before, the trade-off may be regarded as leading to an improvement in cost effectiveness. However, without an adequate logistics-oriented cost accounting system it is extremely difficult to identify the extent to which a particular trade-off is cost-beneficial.

The concept of total cost analysis

Many problems at the operational level in logistics management arise because all the impacts of specific decisions, both direct and indirect, are not taken into account throughout the corporate system. Too often decisions taken in one area can lead to unforeseen results in other areas. Changes in policy on minimum order value, for example, may influence customer ordering patterns and lead to additional costs. Similarly, changes in production schedules that aim to improve production efficiency may lead to fluctuations in finished stock availability and thus affect customer service.

The problems associated with identifying the total system impact of distribution policies are immense. By its very nature logistics cuts across traditional company organization functions with cost impacts on most of those functions. Conventional accounting systems do not usually assist in the identification of these company-wide impacts, frequently absorbing logistics-related costs in other cost elements. The cost of processing orders, for example, is an amalgam of specific costs incurred in different functional areas of the business which generally prove extremely difficult to bring together. Figure 3.6 outlines the various cost elements involved in the complete order processing cycle, each of these elements having a fixed and variable cost component which will lead to a different total cost per order.

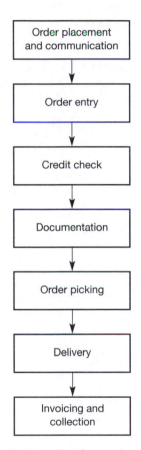

Fig. 3.6 Stages in the order-to-collection cycle

Accounting practice for budgeting and standard-setting has tended to result in a compartmentalization of company accounts; thus budgets tend to be set on a functional basis. The trouble is that policy costs do not usually confine themselves within the same watertight boundaries. It is the nature of logistics that, like a stone thrown into a pond, the effects of specific policies spread beyond their immediate area of impact.

A further feature of logistics decisions that contributes to the complexity of generating appropriate cost information is that they are usually taken against a background of an existing system. The purpose of total cost analysis in this context is to identify the change in costs brought about by these decisions. Cost must therefore be viewed in incremental terms – the change in total costs caused by the change to the system. Thus the addition of an extra warehouse to the distribution network will bring about cost changes in transport, inventory investment and communications. It is the incremental cost difference between the two options that is the relevant accounting information for decision making in this case. Figure 3.7 shows how total logistics costs can be influenced by the addition, or removal, of a depot from the system.

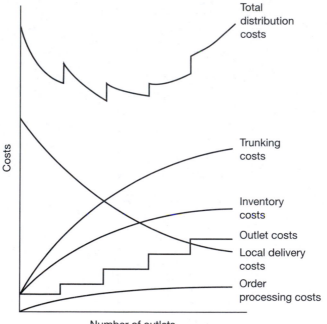

Fig. 3.7 **The total costs of a distribution network**

Principles of logistics costing

It will be apparent from the previous comments that the problem of developing an appropriate logistics-oriented costing system is primarily one of focus. That is the ability to focus upon the output of the distribution system, in essence the provision of customer service, and to identify the unique costs associated with that output. Traditional accounting methods lack this focus, mainly because they were designed with something else in mind.

One of the basic principles of logistics costing, it has been argued, is that the system should mirror the materials flow, i.e. it should be capable of identifying the costs that result from providing customer service in the marketplace. A second principle is that it should be capable of enabling separate cost and revenue analyses to be made by customer type and by market segment or distribution channel. This latter requirement emerges because of the dangers inherent in dealing solely with averages, e.g. the average cost per delivery, since they can often conceal substantial variations either side of the mean.

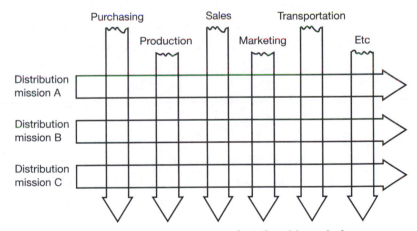

Fig. 3.8 Logistics missions that cut across functional boundaries

To operationalize these principles requires an 'output' orientation to costing. In other words, we must first define the desired outputs of the logistics system and then seek to identify the costs associated with providing those outputs. A useful concept here is the idea of 'mission'. In the context of logistics, a mission is a set of customer service goals to be achieved by the system within a specific product/market context. Missions can be defined in terms of the type of market served, by which products and within what constraints of service and cost. A mission by its very nature cuts across traditional company lines. Figure 3.8 illustrates the concept and demonstrates the difference between an 'output' orientation based upon missions and the 'input' orientation based upon functions.

The successful achievement of defined mission goals involves inputs from a large number of functional areas and activity centres within the firm. Thus an effective logistics costing system must seek to determine the total systems cost of meeting desired logistic objectives (the 'output' of the system) and the costs of the various inputs involved in meeting these outputs. Interest has been growing in an approach to this problem, known as 'mission costing'.[7]

Figure 3.9 illustrates how three distribution missions may make a differential impact upon activity centre/functional area costs and, in so doing, provide a logical basis for costing within the company. As a cost or budgeting method, mission costing is the reverse of traditional techniques: under this scheme a functional budget is determined now by the demands of the missions it serves. Thus in Figure 3.9 the cost per mission is identified horizontally and from this the functional budgets may be determined by summing vertically.

Given that the logic of mission costing is sound, how might it be made to work in practice? This approach requires firstly that the activity centres associated with a particular distribution mission be identified, e.g. transport, warehousing, inventory, etc., and secondly that the incremental costs for each activity centre incurred as a result of undertaking that mission must be isolated. Incremental costs are used because it is important not to take into account 'sunk' costs or costs that would still be incurred even if the mission were abandoned. We can make use of the idea of 'attributable costs'[8] to operationalize the concept:

Attributable cost is a cost per unit that could be avoided if a product or function were discontinued entirely without changing the supporting organization structure.

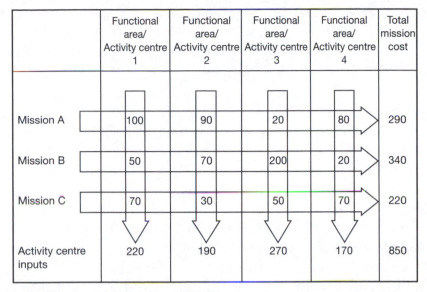

Fig. 3.9 The programme budget (£'000)

In determining the costs of an activity centre, e.g. transport, attributable to a specific mission, the question should be asked: 'What costs would we avoid if this customer/segment/channel were no longer serviced?' These avoidable costs are the true incremental costs of servicing the customer/segment/channel. Often they will be substantially lower than the average cost because so many distribution costs are fixed and/or shared. For example, a vehicle leaves a depot in London to make deliveries in Nottingham and Leeds. If those customers in Nottingham were abandoned, but those in Leeds retained, what would be the difference in the total cost of transport? The answer would be – not very much, since Leeds is further north from London than Nottingham. However, if the customers in Leeds were dropped, but not those in Nottingham, there would be a greater saving of costs because of the reduction in miles travelled.

This approach becomes particularly powerful when combined with a customer revenue analysis, because even customers with low sales offtake may still be profitable in incremental costs terms if not on an average cost basis. In other words the company would be worse off if those customers were abandoned.

Such insights as this can be gained by extending the mission costing concept to produce profitability analyses for customers, market segments or distribution channels. The term 'customer profitability

101

accounting' describes any attempt to relate the revenue produced by a customer, market segment or distribution channel to the costs of servicing that customer/segment/channel. The principles of customer profitability accounting will be explored in detail later in this chapter.

The cost of holding inventory

As we noted, there are many costs incurred in the total logistics process of converting customer orders into cash. However, one of the largest cost elements is also the one that is perhaps least well accounted for and that is inventory. Is it probably the case that many managers are unaware of what the true cost of holding inventory actually is. If all the costs that arise as a result of holding inventory are fully accounted for, then the real holding cost of inventory is probably in the region of 25 per cent per annum of the book value of the inventory.

The reason this figure is as high as it is is that there are a number of costs to be included. The largest cost element will normally be the cost of capital. The cost of capital comprises the cost to the company of debt and the cost of equity. It is usual to use the *weighted cost of capital* to reflect this. Hence, even though the cost of borrowed money might be low, the expectation of shareholders as to the return they are looking for from the equity investment could be high.

The other costs that need to be included in the inventory holding cost are the costs of storage and handling, obsolescence, deterioration and pilferage, as well as insurance and all the administrative costs associated with the management of the inventory (see box).

■ **The true cost of inventory** ■

- Cost of capital
- Storage and handling
- Obsolescence
- Damage and deterioration
- Pilferage/shrinkage
- Insurance
- Management costs

Customer profitability analysis

One of the basic questions that conventional accounting procedures have difficulty answering is: 'How profitable is this customer compared to another?' Usually customer profitability is only calculated at the level of gross profit – in other words the net sales revenue generated by the customer in a period, less the cost of goods sold for the actual product mix purchased. However, there are still many other costs to take into account before the real profitability of an individual customer can be exposed. The same is true if we seek to identify the relative profitability of different market segments or distribution channels.

The significance of these costs that occur as a result of servicing customers can be profound in terms of how logistics strategies should be developed. Firstly, customer profitability analysis will often reveal a proportion of customers who make a negative contribution, as in Figure 3.10. The reason for this is very simply that the costs of servicing a customer can vary considerably – even between two customers who may make equivalent purchases from us.

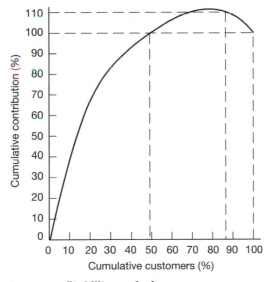

Figure 3.10 Customer profitability analysis
Source: Hill, G.V., *Logistics – The Battleground of the 1990s*, A.T. Kearney.

If we think of all the costs that a company incurs from when it captures an order from a customer to when it collects the payment, is will be apparent that the total figure could be quite high. It will also very likely be the case that there will be significant differences in these costs customer by customer. At the same time, different customers will order a different mix of products so the gross margin that they generate will differ.

As Table 3.1 highlights, there are many costs that need to be identified if customer profitability is to be accurately measured.

Table 3.1 The customer profit and loss account

Revenues	● Net sales value
Less	
Costs	● Cost of sales (actual product mix)
(attributable costs only)	● Commissions
	● Sales calls
	● Key account management time
	● Trade bonuses and special discount
	● Order processing costs
	● Promotional costs (visible and hidden)
	● Merchandising costs
	● Non-standard packaging/unitization
	● Dedicated inventory holding costs
	● Dedicated warehouse space
	● Materials handling costs
	● Transport costs
	● Documentation/communications costs
	● Returns/refusals
	● Trade credit (actual payment period)

The best measure of customer profitability is to ask the question: 'What costs would I avoid and what revenues would I lose if I lost this customer?' This is the concept of 'avoidable' costs and incremental revenue. Using this principle helps circumvent the problems that arise when fixed costs are allocated against individual customers.

■ **The average customer** ■

A study by the consulting company A.T. Kearney suggested that the significance of customer-oriented costs is not their average value, but specifically
how they vary by customer, by order size, by type of order and other key
factors. Whilst the average cost per customer may be easily calculated,
there may be no customer that incurs the average cost to serve. The need is
to be aware of the customers at the extremes of the cost range because, on
the one hand, profits may be eroded by serving them and, on the other,
although high profit is being generated, the business is vulnerable to competitive price-cutting. The table below shows an example of the range of
values of some customer-oriented costs expressed as a percentage of net
sales. This illustrates how misleading the use of averages can be.

Customer costs as a % of net sales

	Low	Average	High
Order processing	0.2	2.6	7.4
Inventory carrying	1.1	2.6	10.2
Picking and shipping	0.3	0.7	2.5
Outbound freight	2.8	7.1	14.1
Commissions	2.4	3.1	4.4

Source: Hill, G.V. and Harland, D.V., 'The Customer Profit Centre', *Focus*, Institute of Logistics and Distribution Management, Vol. 2,
No. 2, 1983.

What sort of costs should be taken into account in this type of analysis?
Figure 3.11 presents a basic model that seeks to identify only those customer-related costs that are avoidable (i.e. if the customer did not exist,
these costs would not be incurred).

The starting point is the gross sales value of the order from which is
then subtracted the discounts that are given on that order to the customer.
This leaves the net sales value from which must be taken the direct production costs or cost of goods sold. Indirect costs are not allocated unless
they are fully attributable to that customer. The same principle applies to
sales and marketing costs as attempts to allocate indirect costs, such as
national advertising, can only be done on an arbitrary and usually
misleading basis. The attributable distribution costs can then be assigned
to give customer gross contribution. Finally any other customer-related
costs, such as trade credit, returns, etc., are subtracted to give a net

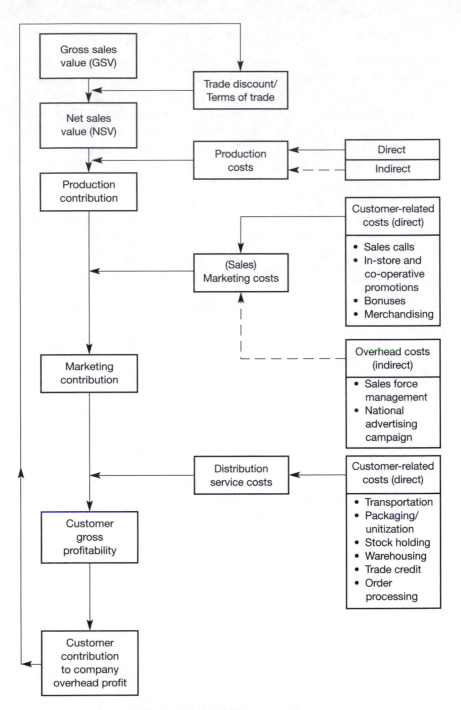

Fig. 3.11 Customer profitability analysis: a basic model

Source: Gattorna, J.L. and Walters, D.W., *Managing the Supply Chain: A Strategic Perspective*, Macmillan Press, 1996.

contribution to overheads and profit. Often the figure that emerges as the 'bottom line' can be revealing as shown, in Table 3.2.

Table 3.2 Analysis of revenue and cost for a specific customer

	£	£
Gross sales value		100,000
Less discount	10,000	
Net sales value		90,000
Less direct cost of goods sold	20,000	
Gross contribution		70,000
Less sales and marketing costs:		
Sales calls	3,000	
Co-operative promotions	1,000	
Merchandising	3,000	
	7,000	
		63,000
Less distribution costs:		
Order processing	500	
Storage and handling	600	
Inventory financing	700	
Transport	2,000	
Packaging	300	
Refusals	500	
	4,600	
Customer gross contribution		58,400
Less other customer-related costs:		
Credit financing	1,500	
Returns	500	
	2,000	
Customer net contribution		56,400

In this case a gross contribution of £70,000 becomes a net contribution of £56,400 as soon as the costs unique to this customer are taken into account. If the analysis were to be extended by attempting to allocate overheads (a step not to be advised because of the problems usually associated with such allocation), what might at first seem to be a profitable customer could be deemed to be the reverse. However, as long as the net contribution is positive and there is no 'opportunity cost' in servicing that customer the company would be better off with the business than without it.

The value of this type of exercise can be substantial. The information could be used, firstly, when the next sales contract is negotiated and, secondly, as the basis for sales and marketing strategy in directing effort away from less profitable types of account towards more profitable business. More importantly it can point the way to alternative strategies for managing customers with high servicing costs. Ideally we require all our customers to be profitable in the medium to long term and where customers currently are profitable we should seek to build and extend that profitability further.

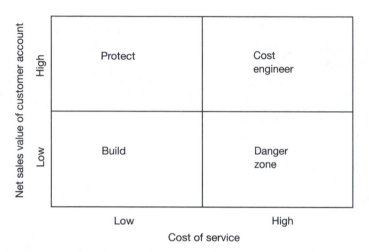

Fig. 3.12 Customer profitability matrix

Figure 3.12 represents a simple categorization of customers along two dimensions: their total net sales value during the period and their cost-to-serve. The suggestion is that there could be a benefit in developing customer-specific solutions depending upon which box of the matrix they fall into. Possible strategies for each of the quadrants are suggested below.

Build

These customers are relatively cheap to service but their net sales value is low. Can volume be increased without a proportionate increase in the costs of service? Can our sales team be directed to seek to influence these customers' purchases towards a more profitable sales mix?

Danger zone

These customers should be looked at very carefully. Is there any medium- to long-term prospect either of improving net sales value or of reducing the costs of service? Is there a strategic reason for keeping them? Do we need them for their volume even if their profit contribution is low?

Cost engineer

These customers could be more profitable if the costs of servicing them could be reduced. Is there any scope for increasing drop sizes? Can deliveries be consolidated? If new accounts in the same geographic area were developed would it make delivery more economic? Is there a cheaper way of gathering orders from these customers, e.g. the Internet.

Protect

The high net sales value customers who are relatively cheap to service are worth their weight in gold. The strategy for these customers should be to seek relationships which make the customer less likely to want to look for alternative suppliers. At the same time we should constantly seek opportunities to develop the volume of business that we do with them whilst keeping strict control of costs.

Ideally the organization should seek to develop an accounting system that would routinely collect and analyze data on customer profitability. Unfortunately most accounting systems are product focused rather than customer focused. Likewise cost reporting is traditionally on a functional basis rather than a customer basis. So, for example, we know the costs of the transport function as a whole or the costs of making a particular product but what we do not know are the costs of delivering a specific mix of product to a particular customer.

There is a pressing need for companies to move towards a system of accounting for customers and marketing as well as accounting for products. As has often been observed, it is customers who make profits, not products!

Direct product profitability

An application of logistics cost analysis that has gained widespread acceptance, particularly in the retail industry, is a technique known as direct product profitability – or more simply 'DPP'. In essence it is somewhat analogous to customer profitability analysis in that it attempts to identify all the costs that attach to a product or an order as it moves through the distribution channel.

The idea behind DPP is that in many transactions the customer will incur costs other than the immediate purchase price of the product. Often this is termed the *total cost of ownership*. Sometimes these costs will be hidden and often they can be substantial – certainly big enough to reduce or even eliminate net profit on a particular item.

For the supplier it is important to understand DPP inasmuch as his ability to be a low-cost supplier is clearly influenced by the costs that are incurred as that product moves through his logistics system. Similarly, as distributors and retailers are now very much more conscious of an item's DPP, it is to the advantage of the supplier equally to understand the cost drivers that impact upon DPP so as to seek to influence it favourably.

Table 3.3 describes the steps to be followed in moving from a crude gross margin measure to a more precise DPP.

Table 3.3 Direct product profit (DPP)

The net profit contribution from the sales of a product after allowances are added and all costs that can be rationally allocated or assigned to an individual product are subtracted = direct product profit.

	Sales
–	Cost of goods sold
=	Gross margin
+	Allowances and discounts
=	Adjusted gross margin
–	Warehouse costs
	Labour (labour model – case, cube, weight)
	Occupancy (space and cube)
	Inventory (average inventory)
–	Transportation costs (cube)
–	Retail costs
	Stocking labour
	Front end labour
	Occupancy
	Inventory
=	Direct product profit

The importance to the supplier of DPP is based on the proposition that a key objective of customer service strategy is 'to reduce the customer's costs of ownership'. In other words the supplier should be looking at his products and asking the question: 'How can I favourably influence the DPP of my customers by changing either the characteristics of the products I sell, or the way I distribute them?'

From pack design onwards there are a number of elements that the manufacturer or supplier may be able to vary in order to influence DPP/square metre in a positive way, for example, changing the case size, increasing the delivery frequency, direct store deliveries, etc.

Cost drivers and activity-based costing

As we indicated earlier in this chapter there is a growing dissatisfaction with conventional cost accounting, particularly as it relates to logistics management. Essentially these problems can be summarized as follows:

- There is a general ignorance of the true costs of servicing different customer types/channels/market segments.
- Costs are captured at too high a level of aggregation.
- Full cost allocation still reigns supreme.
- Conventional accounting systems are functional in their orientation rather than output oriented.
- Companies understand product costs but not customer costs.

The common theme that links these points is that we seem to suffer in business from a lack of visibility of costs as they are incurred through the logistics pipeline. Ideally what logistics management requires is a means of capturing costs as products and orders flow towards the customer.

To overcome this problem it is necessary to change radically the basis of cost accounting away from the notion that all expenses must be allocated (often on an arbitrary basis) to individual units (such as products) and, instead, to separate the expenses and match them to the activities that consume the resources. One approach that can help overcome this problem is 'activity-based costing'.[9] The key to activity-based costing (ABC) is to seek out the 'cost drivers' along the logistics pipeline that cause costs because they consume resources. Thus, for example, if we are concerned to assign the costs of order picking to orders then in the past this may have been achieved by calculating an average cost per order. In fact an activity-based approach might suggest that it is the number of lines on an order that consume the order picking resource and hence should instead be seen as the cost driver. Table 3.4 contrasts the ABC approach with the traditional method.

The advantage of using activity-based costing is that it enables each customer's unique characteristics in terms of ordering behaviour and distribution requirements to be separately accounted for. Once the cost attached to each level of activity is identified (e.g. cost per line item picked, cost per delivery, etc.) then a clearer picture of the true cost-to-serve will emerge. Whilst ABC is still strictly a cost allocation method it uses a more logical basis for that allocation than traditional methods.

Table 3.4 Activity-based costing vs traditional cost bases

Traditional cost bases	£000s	Activity cost bases	£000s	Cost drivers
Salaries	550	Sales order processing	300	Number of orders
Wages	580	Holding inventory	600	Value of shipment
Depreciation	250	Picking	300	Number of order lines
Rent/electricity/		Packing/assembly		
telephone	700	of orders	100	Number of order lines
Maintenance	100	Loading	200	Weight
Fuel	200	Transportation	500	Location of customer
		Delivery at customer	200	Number of drops
		Solving problems	380	Number of order lines
	£2,380		£2,580	

Source: Based upon Simmons, G. and Steeple, D., 'Overhead Recovery – It's as Easy as ABC', *Focus*, Institute of Logistics and Distribution Management, Vol. 10, No. 8, October 1991.

There are certain parallels between activity-based costing and the idea of *mission costing* introduced earlier in this chapter. Essentially mission costing seeks to identify the unique costs that are generated as a result of specific logistics/customer service strategies aimed at targeted market segments. The aim is to establish a better matching of the service needs of the various markets that the company addresses with the inevitably limited resources of the company. There is little point in committing incremental costs where the incremental benefits do not justify the expenditure.

There are four stages in the implementation of an effective mission costing process:

1. *Define the customer service segment*

   Use the methodology described in Chapter 2 to identify the different service needs of different customer types. The basic principle is that because not all customers share the same service requirements and characteristics they should be treated differently.

2. *Identify the factors that produce variations in the cost of service*

   This step involves the determination of the service elements that will directly or indirectly impact upon the costs of service, e.g. the product mix, the delivery characteristics such as drop size and frequency or incidence of direct deliveries, merchandising support, special packs and so on.

3. *Identify the specific resources used to support customer segments*

   This is the point at which the principles of activity-based costing and mission costing coincide. The basic tenet of ABC is that the activities that generate cost should be defined and the specific cost drivers involved identified. These may be the number of lines on an order, the people involved, the inventory support or the delivery frequency.

4. *Attribute activity costs by customer type or segment*

   Using the principle of 'avoidability' the incremental costs incurred through the application of a specific resource to meeting service needs are attributed to customers. It must be emphasized that this is not cost allocation but cost attribution. In other words it is because customers use resources that the appropriate share of cost is attributed to them.

Clearly to make this work there is a prerequisite that the cost coding system in the business be restructured. In other words, the coding system must be capable of gathering costs as they are incurred by customers from the point of order generation through to final delivery, invoicing and collection.

The basic purpose of logistics cost analysis is to provide managers with reliable information that will enable a better allocation of resources to be achieved. Given that logistics management, as we have observed, ultimately is concerned to meet customer service requirements in the most cost-effective way, then it is essential that those responsible have the most accurate and meaningful data possible.

Summary

Because logistics costs can account for such a large proportion of total costs in the business it is critical that they be carefully managed. However, it is not always the case that the true costs of logistics are fully understood. Traditional approaches to accounting based upon full-cost allocation can be misleading and dangerous. Activity-based costing methods provide some significant advantages in identifying the real costs of serving different types of customers or different channels of distribution.

Logistics management impacts not only upon the profit and loss account of the business, but also upon the balance sheet. Logistics is also increasingly being recognized as having a significant impact upon economic value added and hence shareholder value. It is critical that decisions on logistics strategies made based upon a thorough understanding of the impact they will have on the financial performance of the business.

References

1. *State of Logistics Report*, Council for Logistics Management, 2004.
2. Stewart, G.B., *The Quest for Value*, Harper Business, 1991 (EVA is a registered trademark of Stern Stewart & Co).
3. Buffet, W., *Annual Report*, Berkshire Hathaway Corporation, 1994.
4. Srivastava, R. *et al.*, 'Market-Based Assets and Shareholder Value: A Framework for Analysis', *Journal of Marketing*, Vol. 62, No. 1, January 1998, pp. 2–18.
5. *Ibid*.
6. Johnson, H.T. and Kaplan, R.S., *Relevance Lost: The Rise and Fall of Management Accounting*, Harvard Business School Press, 1987.
7. Barrett, T., 'Mission Costing: A New Approach to Logistics Analysis', *International Journal of Physical Distribution and Materials Management*, Vol. 12, No. 7, 1982.
8. Shillinglow, G., 'The Concept of Attributable Cost', *Journal of Accounting Research*, Vol. 1, No. 1, Spring 1963.
9. Cooper, R. and Kaplan, R.S., 'Profit Priorities from Activity-Based Costing', *Harvard Business Review*, May–June 1991.

Creating the responsive supply chain

This chapter:

Highlights the importance of rapid response in markets that are turbulent and volatile.

•

Explores the principles underpinning the agile supply chain and contrasts them with the concept of 'lean' management.

•

Distinguishes between 'push' and 'pull' philosophies of supply chain design and explains the principles of just-in-time.

•

Suggests ways in which 'hybrid' supply chain strategies can be devised combining both lean and agile thinking.

•

Presents a routemap to enable the achievement of higher levels of responsiveness.

One of the biggest challenges facing organizations today is the need to respond to ever increasing levels of volatility in demand. For a variety of reasons product and technology life cycles are shortening, competitive pressures force more frequent product changes and consumers demand greater variety than ever before.

To meet this challenge the organization needs to focus its efforts upon achieving greater agility such that it can respond in shorter time-frames both in terms of volume change and variety change. In other words it needs to be able quickly to adjust output to match market demand and to switch rapidly from one variant to another. To a truly agile business volatility of demand is not a problem; its processes and organizational structure as well as its supply chain relationships enable it to cope with whatever demands are placed upon it.

Agility in the sense of the ability to match supply with demand is not necessarily synonymous with 'leanness'. Much has been written about lean manufacturing – often with reference to the automobile industry.[1] The lean approach to manufacturing seeks to minimize inventory of components and work-in-progress and to move towards a 'just-in-time' environment wherever possible. However, while 'leanness' may be an element of 'agility' in certain circumstances, by itself it will not enable the organization to meet the precise needs of the customer more rapidly. Indeed it could be argued that, at least until recently, the automobile industry, for all its leanness, is one of the least agile industries around. *Webster's Dictionary* makes the distinction clearly when it defines lean as 'containing little fat' whereas agile is defined as 'nimble'.

Agility has many dimensions and the concept applies as much to networks as it does to individual companies. Indeed a key to agile response is the presence of agile partners upstream and downstream of the focal firm. Whilst organizations may have internal processes that are capable of rapid response, their agility will still be constrained if they face long replenishment lead times from suppliers, for example.

Agility, as we have said, is not synonymous with 'leanness' but it can build upon it. Leanness in a sense is about doing more with less. It owes its origins to the Toyota Production System (TPS) and its pre-occupation with the reduction or elimination of waste (*muda*).[2] Lean manufacturing is characterized by 'level schedules', i.e. a forward plan to ensure that the use of resources is optimized.

The backdrop against which lean thinking was originated was the Japanese automobile industry of the 1970s. This was an industrial context typified by the volume manufacture of relatively standard products (i.e. low levels of variety) and a focus on achieving efficiencies in the use of resources and in maximizing economies of scale. In this type of situation, i.e. standard products and relatively predictable demand, experience has shown that lean practices work well.

However, in market environments where demand is uncertain, the levels of variety are high and consequently volume per stock keeping unit (SKU) is low, then a different response is required. Whilst efficiency is always desirable, in the context of unpredictable demand it may have to take second place to 'effectiveness' as the main priority for supply chain management. By effectiveness in this context is meant the ability to respond rapidly to meet the precise needs of an often fragmented market-place. In other words, rather than the emphasis being on producing standard products for mass markets ahead of demand, the requirement becomes one of producing multiple product variants (often customized) for much smaller market segments in response to known demand.

Figure 4.1 reflects the different contexts in which the 'lean' and 'agile' paradigms might work best.

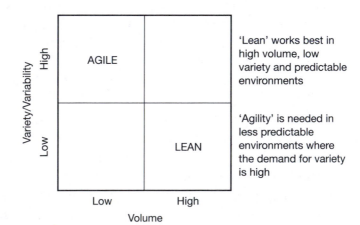

Fig. 4.1 Agile or lean?

In reality, within the same business it is likely that there will exist the need for both lean and agile supply chain solutions since some products will have predictable demand whilst for others demand will be far more volatile. In fact it can be argued that rather than the conventional 'one size fits all' strategy for supply chain design, the need today is for multiple supply chain solutions. One way to identify what types of supply chain strategies might be appropriate in different circumstances is to position the products in an organization's portfolio according to their supply and demand characteristics.

By 'supply characteristic' is meant the lead time of replenishment. This could be replenishment of the product itself if it is bought in (e.g. a retailer) or of components in the case of a manufacturer. Clearly, if replenishment lead times are short then a different supply chain strategy can be employed than when lead times are long.

Demand conditions may be characterized by the predictability of demand. One measure of demand predictability is the variability of demand; by definition demand that does not vary much from one period to another is easier to predict.

Figure 4.2 suggests four broad generic supply chains strategies dependent upon the combination of supply/demand conditions for each product.

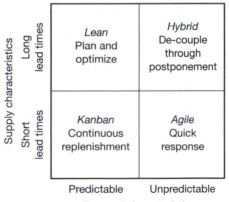

Fig. 4.2 Generic Supply Chain Strategies

In those cases where demand in predictable and replenishment lead times are short, then a 'Kanban' type of solution is indicated. This is a philosophy of continuous replenishment where, at its extreme, as each product is sold or used it is replaced.

In the top left hand box where lead times are long but demand is predictable then a 'lean' type approach will be appropriate. Materials, components or products can be ordered ahead of demand and manu-facturing and transportation facilities can be optimized in terms of cost and asset utilization. Conversely the bottom right hand corner is the real domain of the agile supply chain. Here demand is unpredictable but lead times are short, enabling 'quick response' type solutions – the extreme case being make-to-order (but in very short time-frames).

The top right hand corner presents an interesting situation: lead times are long and demand is unpredictable. In situations such as this, the first priority should be to seek to reduce lead times since the vari-ability of demand is almost certainly outside the organization's control. Lead-time reduction would enable the application of agile solutions. However, if lead times cannot be reduced the next option is to seek to create a hybrid lean/agile solution. These hybrid solutions require the supply chain to be 'de-coupled' through holding strategic inventory in some generic or unfinished form, with final configuration being com-pleted rapidly once real demand is known. This is the classic 'postponement' strategy. An alternative form of postponement where the final physical configuration cannot be delayed is to postpone the actual distribution of the product by holding it in fewer (or even only one) locations and using express transportation to move it to the final market or point of use once actual demand is known.

The goal of a hybrid strategy should be to build an agile response upon a lean platform by seeking to follow lean principles up to the de-coupling point and agile practices after that point.[3] Figure 4.3 illustrates this idea.

A good example of a de-coupling point enabling a lean/agile hybrid strategy is provided by paint manufacturers such as ICI. Today, con-sumers can be offered customized solutions in terms of the colour of paint through the use of paint mixing machines located in retail outlets. The retailers only need to stock a relatively small number of base colours to provide an almost infinite number of final colours. Thus ICI can utilize lean processes in producing base colours in volume but can provide an agile and timely response to end users. This example also illustrates the principle of seeking to reduce *complexity* whilst providing the requisite level of *variety* that the market demands.

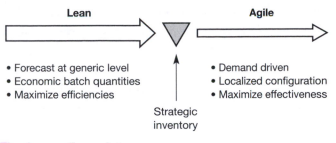

Fig. 4.3 The de-coupling point

To be truly agile a supply chain must possess a number of distinguishing characteristics, as Figure 4.4 suggests.

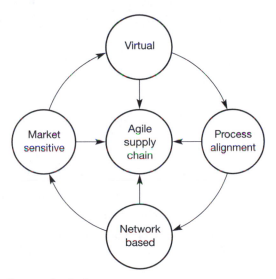

Fig. 4.4 The agile supply chain

Source: Adapted from Harrison, A., Christopher, M. and van Hoek, R., *Creating the Agile Supply Chain,* Chartered Institute of Logistics and Transport, 1999.

Firstly, the agile supply chain is *market-sensitive.* By market-sensitive is meant that the supply chain is capable of reading and responding to real demand. Most organizations are forecast-driven rather than demand-driven. In other words, because they have little direct feed-forward from the marketplace by way of data on actual customer requirements, they are forced to make forecasts based upon past sales or shipments and convert these forecasts into inventory. The breakthroughs of the last decade in the use of information technology to capture data on demand direct from the point-of-sale or point-of-use are now transforming the organization's ability to hear the voice of the market and to respond directly to it.

The use of information technology to share data between buyers and suppliers is, in effect, creating a *virtual* supply chain. Virtual supply chains are information based rather than inventory based.

Conventional logistics systems are based upon a paradigm that seeks to identify the optimal quantities and the spatial location of inventory. Complex formulae and algorithms exist to support this inventory-based business model. Paradoxically, what we are now learning is that once we have visibility of demand through shared information, the premise upon which these formulae are based no longer holds. Electronic Data Interchange (EDI) and now the Internet have enabled partners in the supply chain to act upon the same data, i.e. real demand, rather than be dependent upon the distorted and noisy picture that emerges when orders are transmitted from one step to another in an extended chain.

Supply chain partners can only make full use of shared information through *process alignment*, i.e. collaborative working between buyers and suppliers, joint product development, common systems and shared information. This form of co-operation in the supply chain is becoming ever more prevalent as companies focus on managing their core competencies and outsource all other activities. In this new world a greater reliance on suppliers and alliance partners becomes inevitable and, hence, a new style of relationship is essential. In the 'extended enterprise', as it is often called, there can be no boundaries and an ethos of trust and commitment must prevail. Along with process integration comes joint strategy determination, buyer/supplier teams, transparency of information and even open-book accounting.

This idea of the supply chain as a confederation of partners linked together as a *network* provides the fourth ingredient of agility. There is a growing recognition that individual businesses no longer compete as stand-alone entities but rather as supply chains. Managing networks calls for an entirely difference model than the conventional 'arm's-length' approach to managing customer and supplier relationships.

Clearly a much higher level of collaboration and synchronization is required if the network is to be truly agile. It can be argued that, in today's challenging global markets, the route to sustainable advantage lies in being able to make best use of the respective strengths and competencies of network partners to achieve greater responsiveness to market needs.

Product 'push' versus demand 'pull'

There have been many new ideas and concepts in business management over the last 30 or so years, some of which have endured and others soon discarded. However, perhaps one of the most significant principles to become widely adopted and practised is that of just-in-time. Just-in-time, or JIT, is a philosophy as much as it is a technique. It is based upon the simple idea that wherever possible no activity should take place in a system until there is a need for it.

Thus no products should be made, no components ordered, until there is a downstream requirement. Essentially JIT is a 'pull' concept, where demand at the end of the pipeline pulls products towards the market and behind those products the flow of components is also determined by that same demand. This contrasts with the traditional 'push' system where products are manufactured or assembled in batches in anticipation of demand and are positioned in the supply chain as 'buffers' between the various functions and entities (see Figure 4.5).

The conventional approach to meeting customer requirements is based upon some form of statistical inventory control which typically might rely upon reordering when inventory levels fall to a certain predetermined point – the so-called reorder point (ROP).

Under this approach a reorder point or reorder level is predetermined based upon the expected length of the replenishment lead time (see Figure 4.6). The amount to be ordered may be based upon the economic order quantity (EOQ) formulation which balances the cost of holding inventory against the costs of placing replenishment orders.

Alternative methods include the regular review of stock levels with fixed intervals between orders when the amount to be ordered is determined with reference to a predetermined replenishment level, as in Figure 4.7.

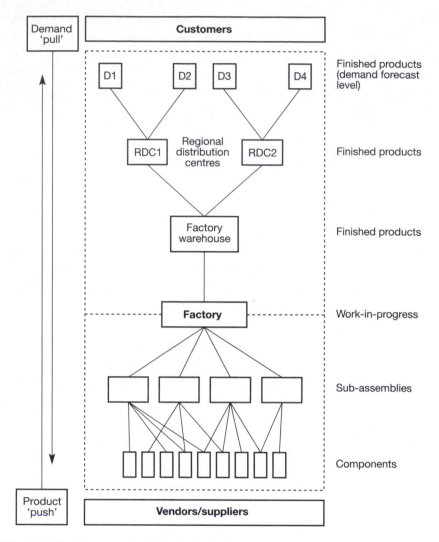

Fig. 4.5 'Push' versus 'pull' in the logistics chain

There are numerous variations on these themes and the techniques have been well documented and practised for many years. However, they all tend to share one weakness, that is they frequently lead to stock levels being higher or lower than necessary, particularly in those cases where the rate of demand may change or occurs in discrete 'lumps'. This latter situation frequently occurs when demand for an item is 'dependent' upon demand for another item, e.g. demand for a

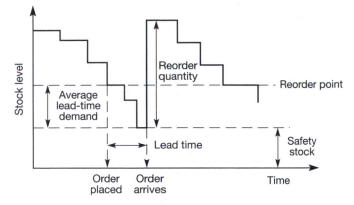

Fig. 4.6 The reorder point method of stock control

TV component is dependent upon the demand for TV sets; or where demand is 'derived', e.g. the demand for TV sets at the factory is determined by demand from the retailer, which is derived from ultimate demand in the marketplace.

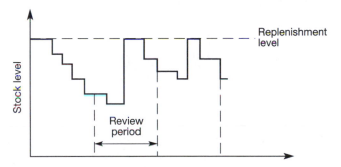

Fig. 4.7 The review period method of stock control

The implications of dependent demand are illustrated in the example given in Figure 4.8, which shows how a regular off-take at the retail level can be converted into a much more 'lumpy' demand situation at the plant by the use of reorder points.

A similar situation can occur in a multi-level distribution system where the combined demand from each level is aggregated at the next level in the system. Figure 4.9 demonstrates such an occurrence.

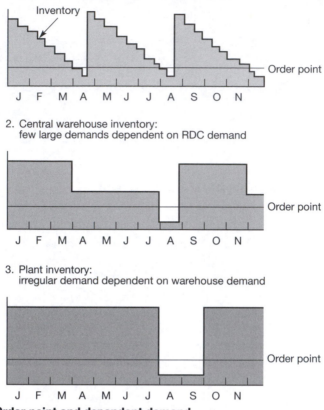

Fig. 4.8 Order point and dependent demand

The common feature of these examples is that demand at each level in the logistics system is dependent upon the demand at the next level in the system. Demand is termed 'dependent' when it is directly related to, or derives from, the demand for another inventory item or product. Conversely, the demand for a given item is termed 'independent' when such demand is unrelated to demand for other items – when it is not a function of demand for other items. This distinction is crucial because whilst independent demand may be forecast using traditional methods, dependent demand must be calculated, based upon the demand at the next level in the logistics chain.

> **Whilst independent demand may be forecast using traditional methods, dependent demand must be calculated, based upon the demand at the next level in the logistics chain.**

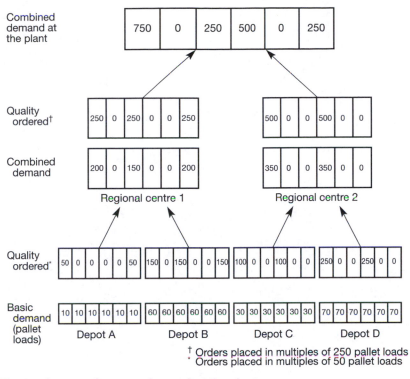

Combined demand at the plant	750	0	250	500	0	250

Fig. 4.9 Causes of uneven demand at the plant

Using the example in Figure 4.9 it would clearly be inappropriate to attempt to forecast demand at the plant using data based upon the pattern of combined demand from the regional centres. Rather it has to be calculated from the identified requirements at each of the preceding levels. It is only at the point of final demand, in this case at the depots, where forecasts can sensibly be made – in fact in most cases demand at the depot would itself be dependent upon retailers' or other intermediaries' demand, but since this is obviously outside the supplier's direct control it is necessary to produce a forecasted estimate of demand.

The classic economic order quantity (EOQ) model has tended to channel our thinking towards the idea that there is some 'optimum' amount to order (and hence to hold in stock). The EOQ model arrives at this optimum by balancing the holding cost of inventory against the cost of issuing replenishment orders and/or the costs of production set-ups (see Figure 4.10).

127

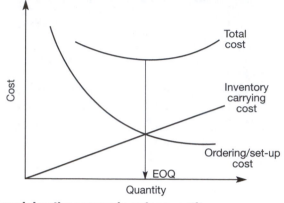

Fig. 4.10 Determining the economic order quantity

The EOQ can be easily determined by the formula:

$$EOQ = \sqrt{\frac{2AS}{i}}$$

where,

> *A* = **Annual usage**
> *S* = **Ordering cost/set-up cost**
> *i* = **Inventory carrying cost**

So, for example, if we use 1,000 units of product X a year, each costing £40, and each order/set-up costs £100 and the carrying cost of inventory is 25 per cent then:

$$EOQ = \sqrt{\frac{2 \times 1000 \times 100}{40 \times 0.25}} = 141$$

The problem is that this reorder quantity means that we will be carrying more inventory than is actually required per day over the complete order cycle (except on the last day). For example, if the EOQ were 100 units and daily usage was 10 units then on the first day of the cycle we will be overstocked by 90 units, on the second day by 80 units and so on.

To compound the problem we have additional inventory in the form of 'safety' stock, which is carried in order to provide a safeguard against demand during the replenishment lead time being greater than expected and/or variation in the lead time itself.

The result is that we end up with a lot of unproductive inventory, which represents a continuing drain on working capital.

The Japanese philosophy

It has often been said that the scarcity of space in industrialized Japan has made the nation conscious of the need to make the most productive use of all physical resources, including inventory – whether this is true is of academic interest only – what is the case is that it is the widely held view in Japan that inventory is waste.

An analogy that is frequently drawn in Japan is that an organization's investment in inventory is like a large, deep lake (see Figure 4.11). Well below the surface of this lake are numerous jagged rocks, but because of the depth of the water, the captain of the ship need have no fear of striking one of them.

The comparison with business is simple: the depth of the water in the lake represents inventory and the rocks represent problems. These problems might include such things as inaccurate forecasts, unreliable suppliers, quality problems, bottlenecks, industrial relations problems and so on. The Japanese philosophy is that inventory merely hides the problems. Their view is that the level of water in the lake should be reduced (say to level 'B' in Figure 4.11). Now the captain of the ship is forced to confront the problems – they cannot be avoided. In the same way if inventory is reduced then management must grasp the various nettles of forecast inaccuracy, unreliable suppliers and so on.

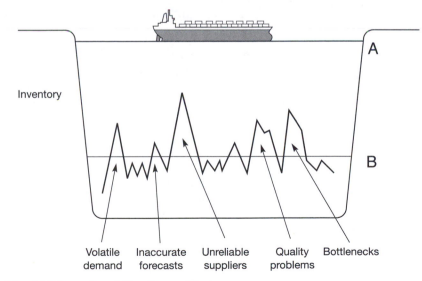

Fig. 4.11 **Inventory hides the problems**

The Japanese developed the so-called Kanban concept as a way of lowering the water in the lake. Kanban originated in assembly-type operations but the principles can be extended across the supply chain and to all types of operations. The name Kanban comes from the Japanese for a type of card that was used in early systems to signal to the upstream supply point that a certain quantity of material could be released.

Kanban is a 'pull' system that is driven by the demand at the lowest point in the chain. In a production operation the aim would be to produce only that quantity needed for immediate demand. When parts are needed on the assembly line they are fed from the next stage up the chain in just the quantity needed at the time they are needed. Likewise this movement now triggers demand at the next work station in the chain and so on.

By progressively reducing the Kanban quantity (i.e. the amount demanded from the supplying work station) bottlenecks will become apparent. Management will then focus attention on the bottleneck to remove it by the most cost-effective means possible. Again the Kanban quantity will be reduced until a further bottleneck is revealed. Hence the Kanban philosophy essentially seeks to achieve a balanced supply chain with minimal inventory at every stage and where the process and transit quantities of materials and stock are reduced to the lowest possible amount. The ultimate aim, say the Japanese, should be the 'economic batch quantity of 1'!

In fact this logic does not necessarily conflict with the traditional view of how the economic batch (or order) quantity is determined. All that is different is that the Japanese are seeking to minimize the batch quantity by shifting the curve that represents the cost of ordering or the cost of set-ups to the left (see Figure 4.12). In other words, they focus on finding ways to reduce set-up costs and ordering costs.

The effect of moving the curve to the left on the economic batch/order quantity is seen in Figure 4.13.

The foundations of agility

It will be apparent that agility is not a single company concept but rather it extends from one end of the supply chain to the other. The concept of agility has significant implications for how organizations within the supply/demand network relate to each other and how they can best work together on the basis of shared information.

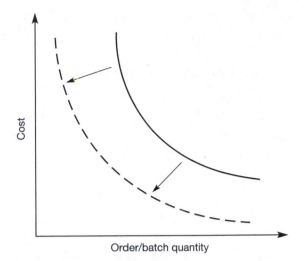

Fig. 4.12 Reducing set-up costs/ordering costs

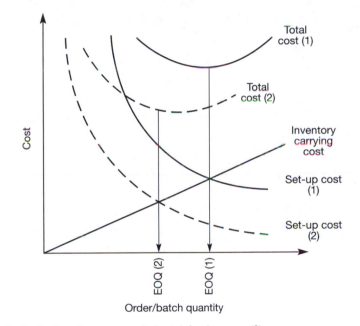

Fig. 4.13 Reducing the economic batch/order quantity

To bring these ideas together, a number of basic principles can be identified as the starting point for the creation of the agile supply chain.

1 Synchronize activities through shared information

Synchronization implies that all parties in the supply chain are 'marching to the same drumbeat'. In other words, through shared information and process alignment there is in effect one set of numbers and a single schedule for the entire supply chain. This somewhat Utopian vision is increasingly becoming reality as web-based technology enables different entities in a network to share information on real demand, inventory and capacity in a collaborative context.

In the fast moving consumer goods (fmcg) sector there is a growing number of examples of supply chain synchronization made possible by the retailers' increasing willingness to share point-of-sale data with manufacturers. One such instance is the web-based system established by the UK's biggest retailer, Tesco. The Tesco Information Exchange (TIE) is an extranet that enables Tesco's suppliers to access their own sales data, item by item. This data is updated several times a day and potentially can provide manufacturers with the means to link their production schedules to Tesco's replenishment requirements.

In the automobile industry most of the volume car manufacturers have established 'seamless' processes with their first tier suppliers based upon providing immediate access to production plans and schedules. This enables just-in-time deliveries to be achieved without the need for major buffers of inventory at the first tier level.

In the US the 'quick response' initiative in the apparel industry has linked retailers to garment manufacturers and also to the fabric producers through shared information. The impact of this collaboration has been a significant improvement in the competitiveness of that industry.

2 Work smarter, not harder

Detailed examination of the processes that together constitute a supply chain inevitably highlights the fact that a large proportion of the end-to-end time is 'non-value-adding'. In other words, time is being spent on activities that typically create cost but do not create a benefit for the customer. Time spent in inventory is a classic example of non-value-adding time. Supply chain mapping can reveal where this idle time

132

occurs; to attack it then requires a review of the processes that precede or follow that idle time. Process time is directly correlated with inventory, e.g. if it takes three weeks from raising a purchase order to receiving the goods, at least three weeks of inventory will be required to buffer ourselves during that lead time.

Business process re-engineering (BPR) is the term frequently applied to the activity of simplifying and reshaping the organizational processes with the goal of achieving the desired outcomes in shorter time-frames at less cost. Many processes in the supply chain are lengthy because the constituent activities are performed in 'series', i.e. in a linear, 'one after the other' way. It is often possible to re-engineer the process so that those same activities can be performed 'in parallel', i.e. simultaneously.

Time compression in a supply chain can be achieved not necessarily by speeding up activities, but rather by doing fewer things – i.e. eliminating where possible non-value adding activities. Many existing practices in business are performed for historical reasons; there was once a justification for those practices but, with changed conditions, that justification may no longer exist.

Supply chains can be transformed in terms of their agility by the rigorous application of process re-engineering principles.

3 Partner with suppliers to reduce in-bound lead times

Conventionally, firms have maintained an arm's-length relationship with suppliers. Suppliers have often been chosen on the basis of price rather than their responsiveness. A major opportunity exists for reducing in-bound lead times through close working with key suppliers. One powerful way in which collaboration can improve responsiveness is through the adoption of Vendor Managed Inventory (VMI) practices.

VMI, which is discussed in more detail in Chapter 6, switches the responsibility for the management and replenishment of inventory from the customer to the supplier. The customer no longer places orders on the supplier but rather shares with them information on sales, rates of usage or consumption. Using this information the supplier is better able to plan and schedule the acquisition, production and delivery of the product. Both parties benefit, the customer through higher levels of availability and reliability and the supplier through a reduction in their need to carry safety stock and, often, a better use of capacity. VMI is a classic instance of the application of the principle of 'substituting information for inventory'.

Increasingly in the defence and aerospace sector the sheer complexity of the products requires a high level of information sharing with suppliers. Thus companies like BAe Systems, Thales and EADS are working with key suppliers to create more responsive supply chains through VMI-type arrangements.

4 Seek to reduce complexity

Complexity comes in many guises in supply chains. Complexity may be generated by multiple variants of the same product, e.g. different pack sizes, or by each product in a family having greatly different Bills of Material, or by frequent product changes, and so on. Complexity can also be generated through cumbersome processes that involve many different stages and hand-offs. Simplification is an obvious remedy for complexity but one which may not always be available. However, there will often be opportunities to reduce complexity by questioning the reasons why things are the way they are.

For example, is the level of product variety greater than the customer actually requires? Often product, proliferation is driven by sales or marketing departments and may not actually achieve additional sales but spread the same total demand over a greater number of stock keeping units (SKUs). The greater the fragmentation of demand the harder it becomes to manage availability in that the variability of demand will tend to be higher.

Simplification can sometimes be achieved through seeking greater commonality of components or sub-assembly across a family of products. For example, in automobile design these days it is increasingly the case that several different models of car are built on the same platform and 'under the skin' share common components and sub-assemblies.

The point about complexity is that it provides a barrier to agility as well as generating cost.

5 Postpone the final configuration/assembly/distribution of products

Postponement refers to the process by which the commitment of a product to its final form or location is delayed for as long as possible. When decisions on the final configuration or pack have to be made ahead of demand there is the inevitable risk that the products that are available are not the ones the customer wants. For example, the customer may want a blue four-door car with air-conditioning but the dealer has a red, two-door with a sunroof. Or, again, there may be a blue four-door available but it is at a different dealer at the other end of the country.

The philosophy of postponement ideally would begin on the drawing board so that products are designed with late configuration in mind. The longer that products can remain as generic 'work in progress' then the more flexibility there will be to ensure the 'right product in the right place at the right time'.

An example of late configuration is provided by Hewlett Packard and its DeskJet printers. These products are designed so that they can be manufactured as generic, but incomplete, units. They are then localized at regional centres where the appropriate power pack, plug and cable, local packaging, etc. are added. In this way inventory is minimized but availability is enhanced.

Postponement may not always be feasible in terms of late configuration but there may be scope for spatial postponement through holding inventory in just a few locations with the ability to ship the product rapidly to the location required when an order is received.

6 Manage processes not just functions

For centuries organizations have followed an organizational logic based upon the 'division of labour' whereby activities take place within functions or departments. Whilst this functionally based organizational concept may ensure the efficient use of resources it is actually inwardly focused and tends to lead to a 'silo' type mentality. It also seems to be the case that these functionally based organizations are slow to respond to changes in the market or business environment. Because there are often multiple 'hand-offs' as things get passed from one function to another there is an inevitable lengthening in the time to respond. In functionally based businesses the new product development activity, for example, is often lengthy as it moves from R&D to product engineering to market research and eventually into production.

On the other hand, those companies who are able to respond rapidly to changing customer requirements tend to focus more upon managing 'processes'. Processes are the horizontal, market-facing sequences of activities that create value for customers. They are cross-functional by definition and are usually best managed through the means of inter-disciplinary teams. The critical business processes that cut across the organization would include innovation, customer relationship management and supplier relationship management.

The way businesses are organized can have a significant impact upon their agility; those companies with cumbersome, multi-level decision-making processes tend to be far slower to respond to market changes than their competitors who give autonomy to self-managed process teams.

A further reason why process management is critical to agility across the wider supply chain is that process alignment between entities in that chain is clearly facilitated if organizational structures are horizontal rather than vertical.

7 Utilize appropriate performance metrics

It is a truism that performance measurement shapes behaviour. This is particularly the case in business organizations where formal measurement systems drive the business. In functionally based organizations these measurements often are based upon departmental budgets and are underpinned by objectives such as cost minimization, asset utilization and efficiency, and productivity improvement. Whilst on the face of it these objectives may appear to be desirable, they will not necessarily encourage agile practices within the organization. If, for example, a manufacturing facility is measured on, say, unit cost of production then the incentive will be to go for big batch sizes to take advantage of economies of scale. However, such actions will probably lead to a loss of flexibility and the creation of additional inventory. If, on the other hand, time-based metrics were to be employed then the focus could be on cycle-time reduction, set-up time reduction and other measures that encourage agile practices.

A further incentive to agility can be created by linking processes to customer-based metrics. One such widely used measure is 'perfect order achievement'. A perfect order is one where the customer gets exactly what they want at the time and place they want it. It will also usually be the case that different customers may well have different requirements and expectations, so the definition of what constitutes a perfect order will have to be specific to each segment, channel or even individual key accounts.

136

A fundamental tenet of agility is customer responsiveness, hence the need to ensure that the primary measures of business performance reflect this imperative. 'Time to market' and 'time to volume' are powerful metrics employed by companies such as Sony and Canon where short life cycles dictate a focus on rapid response to fast-changing technologies and volatile customer demand.

In the past, the focus of many companies was primarily on *efficiency*, i.e. a continuing search for lower costs, better use of capacity, reduced inventories and so on. These are still worthy goals today but the priority has shifted. Now the emphasis must be on *effectiveness*. In other words the challenge is to create strategies and procedures that will enable organizations to become the supplier of choice and to sustain that position through higher levels of customer responsiveness. This is the logic that underpins the concept of the agile supply chains.

A routemap to responsiveness

The shift in the balance of power in the distribution channel has highlighted the need for the business to be driven by the market rather than by its own internal goals. However, for organizations to become truly market-driven, there has to be a sustained focus on responsiveness across the business and its wider supply chain. There are many prerequisites for responsiveness and Figure 4.14 summarizes the key elements.

The responsive business will have agile suppliers and will work very closely with them to align processes across the extended enterprise. It will also be very close to its customers, capturing information on real demand and sharing that information with its partners across the network. Internally the business will also be focused on agility through the way it organizes – breaking through functional silos to create process teams. In terms of its manufacturing and sourcing strategy, the responsive business will seek to marry the lean and agile paradigm through de-coupling its upstream and downstream processes, utilizing the principles of postponement wherever possible.

Those companies that can follow this routemap will be more likely to be the leaders in their field. More often than not, when we look at the successful companies in any market, they tend to be the ones that

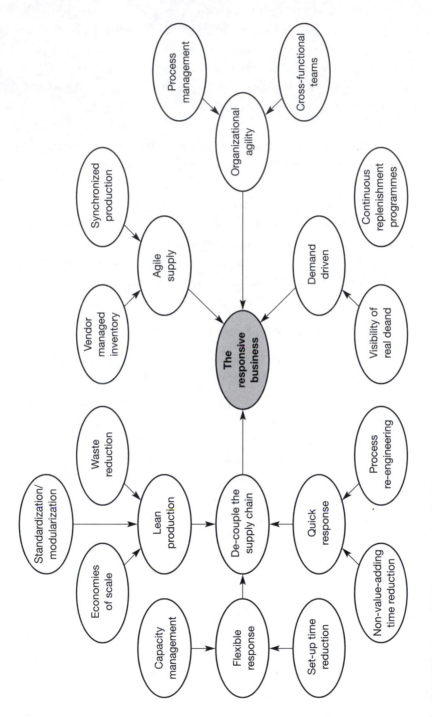

Fig. 4.14 Routemap to the responsive business

have demonstrated their ability to respond more rapidly to the changing needs of their customers. The case study that concludes this chapter underlines the challenges that organizations must confront as they seek to become more responsive to customer needs.

The three-day car programme

Automotive assemblers have for many years led the way with lean production techniques, proving a template for efficiency improvements in many other sectors. They mastered just-in-time supply from first tier suppliers to assembly line, achieved dramatic improvements in terms of better quality, faster throughput and lower production costs. What they did not do was improve end-to-end supply chain efficiency. Nor did they provide customers with exactly the car they wanted when they wanted it, despite producing large stockpiles of unsold finished cars. The problem was identified long ago, and assemblers have been attempting to realize the theoretical goal of a 'stockless' supply chain for many years. Back in 1993 British-based car maker Rover introduced the concept of 'Personal Production', an initiative that aimed to provide prospective buyers and fleet car user-choosers with exactly the car they wanted within 14 days. The project revolved around efforts to link customers' showroom orders directly with production scheduling. Research at the time had underlined the necessity of such a system showing that (industry-wide) only a quarter of all showroom visitors ever got exactly the car they wanted and one in five failed to buy at all.[1] Personal Production eventually foundered, not least because of friction with the dealer network and the difficulties in delivering overseas within the required time-frame; nevertheless, the underlying problem – the lack of agility in automotive supply chains – is more pressing than ever.

Subsequent 'best practice' research, involving eight automotive assembly companies,[2] has shown that speed of supply – and their failure to get it – remains a very significant issue for car buyers, with 65 per cent stating that it was an important factor in their car buying decision. One in five stated that their ideal delivery time was less than one week, not the 40 days they were likely to have to wait for their precisely specified vehicle. Moreover, it was the younger customers who were the most impatient.

▶

▶

Research by specialist teams at Cardiff University and the University of Bath concluded that it was in fact possible for lead times for UK-produced cars for UK customers to be reduced to just three days, if best practice principles were observed. Classic lean production methods, pioneered in the car industry by Toyota, have tended to focus on optimizing flows through a small part of the supply chain – the assembly plant – not the total lead time. Toyota continues to lead the industry in terms of quality and flexible manufacturing systems. Its latest innovations allow up to eight different models to move through the same body shop, making it easier than ever to produce high-margin, low-volume 'boutique' to order.

However, the UK industry research shows that amongst the manufacturers collaborating in the three-day car project, delays in production were minimal, but the batching of orders at dealerships, and delays in transferring this to schedules, more delays with scheduling, together with the unreliability of data sent to suppliers was actually responsible for the bulk of time wasted. Thereafter shortages of components and problems with the quality of paintwork meant the only two-thirds of vehicles were built as scheduled. More delays follow as efforts are made to put together batch loads of finished cars to optimize efficient utilization of high-capacity vehicle transporters.

All of these delays could, in theory, be removed if car manufacturers took some pointers from other retail sectors, notably that demand data in the form of customer orders could be fed in real time directly into production slots. The precise sequence could be determined hourly, but schedules would be frozen 36 hours in advance to provide 12 hours for locally based logistics and first tier component suppliers to deliver inbound supplies. The third and final day is then allowed for delivery of the finished vehicles to the dealerships.

As the three-day car research study is keen to point out, however, some practical hurdles would have to be overcome. First, a different approach to planning would be required. It would be forecast driven, but capacity planning would rely on likely customer orders, segmented by lead-time sensitivity. Private customers would be three-day car customers so scheduling would be based around their orders; orders for 'captive customers', i.e. employees and demonstrators for dealerships, would be used to fill three-day buffer capacity during seasonal dips in demand. The bulk of the production capacity would, however, continue to be assigned to less time-sensitive customers such as fleet buyers who research reveals are willing to wait longer or are better able to place orders well ahead of demand.

A single shared data system, linking dealer showroom all the way through the assembler into first tier suppliers, was deemed essential so that sales staff could check the availability of all component parts for the specified model before the order was formally committed to the production schedule. Then active demand management techniques could be applied to level out serious fluctuations in demand. Some significant sources of demand volatility, such as monthly sales targets, which encourage sales staff to discount heavily at month ends, could be redesigned to take out unnecessary spikes. Other seasonal fluctuations could be levelled to some extent by other 'revenue management' techniques, such as off-peak price promotions. Visibility of component availability would also allow sales staff to steer customers away from some variants where specific component capacity constraints were likely to be problematic.

Back in the assembler's factory common platforms reduce product mix complexity. The researchers found that de-coupling the paint shop from other production processes was key to avoiding in-production delays. The solution was to increase the storage capacity for stocks of unpainted car shells known as 'bodies in white'. Storage capacity levels, currently running at up to 800 bodies, had to be increased. Staffing levels on production lines would also have to be raised. Higher staffing levels, though more costly, allow greater flexibility meaning that all variants could be handled by the same production line, regardless of differences in labour content. In addition employees would themselves be required to be more flexible in terms of working hours, adjusting their working hours in line with fluctuations in demand.

The third and final leg of the process is delivery of the finished vehicle to the appropriate dealership. Ensuring three-day delivery would increase outbound logistics costs, unless the existing model was changed. The solution, according to the three-day car research team, is better information sharing with the logistics providers, together with round the clock, multi-franchise delivery operations, using car

▶

transporters of differing sizes. This would allow the extended enter-prise to optimize the final lead-time component and bring the dream of a stockless supply chain considerably closer.

References

1. Retail Motor Industry Federation, in Towers, J., Transcript of speech delivered at Management Centre Europe, Brussels, 1 February 1996, p. 5.
2. Whiteman, J. *et al.*, 'The Car You Want When You Want It: Summary of the 3-Day Car Programme', ICDP Working Paper 2002, p.32.

Summary

Because markets are volatile and demand uncertain, it is imperative that organizations become more responsive. Responsiveness is characterized by the ability to change more quickly. This change could be in terms of product variety or volume or in the speed of new product introductions.

Agility lies at the heart of the responsive organization. Agile busi-nesses have a number of distinguishing features: they are market sensitive; they are information based and they share that information across their supply network; and, finally, their processes connect easily with those of their supply chain partners.

Whilst 'lean' practices have much to commend them, by themselves they are unlikely to provide levels of responsiveness that the market demand. However, a hybrid lean/agile approach can be adopted or the supply chain can be de-coupled through postponement.

References

1. Womack, J.P., Jones, D.T. and Roos, D., *The Machine that Changed the World*, Macmillan, 1990.
2. Monden, Y., *The Toyota Production System*, Productivity Press, 1983.
3. Christopher, M. and Towill, D., 'An Integrated Model for the Design of Agile Supply Chains', *International Journal of Physical Distribution and Logistics Management*, Vol. 31, No. 4, 2001.

Strategic lead-time management

This chapter:

Explores the 'cost of time' and the drivers of time-based competition: shortening product life cycles, customers' desire for reduced inventories and the dangers of being forecast-dependent in an increasingly volatile marketplace.

●

Examines the concept of lead time, the order-to-deliver cycle, its components and the need to consider the wider context of the order-to-cash cycle.

●

Looks at how the reduction of lead times can impact on the goals of logistics pipeline management.

●

Outlines some of the ways in which inadequate system design can lengthen lead times and engineer costs rather than value into the logistics process.

●

Introduces the concept of the lead-time gap, offering a number of suggestions for lead time reduction.

'Time is money' is perhaps an over-worked cliché in common parlance, but in logistics management it goes to the heart of the matter. Not only does time represent cost to the logistics manager but extended lead times also imply a customer service penalty. As far as cost is concerned there is a direct relationship between the length of the logistics pipeline and the inventory that is locked up in it; every day that the product is in the pipeline it incurs an inventory holding cost. Secondly, long lead times mean a slower response to customer requirements, and, given the increased importance of delivery speed in today's internationally competitive environment, this combination of high costs and lack of responsiveness provides a recipe for decline and decay.

Time-based competition

Customers in all markets, industrial or consumer, are increasingly time-sensitive.[1] In other words they value time and this is reflected in their purchasing behaviour. Thus, for example, in industrial markets buyers tend to source from suppliers with the shortest lead times who can meet their quality specification. In consumer markets customers make their choice from amongst the brands

> Customers in all markets, industrial or consumer, are increasingly time-sensitive.

available at the time; hence if the preferred brand is out of stock it is quite likely that a substitute brand will be purchased instead.

In the past it was often the case that price was paramount as an influence on the purchase decision. Now, whilst price is still important, a major determinant of choice of supplier or brand is the 'cost of time'. The cost of time is simply the additional costs that a customer must bear whilst waiting for delivery or whilst seeking out alternatives.

There are many pressures leading to the growth of time-sensitive markets but perhaps the most significant are:

1. Shortening life cycles
2. Customers' drive for reduced inventories
3. Volatile markets making reliance on forecasts dangerous

1 Shortening life cycles

The concept of the product life cycle is well established. It suggests that for many products there is a recognizable pattern of sales from launch through to final decline (see Figure 5.1).

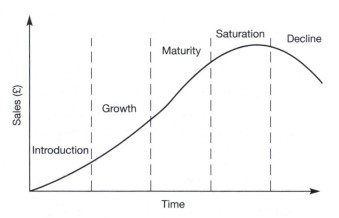

Fig. 5.1 The product life cycle

A feature of the last few decades has been the shortening of these life cycles. Take as an example the case of the typewriter. The early mechanical typewriter had a life cycle of about 30 years – meaning that an individual model would be little changed during that period. These mechanical typewriters were replaced by the electro-mechanical type-writer, which had a life cycle of approximately ten years. The electro-mechanical typewriter gave way to the electronic typewriter with a four-year life cycle. Now personal computers have taken over with a life cycle of one year or less!

In situations like this the time available to develop new products, to launch them and to meet marketplace demand is clearly greatly reduced. Hence the ability to 'fast track' product development, manu-facturing and logistics becomes a key element of competitive strategy. Figure 5.2 shows the effect of being late into the market and slow to meet demand.

146

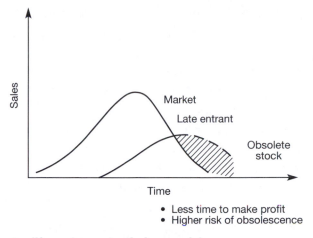

Fig. 5.2 Shorter life cycles make timing crucial

However, it is not just time-to-market that is important. Once a product is on the market the ability to respond quickly to demand is equally important. Here the lead time to re-supply a market determines the organization's ability to exploit demand during the life cycle. It is apparent that those companies that can achieve reductions in the order-to-delivery cycle will have a strong advantage over their slower competitors.

2 Customers' drive for reduced inventories

One of the most pronounced phenomena of recent years has been the almost universal move by companies to reduce their inventories. Whether the inventory is in the form of raw materials, components, work-in-progress or finished products, the pressure has been to release the capital locked up in stock and hence simultaneously to reduce the holding cost of that stock. The same companies that have reduced their inventories in this way have also recognized the advantage that they gain in terms of improved flexibility and responsiveness to their customers.

The knock-on effect of this development upstream to suppliers has been considerable. It is now imperative that suppliers can provide a just-in-time delivery service. Timeliness of delivery – meaning delivery of the complete order at the time required by the customer – becomes the number one order-winning criterion.

Many companies still think that the only way to service customers who require just-in-time deliveries is for them, the supplier, to carry the inventory instead of the customer. Whilst the requirements of such customers could always be met by the supplier carrying inventory close to the customer(s), this is simply shifting the cost burden from one part of the supply chain to another – indeed the cost may even be higher. Instead what is needed is for the supplier to substitute responsiveness for inventory whenever possible.

As we discussed in Chapter 4, responsiveness essentially is achieved through agility in the supply chain. Not only can customers be serviced more rapidly but the degree of flexibility offered can be greater and yet the cost should be less because the pipeline is shorter. Figure 5.3 suggests that agility can enable companies to break free of the classic trade-off between service and cost. Instead of having to choose between either higher service levels or lower costs it is possible to have the best of both worlds.

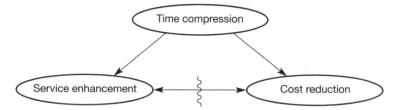

Fig. 5.3 Breaking free of the classic service/cost trade-off

3 Volatile markets make reliance on forecasts dangerous

A continuing problem for most organizations is the inaccuracy of forecasts. It seems that no matter how sophisticated the forecasting techniques employed, the volatility of markets ensures that the forecast will be wrong! Whilst many forecasting errors are the result of inappropriate forecasting methodology, the root cause of these problems is that forecast error increases as lead time increases.

The evidence from most markets is that demand volatility is tending to increase, often due to competitive activity, sometimes due to unexpected responses to promotions or price changes and as a result of intermediaries' reordering policies. In situations such as these there are very few forecasting methods that will be able to predict short-term changes in demand with any accuracy.

All forecasts are prone to error and the further ahead the forecast horizon is the greater the error. Figure 5.4 shows how forecast error increases more than proportionately over time.

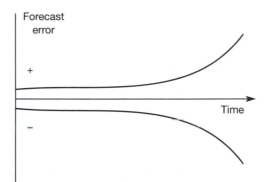

Fig. 5.4 Forecast error and planning horizons

The conventional response to such a problem has been to increase the safety stock to provide protection against such forecast errors. However, it is surely preferable to reduce lead times in order to reduce forecast error and hence reduce the need for inventory.

Many businesses have invested heavily in automation in the factory with the aim of reducing throughput times. In some cases processes that used to take days to complete now only take hours and activities that took hours now only take minutes. However, it is paradoxical that many of those same businesses that have spent millions of pounds on automation to speed up the time it takes to manufacture a product are then content to let it sit in a distribution centre or warehouse for weeks waiting to be sold! The requirement is to look across the different stages in the supply chain to see how time as a whole can be reduced through re-engineering the way the chain is structured.

One of the basic fallacies of management is that long lead times provide security and cover against uncertainty. In fact the reverse is true! Imagine a Utopian situation where a company had reduced its procurement, manufacturing and delivery lead time to zero. In other words, as soon as a customer ordered an item – any item – that product was made and delivered instantaneously. In such a situation there would be no need for a forecast and no need for inventory and at the same time a greater variety could be offered to the customer.

Whilst clearly zero lead times are hardly likely to exist in the real world, the target for any organization should be to reduce lead times, at every stage in the logistics pipeline, to as close to zero as possible. In so many cases it is possible to find considerable opportunity for total lead-time reduction, often through some very simple changes in procedure.

The concept of lead time

From the customer's viewpoint there is only one lead time: the elapsed time from order to delivery. Clearly this is a crucial competitive variable as more and more markets become increasingly time competitive. Nevertheless it represents only a partial view of lead time. Just as important, from the supplier's perspective, is the time it takes to convert an order into cash and, indeed, the total time that working capital is committed from when materials are first procured through to when the customer's payment is received.

Let us examine both of these lead-time concepts in turn.

1 The order-to-delivery cycle

From a marketing point of view the time taken from receipt of a customer's order through to delivery (sometimes referred to as order cycle time (OCT)) is critical. In today's just-in-time environment short lead times are a major source of competitive advantage. Equally important, however, is the reliability or consistency of that lead time. It can actually be argued that reliability of delivery is more important than the length of the order cycle – at least up to a point – because the impact of a failure to deliver on time is more severe than the need to order further in advance. However, because, as we have seen, long lead times require longer-term forecasts, then the pressure from the customer will continue to be for deliveries to be made in ever-shorter time-frames.

What are the components of order cycle time? Figure 5.5 highlights the major elements.

Customer places order	Order entry	Order processing	Order assembly	Transport	Order received

Fig. 5.5 The order cycle

Each of these steps in the chain will consume time. Because of bottle-necks, inefficient processes and fluctuations in the volume of orders handled there will often be considerable variation in the time taken for these various activities to be completed. The overall effect can lead to a substantial reduction in the reliability of delivery. As an example, Figure 5.6 shows the cumulative effect of variations in an order cycle which results in a range of possible cycle times from five days to 25 days.

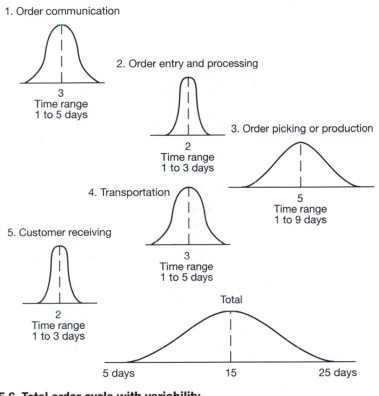

Fig. 5.6 Total order cycle with variability
Source: Stock, J.R. and Lambert, D.M., *Strategic Logistics Management*, 2nd edition, Irwin, 1987.

In those situations where orders are not met from stock but may have to be manufactured, assembled or sourced from external vendors, then clearly lead times will be even further extended, with the possibility of still greater variations in total order-to-delivery time. Figure 5.7 high-lights typical activities in such extended lead times.

151

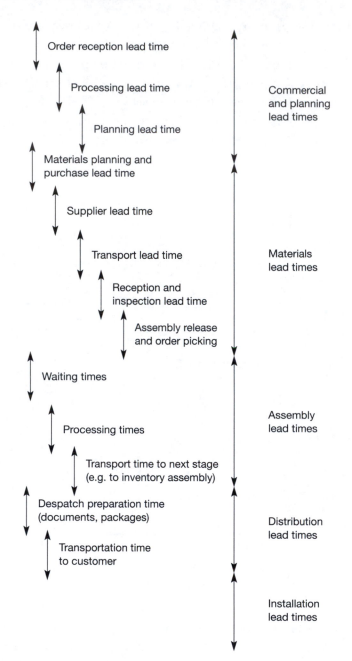

Fig. 5.7 Lead-time components

2 The cash-to-cash cycle

As we have already observed, a basic concern of any organization is: How long does it take to convert an order into cash? In reality the issue is not just how long it takes to process orders, raise invoices and receive payment, but also how long is the pipeline from the sourcing of raw material through to the finished product because throughout the pipeline resources are being consumed and working capital needs to be financed.

From the moment when decisions are taken on the sourcing and procurement of materials and components, through the manufacturing and assembly process to final distribution, time is being consumed. That time is represented by the number of days of inventory in the pipeline, whether as raw materials, work-in-progress, goods in transit, or time taken to process orders, issue replenishment orders, as well as time spent in manufacturing, time in queues or bottlenecks and so on. The control of this total pipeline is the true scope of logistics lead-time management. Figure 5.8 illustrates the way in which cumulative lead time builds up from procurement through to payment.

As we shall see later in this chapter, the longer the pipeline from source of materials to the final user the less responsive to changes in demand the system will be. It is also the case that longer pipelines obscure the 'visibility' of end demand so that it is difficult to link manufacturing and procurement decisions to marketplace requirements. Thus we find an inevitable build-up of inventory as a buffer at each step along

> The longer the pipeline from source of materials to the final user the less responsive to changes in demand the system will be.

the supply chain. An approximate rule of thumb suggests that the amount of safety stock in a pipeline varies with the square root of the pipeline length.

Overcoming these problems and ensuring timely response to volatile demand requires a new and fundamentally different approach to the management of lead times.

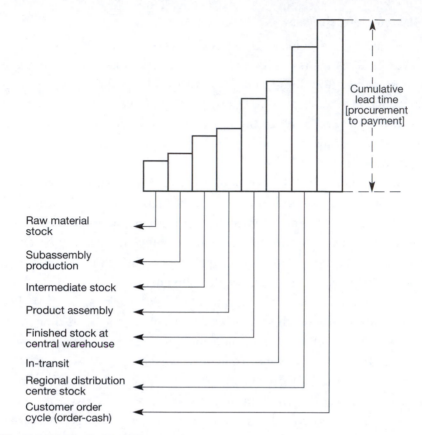

Raw material
stock

Subassembly
production

Intermediate stock

Product assembly

Finished stock at
central warehouse

In-transit

Regional distribution
centre stock

Customer order
cycle (order-cash)

Fig. 5.8 Strategic lead-time management

Logistics pipeline management

The key to the successful control of logistics lead times is pipeline management. Pipeline management is the process whereby manufacturing and procurement lead times are linked to the needs of the marketplace. At the same time, pipeline management seeks to meet the competitive challenge of increasing the speed of response to those market needs.

The goals of logistics pipeline management are:

- Lower costs
- Higher quality
- More flexibility
- Faster response times

The achievement of these goals is dependent upon managing the supply chain as an entity and seeking to reduce the pipeline length and/or to speed up the flow through that pipeline. In examining the efficiency of supply chains it is often found that many of the activities that take place add more cost than value. For example, moving a pallet into a warehouse, repositioning it, storing it and then moving it out in all likelihood has added no value but has added considerably to the total cost.

Very simply, value-adding time is time spent doing something that creates a benefit for which the customer is prepared to pay. Thus we could classify manufacturing as a value-added activity as well as the physical movement of the product and the means of creating the exchange. The old adage 'the right product in the right place at the right time' summarizes the idea of customer value-adding activities. Thus any activity that contributes to the achievement of that goal could be classified as value adding.

On the other hand, non-value-adding time is time spent on an activity whose elimination would lead to no reduction of benefit to the customer. Some non-value-adding activities are necessary because of the current design of our processes but they still represent a cost and should be minimized.

The difference between value-adding time and non-value-adding time is crucial to an understanding of how logistics processes can be improved. Flowcharting supply chain processes is the first step towards understanding the opportunities that exist for improvements in productivity through re-engineering those processes.

> The difference between value-adding time and non-value-adding time is crucial to an understanding of how logistics processes can be improved.

Once processes have been flowcharted, the first step is to bring together the managers involved in those processes to debate and agree exactly which elements of the process can truly be described as value adding. Agreement may not easily be achieved as no one likes to admit that the activity they are responsible for does not actually add any value for customers.

The next step is to do a rough-cut graph highlighting visually how much time is consumed in both non-value-adding and value-adding activities. Figure 5.9 shows a generic example of such a graph.

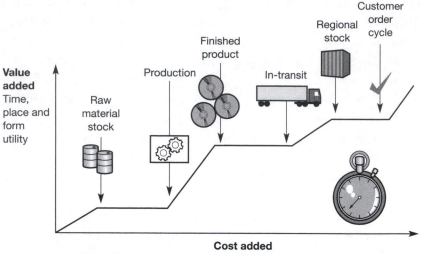

Cost added
Production, storage and transport costs and the time cost of money

Fig. 5.9 Which activities add cost and which add value?

Figure 5.10 shows an actual analysis for a pharmaceutical product where the total process time was 40 weeks and yet value was only being added for 6.2 per cent of that time.

It will be noted from this example that most of the value is added early in the process and hence it is more expensive to hold as inventory. Furthermore, much of the flexibility is probably lost as the product is configured and/or packaged in specific forms early in that process. Figure 5.11 shows that this product started as a combination of three active ingredients but very rapidly became 25 stock keeping units because it was packaged in different sizes, formats, etc., and was then held in inventory for the rest of the time in the company's pipeline.

An indicator of the efficiency of a supply chain is given by its throughput efficiency, which can be measured as:

$$\frac{\text{Value-added time}}{\text{End-to-end pipeline time}} \times 100$$

Throughput efficiency can be as low as 10 per cent, meaning that most time spent in a supply chain is non-value-adding time.

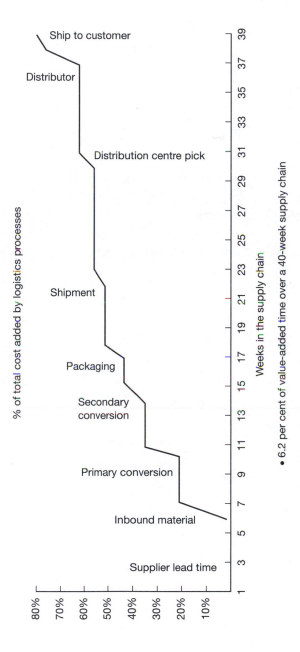

Fig. 5.10 Value added through time

Plot of variety through the supply chain

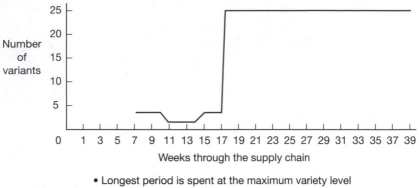

- Longest period is spent at the maximum variety level
- Greatest flexibility is available when the product is generic

Fig. 5.11 Variety through time

Figure 5.12 shows how cost-adding activities can easily outstrip value-adding activities.

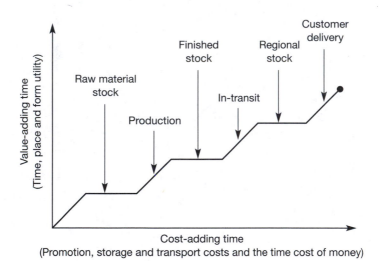

Fig. 5.12 Cost-added versus value-added time

The challenge to pipeline management is to find ways in which the ratio of value-added to cost-added time in the pipeline can be improved. Figure 5.13 graphically shows the goal of strategic lead-time management: to compress the chain in terms of time consumption so that cost-added time is reduced.

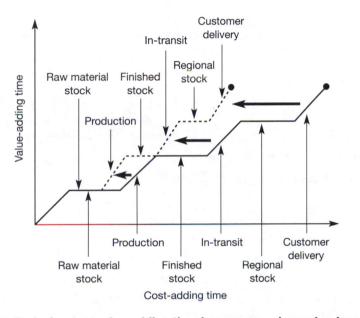

Fig. 5.13 Reducing non-value-adding time improves service and reduces cost

Pipeline management is concerned with removing the blockages and the fractures that occur in the pipeline and which lead to inventory build-ups and lengthened response times. The sources of these block-ages and fractures are such things as extended set-up and change-over times, bottlenecks, excessive inventory, sequential order processing and inadequate pipeline visibility.

To achieve improvement in the logistics process requires a focus upon the lead time as a whole, rather than the individual components of that lead time. In particular the interfaces between the components must be examined in detail. These interfaces provide fertile ground for logistics process re-engineering.

The lead-time gap

Most organizations face a fundamental problem: the time it takes to procure, make and deliver the finished product to a customer is longer than the time the customer is prepared to wait for it.

This is the basis of the lead-time gap. Figure 5.14 highlights the problem.

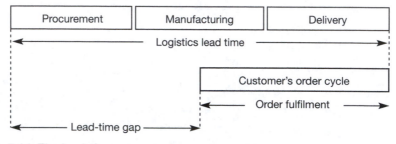

Fig. 5.14 The lead-time gap

The customer's order cycle refers to the length of time that the customer is prepared to wait, from when the order is placed through to when the goods are received. This is the maximum period available for order fulfilment. In some cases this may be measured in months but in others it is measured in hours.

> The competitive conditions of the market as well as the nature of the product will influence the customer's willingness to wait.

Clearly the competitive conditions of the market as well as the nature of the product will influence the customer's willingness to wait. Thus a customer may be willing to wait a few weeks for delivery of a car with particular options but only a day for a new set of tyres.

In the conventional organization the only way to cover the gap between the logistics lead time (i.e. the time taken to complete the process from goods inwards to delivered product) and the customer's order cycle (i.e. the period they are prepared to wait for delivery) is by carrying inventory. This normally implies a forecast. Hence the way most companies address this problem is by seeking to forecast the market's requirements and then to build inventory ahead of demand. Unfortunately all our experience suggests that no matter how sophisticated the forecast, its accuracy is always less than perfect. It has been suggested that all mistakes in forecasting end up as an inventory problem – whether too much or too little!

Whilst improving forecast accuracy will always be a desirable goal it may be that the answer to the problem lies not in investing ever greater sums of money and energy in improving forecasting techniques, but rather in reducing the lead-time gap.

The company that achieves a perfect match between the logistics lead time and the customer's required order cycle has no need of forecasts and no need for inventory.

The challenge for logistics management is to search for the means whereby the gap between the two lead times can be reduced if not closed (see Figure 5.15).

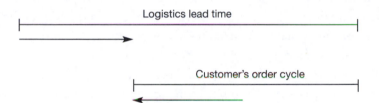

Logistics lead time

Customer's order cycle

Fig. 5.15 Closing the lead-time gap

Reducing the gap can be achieved by shortening the logistics lead time (end-to-end pipeline time) whilst simultaneously trying to move the customer's order cycle closer by gaining earlier warning of requirements through improved visibility of demand.

Reducing logistics lead time

Because companies have typically not managed well the total flow of materials and information that link the source of supply with the ultimate customer, what we find is that there is an incredibly rich opportunity for improving the efficiency of that process.

In those companies that do not recognize the importance of managing the supply chain as an integrated system it is usually the case that considerable periods of time are consumed at the interfaces between adjacent stages in the total process and in inefficiently performed procedures.

Because no one department or individual manager has complete visibility of the total logistics process, it is often the case that major opportunities for time reduction across the pipeline as a whole are not recognized. One electronics company in Europe did not realize for many years that, although it had reduced its throughput time in the factory from days down to hours, finished inventory was still sitting in the warehouse for three weeks! The reason was that finished inventory was the responsibility of the distribution function, which was outside the concern of the production management.

To enable the identification of opportunities for reducing end-to-end pipeline time an essential starting point is the construction of a supply chain map.

A supply chain map is essentially a time-based representation of the processes and activities that are involved as the materials or products move through the chain. At the same time the map highlights the time that is consumed when those materials or products are simply standing still, i.e. as inventory.

In these maps, it is usual to distinguish between 'horizontal' time and 'vertical' time. Horizontal time is time spent in process. It could be in-transit time, manufacturing or assembly time, time spent in production planning or processing, and so on. It may not necessarily be time when customer value is being created but at least something is going on. The other type of time is vertical time, which is time when nothing is happening and hence the material or product is standing still as inventory. No value is being added during vertical time, only cost.

The labels 'horizontal' and 'vertical' refer to the maps themselves where the two axes reflect process time and time spent as static inventory respectively. Figure 5.16 depicts such a map for the manufacture and distribution of men's underwear.

From this map it can be seen that horizontal time is 60 days. In other words, the various processes of gathering materials, spinning, knitting, dyeing, finishing, sewing and so on take 60 days to complete from start to finish. This is important because horizontal time determines the time that it would take for the system to respond to an increase in demand. Hence, if there were to be a sustained increase in demand, it would take that long to 'ramp up' output to the new level. Conversely, if there was a downturn in demand then the critical measure is pipeline

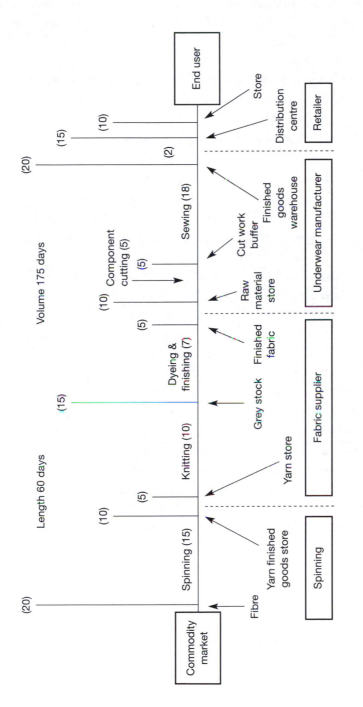

Fig. 5.16 Supply chain mapping – an example

Source: Scott, C. and Westbrook, R., 'New Strategic Tools for Supply Chain Management', *International Journal of Physical Distribution & Logistics Management*, Vol. 21, No. 1., 1991.

volume, i.e. the sum of both horizontal and vertical time. In other words it would take 175 days to 'drain' the system of inventory. So in volatile fashion markets, for instance, pipeline volume is a critical determinant of business risk.

Pipeline maps can also provide a useful internal benchmark. Because each day of process time requires a day of inventory to 'cover' that day then, in an ideal world, the only inventory would be that needed to cover during the process lead time. So a 60-day total process time would result in 60 days' inventory. However, in the case highlighted here there are actually 175 days of inventory in the pipeline. Clearly, unless the individual processes are highly time variable or unless demand is very volatile, there is more inventory than can be justified.

It must be remembered that in multi-product businesses each product will have a different end-to-end pipeline time. Furthermore, where products comprise multiple components, packaging materials or sub-assemblies, total pipeline time will be determined by the speed of the slowest moving item or element in that product. Hence in procuring materials for and manufacturing a household aerosol air freshener, it was found that the replenishment lead time for one of the fragrances used was such that weeks were added to the total pipeline.

Mapping pipelines in this way provides a powerful basis for logistics re-engineering projects. Because it makes the total process and its associated inventory transparent, the opportunities for reducing non-value-adding time become apparent. In many cases much of the non-value-adding time in a supply chain is there because it is self-inflicted through the 'rules' that are imposed or that have been inherited. Such rules include: economic batch quantities, economic order quantities, minimum order sizes, fixed inventory review periods, production planning cycles and forecasting review periods.

The importance of strategic lead-time management is that it forces us to challenge every process and every activity in the supply chain and to apply the acid test of 'does this activity add value for a customer or consumer or does it simply add cost?'

The basic principle to be noted is that every hour of time in the pipeline is directly reflected in the quantity of inventory in the pipeline and thus the time it takes to respond to marketplace requirements.

A simple analogy is with an oil pipeline. Imagine a pipeline from a refinery to a port that is 500 kilometres long. In normal conditions there will be 500 kilometres equivalent of oil in the pipeline. If there is a change in requirement at the end of the pipeline (say, for a different grade of oil) then 500 kilometres of the original grade has to be pumped through before the changed grade reaches the point of demand.

In the case of the logistics pipeline it is the case that time is consumed not just in slow-moving processes but also in unnecessary stock holding – whether it be raw materials, work-in-progress, waiting at a bottleneck or finished inventory.

Bottleneck management

All the logistics processes can be viewed as a network of inter-linked activities that can only be optimized as a whole by focusing on total throughput time. Any attempt to manage by optimizing individual elements or activities in the process will lead to a less-than-optimal result overall. A significant contribution to the way we view logistics processes has been made by Goldratt,[2] who developed the theory of constraints more usually known as Optimized Production Technology (OPT).

The essence of OPT is that all activities in a logistics chain can be categorized as either 'bottlenecks' or 'non-bottlenecks'. A bottleneck is the slowest activity in a chain and whilst it may often be a machine, it could also be a part of the information flow such as order processing. The throughput time of the entire system is determined by bottleneck activities. It follows therefore that to speed up total system throughput time it is important to focus on the bottlenecks, to add capacity where possible and to reduce set-ups and set-up times if applicable.

Equally important, however, is the realization that non-bottlenecks should not be treated in the same way. It is unnecessary to improve throughput at non-bottlenecks as this will only lead to the build-up of unwanted inventory at the bottleneck. Consequently, the output of non-bottlenecks that feed bottlenecks must be governed by the requirements of the bottlenecks they serve.

These ideas have profound implications for the re-engineering of logistics systems where the objective is to improve throughput time overall, whilst simultaneously reducing total inventory in the system. The aim is to manage the bottlenecks for throughput efficiency, which implies larger batch quantities and fewer set-ups at those crucial points, whereas non-bottlenecks should minimize batch quantities even though more set-ups will be involved. This has the effect of speeding up the flow of work-in-progress and these 'transfer batches' merge into larger 'process batches' at the bottlenecks, enabling a faster flow through the bottleneck. It follows that idle time at a non-bottleneck need not be a concern, indeed it should be welcomed if the effect is to reduce the amount of work-in-progress waiting at a bottleneck.

Emerging from the theory of constraints is the idea of 'drum-buffer-rope'. The drum is beating the pace at which the system as a whole should work. The buffer is placed before the bottleneck to ensure that this limiting factor in the system is always working to its full capacity. The rope is drawn from an analogy with a column of marching soldiers where the slowest man sets the pace. The rope attaches the leader of the column to the slowest man – in a supply chain the rope is the means by which replenishment quantities of materials, components, etc., are communicated to suppliers.

Improving visibility of demand

The idea that it could be possible to 'extend' the customer's order cycle may at first sight seem implausible. Certainly it is unrealistic to expect that customers could be persuaded to wait longer for delivery of their order – if anything, as we have seen, the pressure is on to reduce order cycle times.

No, what is meant by extending the customer's order cycle is that we should seek to obtain significantly earlier warnings of the customer's requirements. What we frequently find is that, firstly, the *demand penetration point* is too far down the pipeline and that, secondly, real demand is hidden from view and all we tend to see are orders. Both these points need further explanation; we will deal with the concept of the demand penetration point first.

The simplest definition of the demand penetration point is that it occurs at that point in the logistics chain where real demand meets the plan. Upstream from this point everything is driven by a forecast and/or a plan. Downstream we can respond to customer demand. Clearly in an ideal world we would like everything to be demand-driven so that nothing is purchased, manufactured or shipped unless there is a known requirement.

A key concern of logistics management should be to seek to identify ways in which the demand penetration point can be pushed as far as possible upstream. This might be achieved by the use of information so that manufacturing and purchasing get to hear of what is happening in the marketplace faster than they currently do. Figure 5.17 illustrates a range of possible demand penetration points in different industrial and market contexts.

Perhaps the greatest opportunity for extending the customer's order cycle is by gaining earlier notice of their requirements. In so many cases the supplying company receives no indication of the customer's actual usage until an order arrives. For example, the customer may be using ten items a day but because they order only intermittently the supplier sometimes receives an order for 100, sometimes for 150 and sometimes for 200. If the supplier could receive 'feed-forward' on what was being consumed they would anticipate the customer's requirement and better schedule their own logistics activities.

In a sense the information we receive, if we only have the order to rely on, is like the tip of an iceberg. Only a small proportion of the total iceberg is visible above the surface. Likewise the order cycle time (i.e. the required response time from order to delivery) may only be the visible tip of the 'information iceberg' (see Figure 5.18).

The area below the surface of the iceberg represents the ongoing consumption, demand or usage of the product which is hidden from the view of the supplier. It is only when an order is issued that demand becomes transparent.

There are now signs that buyers and suppliers are recognizing the opportunities for mutual advantage if information on requirements can be shared on a continuing basis. If the supplier can see right to the end of the pipeline then the logistics system can become much more responsive to actual demand. Thus, whilst the customer will still require ever swifter delivery, if an ongoing feed-forward of information on demand or usage can be established there is a greater chance that the service to the customer will be enhanced and the supplier's costs reduced.

This twin-pronged approach of simultaneously seeking to reduce the logistics lead time whilst extending the customer's order cycle may never completely close the lead-time gap. However, the experience of a growing number of companies is that substantial improvements can be made both in responsiveness and in the early capture of information on demand – the end result of which is better customer service at lower cost.

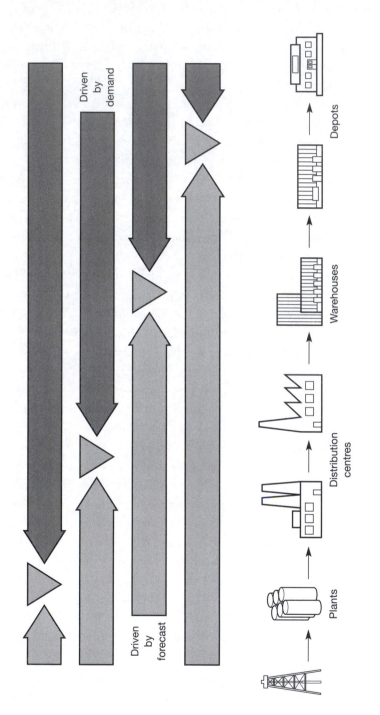

Fig. 5.17 Demand penetration points and strategic inventory

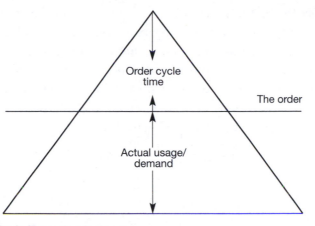

Fig. 5.18 The information iceberg

The supply chain fulcrum

At its simplest the purpose of the supply chain is to balance supply and demand. Traditionally, as we have noted, this has been achieved through forecasting ahead of demand and creating inventory against that forecast. Alternatively, additional capacity might be maintained to cope if demand turned out to be greater than forecast. Either way, demand was balanced with supply. Figure 5.19(a) illustrates a balance with the box marked 'D' representing demand and the boxes 'I' and 'C' representing inventory and capacity respectively.

Fig. 5.19(a) Balancing supply and demand

In other words there must be enough capacity and/or inventory to meet anticipated demand.

Now imagine that the fulcrum is moved closer to the box marked 'D' as in Figure 5.19(b). Obviously the same amount of demand can be balanced with less inventory and/or less capacity.

Fig. 5.19(b) Balancing supply and demand

What does the fulcrum represent in a supply chain? The fulcrum is the point at which we commit to source/produce/ship the product in its final form and where decisions on volume and mix are made. The idea being that if that point of commitment can be delayed as long as possible then the closer we are to make-to-order with all the benefits that brings.

The problem for many companies is that the fulcrum in their supply chains is more like that shown in Figure 5.19(c).

Fig. 5.19(c) Balancing supply and demand

Here the fulcrum is a long way from demand, i.e. the forecasting horizon is long, necessitating more inventory and capacity to balance against demand.

How in reality do we move the fulcrum closer to demand? The answer in effect is to improve *visibility* of demand along with enhancing the *velocity* of the supply chain. In other words, if we can have a clearer view of real demand in the final marketplace, rather than the distorted picture that more typically is the case, and if we can respond more rapidly, then a more effective matching of supply and demand can be achieved.

Thus it can be argued that visibility and velocity are the foundations for a responsive supply chain.

Figure 5.20 indicates some of the key drivers of velocity and visibility in a supply chain. Some of these drivers have already been discussed in this and earlier chapters. The remaining elements are addressed in subsequent chapters.

The case of Cisco Systems, described below, illustrates how reliance on forecasts and lack of visibility of real demand can have a dramatic impact upon a company's operations.

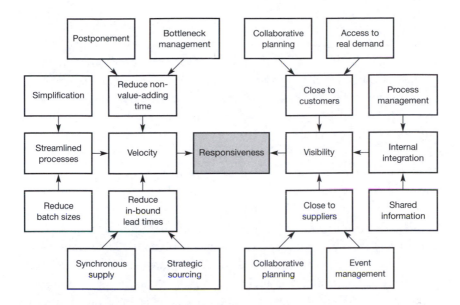

Fig. 5.20 Velocity and visibility drive responsiveness

What went wrong at Cisco Systems?

In 2000 Cisco Systems was the world's foremost e-business and the most valuable quoted company on the planet, more valuable even than Microsoft, with a market capitalization of $579bn. 'I have never been more optimistic about the future of our industry as a whole or of Cisco', CEO John Chambers declared in December 2000, projecting 50 per cent annual growth for the coming year. Chambers' optimism was not shared by others in industry. Less technologically sophisticated competitors also believed that the Internet boom was over and a downturn was deepening. They were cutting back inventory levels in anticipation, unlike the bullish Cisco. Cisco was wrong, its competitors were right. The markets were in turmoil.

In April 2001 Cisco announced its first quarterly decline in revenues since it was founded in 1985, along with over 8000 redundancies, a restructuring of the business and a rationalization of its portfolio of routers, switches and other equipment that powers the Internet and large corporate networks. Some of Cisco's largest customers, the

▶

telecoms companies, were going bankrupt and market research consultants Forrester Research reported that 41 per cent of US companies had postponed e-business projects as a result of the economic downturn.[1]

Cisco's own results for the quarter ending 27 January 2001 had already confirmed that something was going badly wrong. It showed that the level of inventory (finished and semi-finished goods) on its books had more than doubled from $1.2bn to $2.5bn over the preceding six months. The cost of financing its inventory had shot up from $25m to $645m in just one year. The inventory overhang was translated into a $2.2bn write down. Its shares lost 88 per cent of their value in a year.[2] So what went wrong at Cisco?

Cisco's optimism was born out of its combination of denial, technological wizardry and the success of its business model. Its technological lead came first from the operating software it developed to route large amounts of data from one computer to another, using specially designed microprocessors. Its operational capabilities came from its online supply chain management system – the most advanced in the world. From the mid-1990s Cisco's 'Networked Strategy' used the Internet to create interactive relationships, linking employees, partners, suppliers and customers together. The links enabled Cisco itself to concentrate on product design, while other tasks were outsourced to suppliers and contract manufacturers. Cisco's sophisticated automatic testing software meant that much of the production could be outsourced to suppliers without any danger of quality problems going undetected.

The company had always made customer service and on-time order fulfilment key performance indicators internally and throughout its extended enterprise. The Internet-based network allowed customers to order and configure online, and contract manufacturers to begin building systems within 15 minutes of receipt of the order. Third-party logistics suppliers were also linked in to the system, enabling Cisco to provide customers with information on the status of their orders at any time. The Network Strategy facilitated direct fulfilment, which led to a reduction in inventories, labour and shipping costs, saving Cisco $12m per year. Cycle times were further shortened by online prototype testing of customers' new systems, allowing lead times to be reduced from weeks to days. To the delight of the investment community, this completely networked environment allowed Cisco to monitor demand and revenues on an hour-by-hour basis. This 'virtual close' facility not only helped Cisco to run its own business, but also became a useful marketing tool to promote its systems to customers.

Real world problems began to impinge on Cisco's virtual idyll in June 2000, when a booming market led to component shortages, delaying deliveries of customer orders by three to four weeks.[3] It was by then becoming apparent that there were also communication and forecasting problems between Cisco and lower tiers of subcontractors in the network. The problem was quickly addressed by the introduction of Cisco Connection Online, linking in all subcontractors. Another innovation – the Integrated Commerce Solution (ICS) – was introduced soon afterwards, connecting in any remaining larger customers (mainly telecoms equipment distributors or operators) who had previously been unable to link up. Thus all parties were connected in real time to the network.

To overcome the problem of component shortages, Cisco entered into long-term contractual agreements with key suppliers of scarce components. The forecasts for these orders were based on the projections of sales staff. These were in turn based on indications of demand from suppliers and partners (systems integration consultants) and customer orders. What Cisco's real-time systems failed to recognize was that waning confidence in delivery lead times was prompting buyers to over-order. Customers were placing multiple orders with several suppliers, accepting only the first to deliver. Cisco was itself actioning orders that would never be confirmed and its suppliers – who were also receiving multiple orders from other manufacturers – would interpret and duly report this as a surge in demand. Cisco's inventory cycle rose from 53.9 days to over 88. The problem was eventually recognized towards the end of 2000, when Cisco began hurried implementation of its e-hub solution, which would automatically cancel any unconfirmed order within two hours. But the task of implementing the e-hub proved more costly, complex and time consuming than expected. When the bubble burst Cisco was left holding the inventory.

The company's executives later explained that the scale of the inventory write down was partly due to the need to maintain relationships with its supply chain partners – notably the semiconductor manufacturers – by honouring long-term contractual commitments. They were also keen to stress that the company had in fact experienced the forecasting equivalent of 'the 100-year flood' and, less convincingly, they

▶

▶ continued to insist that their systems had enabled them to respond faster than anyone to this unprecedented downturn.

References

1. Luce, E. and Kehoe, L., 'Cisco has a Fighting Chance', *Financial Times*, 5 April 2001.
2. Chara, R. and Useem, J., 'Why Companies Fail', *Fortune*, 27 May 2002, pp. 36–44.
3. Mukund, A. and Subhadra, K., *Cisco Systems – The Supply Chain Story*, ICFAI, Centre for Management, Hyderabad, 2002.

Summary

In a world of shortening product life cycles, volatile demand and constant competitive pressure, the ability to move quickly is critical. It is not just a question of speeding up the time it takes to get new products to market, but rather the time it takes to replenish existing demand. Markets today are often 'time-sensitive' as well as 'price-sensitive', thus the search is for logistics solutions that are more responsive but low-cost.

Time compression in the pipeline has the potential both to speed up response times and to reduce supply chain cost. The key to achieving these dual goals is through focusing on the reduction of non-value-adding time – and particularly time spent as inventory. Whereas in the past logistics systems were very dependent upon a forecast, with all the problems that entailed, now the focal point has become lead-time reduction.

References

1. Stalk, G. and Hout, T.M., *Competing Against Time*, The Free Press, 1990.
2. Goldratt, E.M., *Theory of Constraints*, North River Press, 1990.

The synchronous supply chain

This chapter:

Introduces the idea of synchronization across a series of connected businesses to create an 'extended enterprise'.

●

Examines the role of the logistics information system in enabling the sharing of supply and demand data across the network.

●

Highlights the benefits of implementing 'quick response' logistics processes based upon enhanced pipeline visibility.

●

Outlines the 'Forrester Effect' and 'acceleration effect' as key concepts from the field of industrial dynamics, explaining their significance.

●

Emphasizes the importance of collaborative working and 'co-makership' as the foundation for the creation of synchronous supply chains.

In conventional supply chains each stage in the chain tends to be disconnected from the others. Even within the same company the tendency is for separate functions to seek to optimize their own performance. As a result the interfaces between organizations and between functions within those organizations need to be buffered with inventory and/or time lags. The effect of this is that end-to-end pipeline times are long, responsiveness is low and total costs are high.

To overcome these problems it is clear that the supply chain needs to act as a synchronized network – not as a series of separate islands. Synchronization implies that each stage in the chain is connected to the other and that they all 'march to the same drumbeat'. The way in which entities in a supply chain become connected is through shared information.

The information to be shared between supply chain partners includes demand data and forecasts, production schedules, new product launch details and bill of material changes.

To enable this degree of visibility and transparency, synchronization requires a high level of *process alignment*, which itself demands a higher level of collaborative working. These are issues to which we shall return. The box below indicates some of the key processes that need to be linked, upstream and downstream, to provide the foundation for supply chain synchronization.

- **Planning and scheduling**: Material positioning/visibility, advanced planning, scheduling, forecasting, capacity management.
- **Design**: Mechanical design, electrical design, design for supply chain, component selection.
- **New product introduction**: Bill of materials management, prototyping, design validation, testing, production validation, transfer to volume.
- **Product content management**: Change generation, change impact assessment, product change release, change cut-in/phase-out.
- **Order management**: Order capture/configuration, available to promise, order tracking, exception management.

▶

● **Sourcing and procurement**: Approved vendor management, strategic sourcing, supplier selection, component selection.

Source: Cookson, C. 'Linking Supply Chains to Support Collaborative Manufacturing', *Ascet*, Vol. 3, 2001, www.ascet.com

Figure 6.1 depicts the difference between the conventional supply chain with limited transfer of information and the synchronous supply chain with network-wide visibility and transparency.

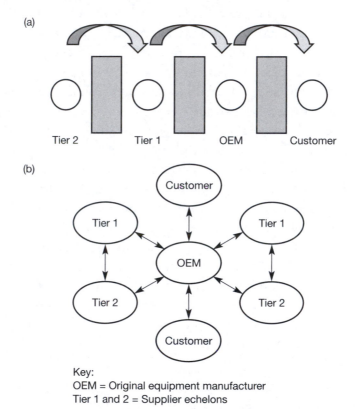

Fig. 6.1 **Achieving synchronization through shared information: (a) before synchronization; (b) after synchronization**

The extended enterprise and the virtual supply chain

The nature of business enterprise is changing. Today's business is increasingly 'boundaryless', meaning that internal functional barriers are being eroded in favour of horizontal process management and externally the separation between vendors, distributors, customers and the firm is gradually lessening. This is the idea of the *extended enterprise*, which is transforming our thinking on how organizations compete and how value chains might be reformulated.

Underpinning the concept of the extended enterprise is a common information 'highway'. It is the use of shared information that enables cross-functional, horizontal management to become a reality. Even more importantly it is information shared between partners in the supply chain that makes possible the responsive flow of product from one end of the pipeline to another. What has now come to be termed the virtual enterprise or supply chain is in effect a series of relationships between partners that is based upon the *value-added exchange of information*. Figure 6.2 illustrates the concept.

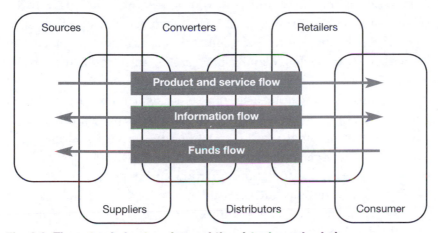

Fig. 6.2 The extended enterprise and the virtual supply chain
Source: A. T. Kearney.

The notion that partnership arrangements and a mentality of co-operation are more effective than the traditional arm's-length and often adversarial basis of relationships is now gaining ground. Thus the supply chain is becoming a confederation of organizations that agree common goals and who bring specific strengths to the overall value creation and value delivery system. This process is being accelerated as the trend towards outsourcing continues. Outsourcing should not be confused with 'subcontracting' where a task or an activity is simply handed over to a specialist. In a way it would be better to use the term 'in-sourcing' or 're-sourcing', when we refer to the quite different concept of partnering that the virtual supply chain depends upon. These partnerships may not be for all time – quite possibly they exist only to exploit a specific market opportunity – but they will be 'seamless' and truly synergetic.

The role of information in the virtual supply chain

Leading organizations have long recognized that the key to success in supply chain management is the information system. However, what we are now learning is that there is a dimension to information that enables supply and demand to be matched in multiple markets, often with tailored products, in ever-shorter time-frames.

This extension of the information system beyond the classical dimensions of simple planning and control enables time and space to be collapsed through the ability to link the customer directly to the supplier and for the supplier to react, sometimes in real time, to changes in the market. Rayport and Sviokla[1] have coined the term 'marketspace' to describe the new world of electronic commerce, internets and virtual supply chains. In the marketspace, customer demand can be identified as it occurs and, through CAD/CAM and flexible manufacturing, products created in minimal batch sizes. Equally, networks of specialist suppliers can be joined together to create innovative yet cost-effective solutions for complex design and manufacturing problems. The way that Airbus now designs and assembles its advanced aeroplanes, for example, would not be possible without the use of global information networks that link one end of the value chain to the other.

The Internet has in many ways transformed the ways in which supply chain members can connect with each other.[2] It provides a perfect vehicle for the establishment of the virtual supply chain. Not only does it enable vast global markets to be accessed at minimal cost and allow customers to shorten dramatically search time and reduce transaction costs, but it also enables different organizations in a supply chain to share information with each other in a highly cost-effective way. *Extranets* as they have come to be termed are revolutionizing supply chain management. Organizations with quite different internal information systems can now access data from customers on sales or product usage and can use that information to manage replenishment and to alert their suppliers of forthcoming requirements.

One of Britain's major retailers, Tesco, is using an extranet to link with its suppliers to share point-of-sale data. At the same time the company is successfully running a home shopping and delivery system for consumers over the Internet. Within the business, *intranets* are in place that enable information to be shared between stores and to facilitate communication across the business. We are probably even now only scraping the surface in terms of how the Internet and its associated technologies can be used to further exploit the virtual supply chain. Figure 6.3 highlights some of the current applications of Internet-based concepts to supply chain management.

The IT solutions now exist to enable supply chain partners to share information easily and at relatively low cost. A major benefit that flows from this greater transparency is that the internal operations of the business can become much more efficient as a result. For example, by capturing customer demand data sooner, better utilization of production and transport capacity can be achieved through better planning or scheduling. Figure 6.4 indicates some of the uses to which improved logistics information can be put.

Increasingly, it seems that successful companies have one thing in common – their use of information and information technology to improve customer responsiveness. Information systems are reshaping the organization and also the nature of the linkages between organizations. Information has always been central to the efficient management of logistics but now, enabled by technology, it is providing the driving force for competitive logistics strategy.

We are now starting to see the emergence of integrated logistics systems that link the operations of the business, such as production and distribution, with the supplier's operations on the one hand and the customer on the other.[3] Already it is the case that companies can literally link the replenishment of product in the marketplace with their upstream operations and those of their suppliers through the use of shared information. The use of these systems has the potential to convert supply chains into demand chains in the sense that the system can now respond to known demand rather than having to anticipate that demand through a forecast. Figure 6.5 describes the architecture of such a system.

Customer service

- Information and support products and services
- Electronic help desk
- Mass customization and order processing

Marketing channel

- Public relations and advertising
- Market research and test
- Electronic mails and catalogues

Information retrieval

- Online news
- Statistics, reports and databases
- Data mining
- Competitive analysis

Supplier relationships

- Logistics
- Product search
- Electronic data interchange
- Ordering and payment
- Supply chain integration

Financial transactions

- Selling and payment
- Managing accounts
- Credit card payments

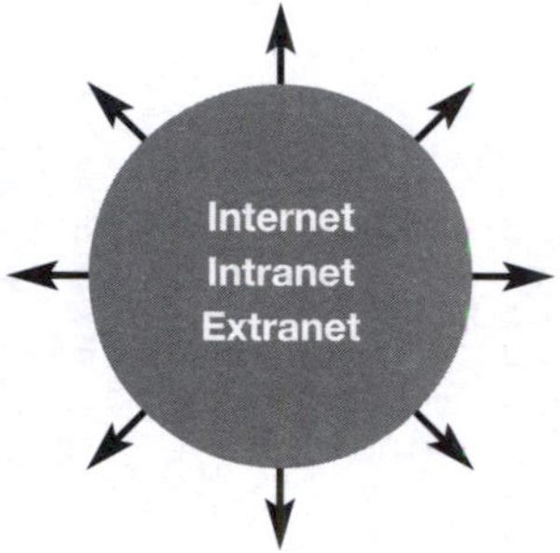

Building strategic alliances

- Newsletters, bulletin boards, discussion databases
- Sharing knowledge and experience

Electronic distribution

- Product, data, information

Internal communications

- Complete internal, external, vertical and horizontal communications
- Groupware
- E-mail
- Collaboration
- Knowledge transfer
- Telecommuting

Human resources and employee relations

- Job opening posting
- Expert search
- Employee training and support
- Distance learning

Sales force automation

- On-site configuration and order processing
- Sales process transformation

Internet
Intranet
Extranet

Fig. 6.3 Internet applications and the supply chain

Source: A. T. Kearney.

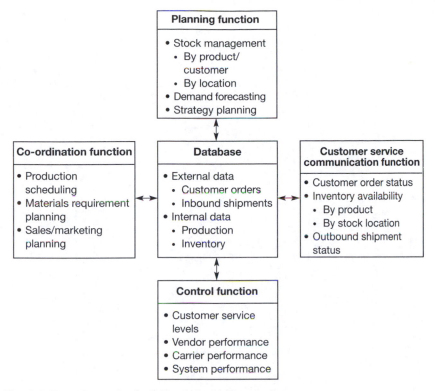

Fig. 6.4 Functions of a logistics information system

Implications for logistics

In the same way that the conventional wisdom in production and manufacturing was to maximize batch quantities, similar thinking could be found in the rest of the supply chain. Thus we used to seek to ship by the container or truck load, customers were discouraged from ordering in smaller quantities by price penalties and delivery schedules were typically based on optimizing the efficiency of routes and the consolidation of deliveries. Clearly such an approach runs counter to the requirements of a synchronous supply chain. Under the synchronization philosophy the requirement is for small shipments to be made more frequently and to meet the precise time requirements of the customer.

The challenge to logistics management is to find ways in which these changed requirements can be achieved without an uneconomic escalation of costs. There may have to be trade-offs but the goal must be to improve total supply chain cost effectiveness. The Smart Car case study

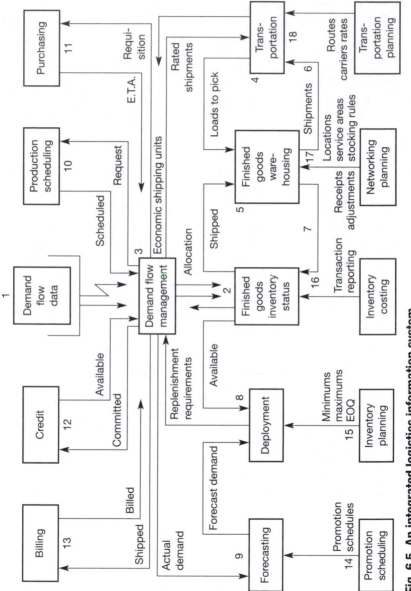

Fig. 6.5 An integrated logistics information system

Source: Digital Equipment Corporation.

below demonstrates what can be achieved if the partners in the supply chain are closely linked to each other.

Smart Car's synchronous supply chain

At the 1998 Geneva Motor Show, the car that everyone wanted to see was the eagerly awaited 'Smart Car', the tiny, relatively cheap, two-seater run-around produced by Micro Compact Car (MCC). Originally conceived as an unlikely joint venture project between Germany's Daimler-Benz and Swiss watchmakers, SMH, MCC was soon taken over to be wholly run by Daimler-Benz. The innovative little car it produced was meant to be unlike any other car currently on the road. Designed to appeal to the young urban drivers of continental Europe, it forms part of a wider urban mobility concept that includes space-saving parking, pool leasing and networking with public transport systems. The public were intrigued by the concept, the car's odd appearance and the prospect of using multi-media systems to allow them to order on-screen their own individually configured vehicles. Other car makers were much more interested in MCC's manufacturing systems.

At launch in 1998 the Smart Car could be built in only seven and a half hours, beating the industry's leading performers by some two and a half hours.[1] The difference in performance was due to the fact that MCC was a very different kind of car company with a radically different approach to vehicle development and manufacturing. The first Smart Cars were produced in a region with no previous history of automotive manufacturing, at a single site factory complex at Hambach in eastern France. At the heart of the complex a large cruciform building houses the main assembly line. Radiating off each arm of the cruciform are a number of smaller structures, containing one of MCC's seven first tier suppliers or 'system partners'. The systems partners, a multinational collection of specialist companies, are subcontracted to undertake large portions of the assembly process. Most were involved in the car's development right from the earliest concept stage. Unlike conventional suppliers, they provide entire subassemblies including the five 'super modules' – chassis, power train, doors and roof, electronics and cockpit. The remaining parts are supplied by a further 16 less-integrated suppliers, some located at quite a distance from the plant.

▶

▶

The cars are constructed around an integral body frame, known as the 'Tridion' to which the modular subassemblies are attached. These are delivered to the production lines on conveyor belts in sequence with the line, from the systems partners who are linked into MCC's order and production scheduling systems, allowing their operations and those of their webs of suppliers to be fully integrated in real time into a single synchronous supply chain.[2] Learning how to produce subassemblies in lock-step with a production line that moved 88 feet per minute was one of the toughest challenges the systems partners had to overcome. As one MCC executive observed: 'Some suppliers underestimated what they had to do in project management. It's a different job to produce a component than to be the manager of a big module like a cockpit.' Nevertheless, by 2002 the processes had bedded in and build times had been reduced to just four hours, with a new Smart rolling off the Hambach production line every 90 seconds. All were sold and each was different from the last.

The super modules originally accounted for around 70 per cent of the engineering work on the car, but not all of the systems partners managed to stay the course. One company hired to build complete doors had to be replaced and another stopped building the front end module when it became clear that it could be assembled on the production line at less cost. Nevertheless, if the three logistics companies involved in the movement of materials and cars are included into the calculations, only ten suppliers are responsible for 85 per cent of the cost of goods.[3] The systems partners' involvement in modular subassemblies reduces the final assembler's capital costs and the amount of working capital tied up in stocks, as suppliers are only paid once the modules are used. Some of the modules, such as the power train and cockpit, contain complex subassemblies that are necessarily assembled in advance by the suppliers.

Smart Car's integrated manufacturing site is in fact a logical extension of the 1990s trend that saw clusters of first tier suppliers opening dedicated facilities in industrial parks adjacent to large automotive customers' plants. It is also indicative of a wider trend towards integrated suppliers actually installing parts on the line, which totally blurs the distinction between the car manufacturer's own employees and those of its systems suppliers. At Hambach over half of the 1900 people working in the complex and two-thirds of all production workers are not on MCC's payroll. Ownership of the factory buildings and the site's facilities management are also outsourced to specialist providers. In addition, programme management and information technology operations have all been passed over to consultants Accenture on a long-term contract.

Accenture were also contracted to develop and implement the business and vehicle production processes and oversee Smart Car's introduction to the market.[4] The cars are sold through a network of dealerships located in special 'lifestyle centres' within shopping complexes or other frequently visited urban locations, increasingly through satellite branches Mercedes dealerships. To retain maximum flexibility, it was also decided that some elements of product customization should take place between factory and dealer at the distribution centre, where stocks of easily interchangeable modules and body parts are held so that other features can be changed or added as required, without introducing unnecessary complexity on the production line.

References
1. Simonian, Haig, 'Carmakers' Smart Move', *Financial Times*, 1 July 1997.
2. Siekman, Philip, 'The Smart Car is Looking More so', *Fortune*, 15 April 2002, p. 310; Van Hoek, Remko and Weken, Harm, 'How Modular Production can Contribute to Integration in Inbound and Outbound Logistics', *Proceedings of the Logistics Research Network Conference*, University of Huddersfield, 16–17 September 1997.
3. Van Hoek, Remko, 'E-supply Chains – Virtually Non-existing', *Supply Chain Management: An International Journal*, Vol. 6, No. 1, 2001, pp. 21–28.
4. Reuter News Service, 'Andersen Consulting joins Smart Car Project', Reuter News Service – Western Europe, *Reuter Textline*, 18 February 1997 (Q2:23).

The basic principle of synchronization is to ensure that all elements of the chain act as one and hence there must be early identification of shipping and replenishment requirements and, most importantly of all, there must be the highest level of planning discipline.

In a synchronous supply chain the management of in-bound materials flow becomes a crucial issue. In particular the search for consolidation opportunities has to be a priority. Thus, for example, rather than one supplier making a series of deliveries in small quantities to a customer, the orders from a number of suppliers are combined into a single delivery. It is perhaps not surprising that the emergence of synchronous supply chains as a management philosophy has coincided with the growth of third-party distribution and logistics companies specializing in providing an in-bound consolidation service.

These logistics service companies can manage the pick-up of materials and components from suppliers on a 'milk round' basis, using a central 'hub' or transhipment centre for re-sorting and consolidating for in-bound delivery. They may also perform certain value-adding activities such as quality control, kitting, sequencing or final finishing.

A good example of such a third-party service is that provided in the UK by TNT on behalf of the Rover Group car company. Here both suppliers and TNT deliver consolidated loads to a specially designed transhipment centre owned and operated by TNT near to Rover's factory. Components and subassemblies are then sequenced for delivery to the point of use on the assembly line in the required quantities at the required time. This enables the smooth flow of in-bound material with no congestion of delivery vehicles at the plant.

In complex assembly operations such as motor manufacture the prior sequencing of parts and components prior to assembly is a crucial activity (see the example below of seat delivery to Nissan's assembly line in north-east England).

■ Synchronized delivery ■

How Nissan Motors UK receives vehicle seats

Elapsed hours

0 – Painted body passes to trim line in Nissan
  – Precise vehicle specifications of next 12 vehicles transmitted by computer from Nissan to seat suppliers
  – Supplier transfers information to picking lists
  – Seat covers selected from range

1 – Covers prepared for assembly (in reverse order)
  – Seat assembly from synchronized manufacture of subassemblies (frames, foams, finishers, plastic parts)

2 – Quality audit and load
  – Delivery of seats to stock holding point by special purpose vehicle
  – Stock to lineside

3 – Rear seats fitted followed by front seats (waiting stillages returned to empty wagon)
  – Delivery frequency now every 15–20 minutes

Similar developments have enabled the transformation of retail logistics. The idea of 'stockless distribution centres' or 'cross-docking' enables a more frequent and efficient replenishment of product from manufacture to individual stores. Cross-docking, often facilitated by a logistics service provider, is a single, but powerful, concept. Point-of-sale data from individual stores is transmitted to the retailer's head office to enable them to determine replenishment requirements. This information is then transmitted directly to the suppliers who assemble orders for specific stores and the pallets or cases are then bar-coded (or increasingly electronically tagged). On a pre-planned basis these store orders are then collected by the logistics service provider and are taken to a transhipment centre (the 'cross-dock' facility) – possibly operated by the logistics service provider – where they are sorted for store delivery along with other suppliers' orders. In effect, a just-in-time delivery is achieved, which enables minimum stock to be carried in the retail stores, and yet transport costs are contained through the principles of consolidation (see Figures 6.6 and 6.7).

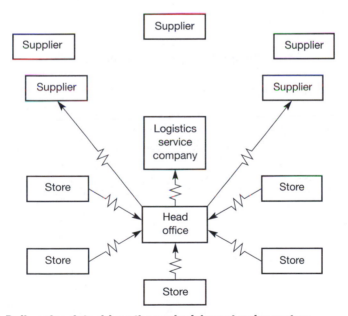

Fig. 6.6 Daily sales data drives the replenishment order system

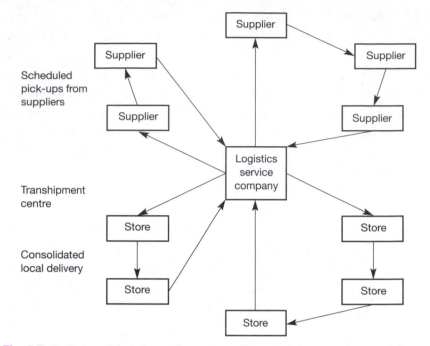

Fig. 6.7 Acting on this information a consolidated pick-up and store delivery sequence is activated

'Quick response' logistics

An outgrowth of the synchronization philosophy has emerged in recent years under the banner of 'quick response' logistics.[4] The basic idea behind quick response (QR) is that in order to reap the advantages of time-based competition it is necessary to develop systems that are responsive and fast. Hence QR is the umbrella term for the information systems and the logistics systems that combine to provide 'the right product in the right place at the right time'.

> The basic idea behind quick response (QR) is that in order to reap the advantages of time-based competition it is necessary to develop systems that are responsive and fast.

What has made QR possible is the development of information technology and in particular the rise of Internet-enabled data exchange, bar coding, the use of electronic point of sale (EPOS) systems with laser scanners and so on.

Essentially the logic behind QR is that demand is captured in as close to real-time as possible and as close to the final consumer as

190

possible. The logistics response is then made directly as a result of that information. An example of such an approach is provided in the United States by Procter & Gamble who receive sales data directly from the check-out counters of North America's largest retailer, Wal-Mart. Making use of this information P&G can plan production and schedule delivery to Wal-Mart on a replenishment basis. The result is that Wal-Mart carries less inventory yet has fewer stock-outs and P&G benefit because they get better economies in production and logistics as a result of the early warning and – most importantly – they have greatly increased their sales to Wal-Mart. Whilst the investment in the information system is considerable, so too is the payback. Early experience with QR suggests that paybacks of less than two years can be expected.

QR is obviously a classic case of the substitution of information for inventory. Figure 6.8 indicates the relative advantage of QR when higher service levels are demanded. Whilst QR may have a high fixed cost the incremental costs of service improvements are relatively low.

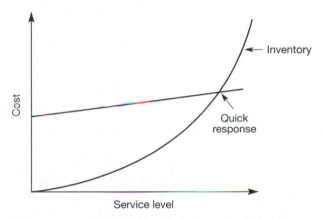

Fig. 6.8 Quick response system versus inventory-based system

A further feature in favour of QR systems is that by speeding up processing time in the system, cumulative lead times are reduced. This can then result in lower inventory (see Figure 6.9) and thus further reduce response times. In effect a 'virtuous circle'!

Quick response systems have begun to emerge in the fashion and apparel industry where the costs of traditional inventory-based systems based upon buyers' prior purchase decisions (in effect a 'push' system)

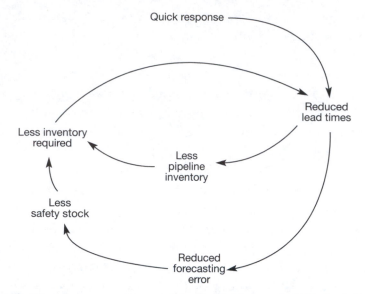

Fig. 6.9 Quick response system can trigger a 'virtuous circle' in logistics

can be considerable. In the United States it is estimated that the annual costs to the US textile and apparel industry of conventional logistics systems is $25 billion. This comprises the following elements:

Forced markdowns	$14.08bn
Stock-outs	$6.08bn
Inventory carrying costs	$5.08bn
Total:	**$25.24bn**

There could be massive advantages to be gained by all parties in the supply chain if the concept of QR was adopted throughout the chain. Thus in the case of fashion garments the aim should be to link retail sales with the apparel manufacturers, who in turn are linked to the textile producers who themselves are linked to the suppliers of fibres. One such reported case is the linkage through shared information of the US textile company Milliken with the Seminole Manufacturing Company (a manufacturer of men's slacks) and the retailer Wal-Mart. Information on end-user demand was captured at the point of sale and rapidly fed back up the supply chain, enabling dramatic reductions in lead times to be achieved and hence substantial reductions in inventory.

Another case from the US is provided by the chain of retail fashion stores, The Limited. Each of the several thousand stores in the chain tracks consumer preferences daily using their point-of-sale data. Based upon this, orders are sent by satellite links to the suppliers around the world. Using Hong Kong as a consolidation centre, goods are flown back to The Limited's distribution centre in Columbus, Ohio. At the distribution centre the goods are price-marked and re-sorted for immediate onward shipment by truck and plane to the retail stores. The whole cycle from reorder to in-store display can be achieved in six weeks. Conventional systems take more like six months.

Production strategies for quick response

As the demand by all partners in the supply chain for a quick response increases, the more will be the pressure placed upon manufacturing to meet the customer's needs for variety in shorter and shorter time-frames.

The answer has to lie in flexibility. As we have already observed, if it were possible to reduce manufacturing and logistics lead times to zero then total flexibility could be achieved. In other words the organization could respond to any request that was technologically feasible in any quantity. Whilst zero lead times are obviously not achievable, the new focus on flexible manufacturing systems (FMS) has highlighted the possibility of substantial progress in this direction.

The key to flexibility in manufacturing is not just new technology, e.g. robotics, although this can contribute dramatically to its achievement. The main barrier to flexibility is the time taken to change; to change from one level of volume to another and to change from making one variant to another. Typically we call this 'set-up time'. It will be apparent that if set-up times can be driven as close as possible to zero then flexible response to customer requirements presents no problem.

The Japanese, not surprisingly, have led the way in developing techniques for set-up time reduction. 'Single minute exchange of die', or SMED, is the goal in many Japanese plants. In other words continuous attention by management and the workforce is focused upon the ways in which set-up times can be reduced. Sometimes it will involve new technology, but more often than not it is achieved through taking a totally different look at the process itself. In many cases set-up times have been reduced from hours down to minutes, simply by questioning the conventional wisdom.

What in effect we are seeing is a fundamental shift away from the economies of scale model, which is volume based and hence implies long production runs with few change-overs, to the economies of scope model, which is based upon producing small quantities of a wider range, hence requiring more change-overs.

It has been suggested that under the economies of scope model:

> ...a single plant can produce a variety of output at the same cost as (if not lower than) a separate plant, dedicated to producing only one type of product at a given level. In other words an economic order quantity (EOQ) of one unit, and specific production designs, engender no additional costs. Economies of scope change the materials-driven, batch-system technology into a multi-functional, flow system configuration.[5]

The marketing advantages that such flexibility brings with it are considerable. It means that in effect the company can cater for the precise needs of multiple customers, and instead of the old Henry Ford Model 'T' motto – 'Any colour you like, as long as it's black' – we can offer even higher levels of customization. In today's marketplace where customers seek individuality and where segments or 'niches' are getting ever smaller, a major source of competitive advantage can be gained by linking production flexibility to customers' needs for variety.

A classic example is provided by Benetton, the Italian fashion goods manufacturer and distributor, who have created a worldwide business based upon responsiveness to fashion changes – with a particular emphasis upon colour. By developing an innovative process whereby entire knitted garments can be dyed in small batches, they reduced the need to carry inventory of multiple colours, and because of the small batch sizes for dying they greatly enhanced their flexibility. Benetton's speed of response is also assisted by the investment that they have made in high-speed distribution systems, which are themselves aided by rapid feedback of sales information from the marketplace.

Many companies are now seeking to construct supply chains to enable them to support a marketing strategy of *mass customization*. The idea behind this is that today's customers in many markets are increasingly demanding tailored solutions for their specific requirements. The challenge is to find ways of achieving this marketing goal without increasing finished goods inventory and without incurring the higher costs of production normally associated with make-to-order.

Often this can be achieved by postponing the final configuration or assembly of the product until the actual customer requirement is known – a strategy pursued by Dell and Hewlett Packard for example.

In other cases high technology in the form of computer-aided design/computer-aided manufacturing (CAD/CAM) can provide the means for this mass customization.

Logistics systems dynamics

One of the major advantages of moving to QR and synchronous supply chain strategies is that, by reducing lot quantities and increasing the rate of throughput in the logistics system, modulations in the level of activity in the pipeline can be reduced.

Logistics systems are prone to what has been called the 'Bullwhip' or 'Forrester Effect', after Jay Forrester, who developed a set of techniques known as Industrial Dynamics.[6] Forrester defined industrial dynamics as:

> The study of the information feedback characteristics of industrial activity to show how organizational structure, amplification (in policies) and time delays (in decisions and returns) interact to influence the success of the enterprise. It treats the interactions between the flows of information, money, orders, materials, personnel, and capital equipment in a company, an industry or a national economy.

> Industrial dynamics provides a single framework for integrating the functional areas of management – marketing, production, accounting, research and development and capital investment.

Using a specially developed computer simulation language, DYNAMO, Forrester built a model of a production/distribution system involving three levels in the distribution channel: a retailer's inventory, a distributor's inventory and a factory inventory. Each level was interconnected through information flows and flows of goods. The model used real world relationships and data and included parameters such as order transmission times, order processing times, factory lead times and shipment delivery times. Management could then examine the effects on the total system of, say, a change in retail sales or the impact of changing production levels or any other policy change or combination of changes.

What becomes apparent from this modelling of complex systems is that small disturbances in one part of the system can very quickly become magnified as the effect spreads through the pipeline.

For example, many consumer product companies that are heavy spenders on trade promotions (e.g. special discounts, incentives, etc.) do not realize what the true costs of such activities are. In the first instance there is the loss of profit through the discount itself, and then there is the hidden cost of the disturbance to the logistics system. Consider first the loss of profit. When a discount is offered for a limited period then that discount obviously will apply to all sales – not just any incremental sales. So if sales during the promotional period are, say, 1100 cases but without the promotion they would have been 1000, then whilst the incremental revenue comes only from the additional 100 cases, the discount applies to all 1100. Additionally the retailer may decide to take advantage of the discount and 'forward order'; in other words buy ahead of requirement to sell at a later time at the regular price. One study[7] found that for these reasons only 16 per cent of promotions were profitable, the rest only 'bought sales' at a loss.

The second impact of promotional activity on profit is the potential it provides for triggering the 'acceleration effect' and hence creating a Forrester-type surge throughout the logistics pipeline. This is because in most logistics systems there will be 'leads and lags', in other words the response to an input or a change in the system may be delayed. For example, the presence of a warehouse or a stock holding intermediary in the distribution channel can cause a substantial distortion in demand at the factory. This is due to the 'acceleration effect', which can cause self-generated fluctuations in the operating characteristics of a system.

As an example, imagine a retailer who has an inventory management reordering strategy based on starting each week with the equivalent of three weeks' demand in stock. So if weekly demand were 100 units for a particular item the target starting inventory would be 300 (i.e. 100×3). Now let us assume that as a result of a promotion demand increases by 10 per cent to 110. This means that the system would place an order to bring the next week's starting inventory up to 330 (i.e. 110×3). So the re-order quantity would have to be 140 (i.e. the 110 units sold to consumers plus the extra 30 required to meet the new starting level).

In this particular case an increase in consumer demand of 10 per cent leads to a one-off increase in demand on the supplier of 40 per cent!

If in the next period consumer demand were to fall back to its old level then the same effect would happen in reverse.

It is not unusual for companies undertaking frequent promotional activity to experience considerable upswings and downswings in factory shipments on a continuing basis. Figure 6.10 illustrates the lagged and magnified effect of such promotional activity upon the factory. It can be imagined that such unpredictable changes in production requirement add considerably to the unit costs of production. In the case of US retailer Kmart previously described (see page 93), it has been suggested that high levels of promotional activity led to a loss of control of their supply chain and hence to their cash flow crisis.

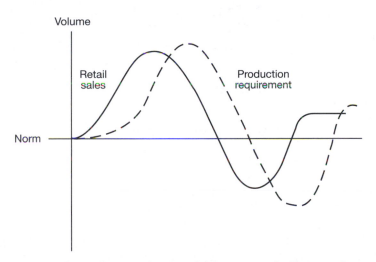

Fig. 6.10 The impact of promotional activity upon production requirement

In the grocery industry, where much of this promotional activity is found, there is a growing recognition of the need to achieve a closer linkage between the ordering policies of the retail trade and the manufacturing schedules of the supplier. In the United States it was estimated that the time from the end of the production line to purchase by the consumer in a retail store was 84 days for a typical dry grocery product (see Figures 6.11 and 6.12).

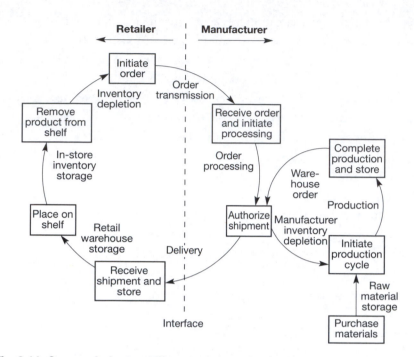

Fig. 6.11 Grocery industry delivery system order cycle
Source: Grocery Manufacturers Association of America.

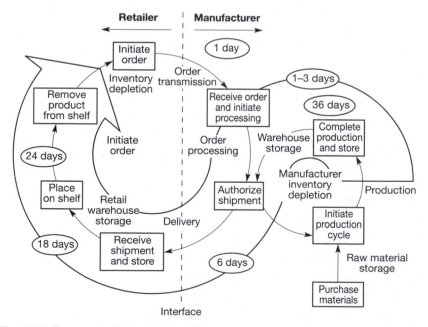

Fig. 6.12 Grocery industry product flow
Source: Grocery Manufacturers Association of America.

This means that the 'tidal wave' effect of changes in demand can be considerably magnified as they pass through all the intermediate stock holding and reorder points. One of the benefits of a quick response system is that by linking the retail check-out desk to the point of production through electronic data transfer, the surge effect can be dramatically reduced. This fact alone could more than justify the initial investment in linked buyer/supplier logistics information systems.

Collaboration in the supply chain

It will be clear that none of the benefits of synchronous supply can be achieved without high levels of collaboration across the network.

The benefits of collaboration are well illustrated by the often quoted example of the 'prisoner's dilemma'. The scenario is that you and your partner have been arrested on suspicion of robbing a bank. You are both put in separate cells and not allowed to communicate with each other. The police officer tells you both independently that you will be leniently treated if you confess, but less well so if you do not!

In fact the precise penalties are given to you as follows:

Option 1: You confess but your partner doesn't.
Outcome: You get one year in jail for co-operating but your partner gets five years.

Option 2: You don't confess but your partner does.
Outcome: You get five years in jail and your partner gets only one year for co-operating.

Option 3: Both of you confess.
Outcome: You get two years each.

Option 4: Neither of you confess.
Outcome: You both go free.

These options and outcomes can be summarized in the matrix in Figure 6.13.

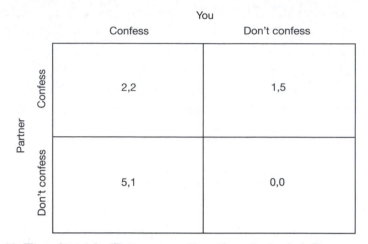

Fig. 6.13 The prisoner's dilemma: penalty options (years in jail)

What is the most likely outcome? If neither you nor your partner really trusts the other, particularly if previous experience has taught you to be wary of each other, then both of you will confess. Obviously the best strategy is one based on trust and hence for neither party to confess!

This simple example provides a good analogy with the real world. The conventional wisdom of purchasing has tended towards the view that multiple sources of supply for a single item are to be preferred. In such situations, it is argued, one is unlikely to become too reliant upon a single source of supply. Furthermore we can play one supplier off against another and reduce the cost of purchases. However, such relationships tend to be adversarial and, in fact, sub-optimal.

One of the first things to suffer when the relationship is based only upon negotiations about price is quality. The supplier seeks to minimize his costs and to provide only the basic specification. In situations like this the buyer will incur additional costs on in-bound inspection and re-work. Quality in respect of service is also likely to suffer when the supplier does not put any particular priority on the customer's order.

At a more tangible level those customers who have moved over to synchronous supply with the consequent need for JIT deliveries have found that it is simply impractical to manage in-bound shipments from multiple suppliers. Similarly the communication of orders and replenishment instructions is so much more difficult with multiple suppliers.

The closer the relationship between buyer and supplier the more likely it is that the expertise of both parties can be applied to mutual benefit. For example, many companies have found that by close co-operation with suppliers they can improve product design, value-engineer components, and generally find more efficient ways of working together.

This is the logic that underlines the emergence of the concept of 'co-makership' or 'partnership sourcing'. Co-makership may be defined as:

The development of a long-term relationship with a limited number of suppliers on the basis of mutual confidence.

The basic philosophy of co-makership is that the supplier should be considered to be an extension of the customer's operations with the emphasis on continuity and a 'seamless' end-to-end pipeline. As the trend to outsourcing continues so must the move towards co-makership. Nissan Motors in the UK have been one of the leading advocates of this concept. A key element of their approach is the use of 'supplier development teams', which are small groups of Nissan specialists who will help suppliers to achieve the requirements that Nissan places upon them. The overall objective of the supplier development team is to reduce the costs and increase the efficiency for both parties – in other words a 'win-win' outcome. Because the cost of materials in an automobile can be as high as 85 per cent, anything that can reduce the costs of purchased supplies can have a significant effect on total costs.

Figure 6.14 depicts a not-untypical situation where a car manufacturer's purchased materials are 85 per cent of total costs. This is then exploded further where it is shown that the material costs of the component supplier are a figure closer to the average for manufacturing industry of 40 per cent. Of the remaining 60 per cent ('supplier value added'), 80 per cent of that figure might be accounted for by overheads, of which typically 30 per cent or so would be accounted for by the supplier's logistics costs (i.e. inventory, set-up costs transport, warehousing, etc.).

What this implies is that approximately 12 per cent of the cost of materials to the car manufacturer are accounted for by the supplier's logistics costs (i.e. 85 per cent × 60 per cent × 80 per cent × 30 per cent). When it is realized that a proportion of the supplier's logistics costs are caused by the lack of integration and partnership between the car manufacturer and the supplier, it becomes apparent that a major opportunity for cost reduction exists.

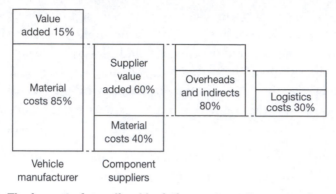

Fig. 6.14 The impact of suppliers' logistics costs on the costs of a car

Under the traditional adversarial relationship the vehicle manufacturer would seek to reduce his material cost by squeezing the profit margin of the component suppliers. The co-makership approach is quite different – here the vehicle manufacturer seeks to reduce a supplier's costs, not his profits. Through collaboration and closely integrated logistics planning mechanisms the two parties seek to achieve a situation where there are benefits to both parties. Companies like Nissan Motors in the UK have shown that this is not a Utopian dream but can be a practical reality.

The principle of co-makership can be extended in both directions in the supply chain – upstream to suppliers and downstream to distributors, retailers and even end users. The prizes to be won from successful co-makership potentially include lower costs for all parties through reduced inventories and lower set-up costs as a result of better schedule integration. The implications for competitive strategy are profound. The new competitive paradigm is that supply chain competes with supply chain and the success of any one company will depend upon how well it manages its supply chain relationships.

> The new competitive paradigm is that supply chain competes with supply chain and the success of any one company will depend upon how well it manages its supply chain relationships.

One example of collaboration in the supply chain that is increasingly encountered is the concept of Vendor Managed Inventory.

Vendor Managed Inventory

Traditionally, customers place orders on their suppliers. Whilst the logic of this might seem obvious, the inherent inefficiencies are significant. Firstly, the supplier has no advance warning of requirements – they are forced to make forecasts and, as a result, carry unnecessary safety stocks. Secondly, the supplier is often faced with unexpected short-term demands for products, which leads to frequent changes to their production and distribution schedules and thus additional cost. The paradoxical end result is that customer service suffers because of the inevitably higher level of stock-outs.

There is now emerging an alternative way of managing demand. In this revised model the customer no longer places orders but instead shares information with the vendor. This information relates to the actual usage or sales of their product, their current on-hand inventory and details of any additional marketing activity such as promotions.

On the basis of this information, the supplier takes responsibility for replenishment of the customer's inventory. No orders are received, but instead an indication is given by the customer of the upper and lower limits of stock that they wish to keep on hand.

It is the responsibility of the supplier to maintain the customer's inventory within the specified stock bands.

The benefit to the customer is that inventory levels can be significantly reduced whilst the risk of stock-outs diminishes. Furthermore it is often the case that the customer does not pay for the inventory until after it has been sold or used – so there is a considerable cash flow benefit. The advantage to the supplier is that because they have direct access to information on real demand, usually transmitted through Electronic Data Interchange (EDI) or web-based systems, they can much better plan and schedule production and distribution – thus improving capacity utilization – and at the same time the requirement for safety stock is considerably reduced.

This system of demand management and replenishment is known as *Vendor Managed Inventory* (VMI). However, because such arrangements are usually based upon close co-operation between the customer and the supplier, the term *Co-managed Inventory* (CMI) is probably more appropriate.

Summary

The key to supply chain responsiveness is synchronization. Synchronization implies that each entity in the network is closely connected to the others and that they share the same information. In the past there was often limited visibility, either upstream or downstream, meaning that organizations were forced to act independently, making their own forecasts, and, as a result, inevitably relying upon a 'push' rather than a 'pull' philosophy.

Underpinning successful supply chain synchronization is, firstly, the information systems capability to capture data on supply and demand and, secondly, a spirit of co-operation across the so-called 'extended enterprise'. In practice it is the latter issue that tends to limit the extent to which synchronization can be achieved.

Nevertheless, as more examples of the financial benefits of ideas like quick response and Vendor Managed Inventory come to be publicised, the likelihood is that supply chain synchronization will come to be more widely practised.

References

1. Rayport, J.F. and Sviokla, J.J., 'Managing in the Marketspace', *Harvard Business Review*, November–December 1994.
2. Chandrashekar, A. and Schary, P., 'The Virtual Web-Based Supply Chain', in Franke, U. (ed.), *Managing Virtual Web Organizations in the 21st Century*, Idea Group Publishing, 2002.
3. Heinrich, C., *Adapt or Die: Transforming your Supply Chain into an Adaptive Business Network*, John Wiley & Sons, 2003.
4. Lowson, R., King, R. and Hunter, A., *Quick Response: Managing the Supply Chain to Meet Consumer Demand*, John Wiley & Sons, 1999.
5. Lei, D. and Goldhars, J.D., 'Computer-Integrated Manufacturing: Redefining the Manufacturing Firm into a Global Service Business', *International Journal of Operations & Production Management*, Vol. 11, No. 10, 1991.
6. Forrester, J., *Industrial Dynamics*, MIT Press, 1961.
7. Abraham, M.M. and Lodish, L.M., 'Getting the Most out of Advertising and Promotion', *Harvard Business Review*, May–June 1990.

Managing the global pipeline

This chapter:

Discusses the globalization of industry, the emergence of global companies and the trend towards global production, distribution and marketing strategies.

●

Explores the implications of some of the most significant aspects of globalization in the supply chain: focused factories, centralization of inventories and postponement and localization.

●

Identifies the most pressing challenges for logistics managers arising from the globalization of supply chains.

●

Considers how managers might structure and manage a global logistics network, balancing the benefits of centralized logistics planning with the need to meet localized customer demands.

●

Raises issues of outsourcing and the co-ordination of network partners and the critical role of logistics information in managing a global logistics pipeline.

Global brands and companies now dominate most markets. Over the last two decades there has been a steady trend towards the worldwide marketing of products under a common brand umbrella – whether it be Coca-Cola or Marlborough, IBM or Toyota. At the same time the global company has revised its previously localized focus, manufacturing and marketing its products in individual countries, and now instead will typically source on a worldwide basis for global production and distribution.

The logic of the global company is clear: it seeks to grow its business by extending its markets whilst at the same time seeking cost reduction through scale economies in purchasing and production and through focused manufacturing and/or assembly operations.

However, whilst the logic of globalization is strong, we must recognize that it also presents certain challenges. Firstly, world markets are not homogeneous, there is still a requirement for local variation in many product categories. Secondly, unless there is a high level of co-ordination the complex logistics of managing global supply chains may result in higher costs and extended lead times.

These two challenges are related: on the one hand, how to offer local markets the variety they seek whilst still gaining the advantage of standardized global production and, on the other, how to manage the links in the global chain from sources of supply through to end user. There is a danger that some global companies in their search for cost advantage may take too narrow a view of cost and only see the purchasing or manufacturing cost reduction that may be achieved through using low-cost supply sources. In reality it is a total cost trade-off where the costs of longer supply pipelines may outweigh the production cost saving. Figure 7.1 illustrates some of the potential cost trade-offs to be considered in establishing the extent to which a global strategy for logistics will be cost-justified. Clearly a key component of the decision to go global must be the service needs of the marketplace. There is a danger that companies might run the risk of sacrificing service on the altar of cost reduction through a failure to fully understand the service needs of individual markets.

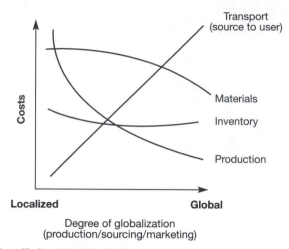

Degree of globalization
(production/sourcing/marketing)

Fig. 7.1 Trade-offs in global logistics

The trend towards global organization of both manufacturing and marketing is highlighting the critical importance of logistics and supply chain management as the keys to profitability. The complexity of the logistics task appears to be increasing exponentially, influenced by such factors as the increasing range of products, shorter product life cycles, marketplace growth and the number of supply/market channels.

> The trend towards global organization of both manufacturing and marketing is highlighting the critical importance of logistics and supply chain management as the keys to profitability.

There is no doubting that the globalization of industrial activity has become a major issue in business. Articles in the business press, seminars and academic symposia have all focused upon the emerging global trend. The competitive pressures and challenges that have led to this upsurge of interest have been well documented. What are less well understood are the implications of globalization for operations management in general and specifically for logistics management.

At the outset it is important that we define the global business and recognize its distinctiveness from an international or a multinational business. A global business is one that does more than simply export. The global business will typically source its materials and components in more than one country. Similarly it will often have multiple assembly or manufacturing locations geographically dispersed. It will subsequently market its products worldwide. A classic example is the Singer

208

Sewing Machine Company (SSMC). It buys its sewing machine shells from a subcontractor in the United States, the motors from Brazil, the drive shafts from Italy and assembles the finished machine in Taiwan. It then markets the finished machines in most countries of the world.

The trend towards globalization and offshore sourcing has been growing rapidly for some years. What some have called the 'hollow corporation'[1] is in reality part of a worldwide move towards recognizing the interdependence of suppliers, manufacturers and customers in what is truly becoming a 'global village'.

Early commentators like Levitt[2] saw the growth of global brands and talked in terms of the growing convergence of customer preferences that would enable standardized products to be marketed in similar fashion around the world. However, the reality of global marketing is often different, with quite substantial differences in local requirements still very much in evidence. Thus, whilst the brand may be global, the product may need certain customization to meet specific country needs, whether it be left or right hand drive cars or different TV transmission standards or local tastes.

The trend towards globalization in the supply chain

The growth in world trade continues to outstrip growth in most countries' gross national product and looks set to continue for the foreseeable future (see Figure 7.2). In part this trend is driven by expanding demand in new markets but also the liberalization of international trade through World Trade Organization (WTO) accords has had a significant effect.

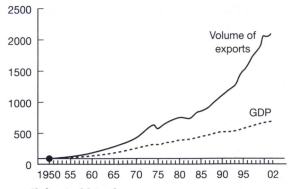

Fig. 7.2 The growth in world trade
Source: World Trade Organization.

Once, companies established factories in overseas countries to manufacture products to meet local demand. Now, with the reduction of trade barriers and the development of a global transportation infrastructure, fewer factories can produce in larger quantities to meet global, rather than local, demand.

Paradoxically, as the barriers to global movement have come down so the sources of global competition have increased. Newly emerging economies are building their own industries with global capabilities. At the same time technological change and production efficiencies mean that most companies in most industries are capable of producing in greater quantity at less cost. The result of all of this is that there is now overcapacity in virtually every industry, meaning that competitive pressure is greater than ever before.

To remain competitive in this new global environment, companies will have to continually seek ways in which costs can be lowered and service enhanced, meaning that supply chain efficiency and effectiveness will become ever more critical. See the Nike case study below.

Nike: The logistics challenge of global business

In little more than the time needed to raise just one generation of rebellious youth, US-based sports company Nike Inc. reinvented the concept of sports shoes. It transformed the cheapest of mass-market footwear into high-tech, high-performance products – imbued with all the cachet of haute couture and carrying price tags to match. Technologically, Nike's products are leading edge, as is its brand-led marketing which successfully used sporting superstar endorsement and advertisements with 'attitude' to establish the brand as an icon of youth subculture. However, as in any global organization, logistics and the management of the supply chain is a crucial strategic issue at Nike.

From its headquarters in Beaverton, Oregon, Nike operates a globe-spanning virtual enterprise. At its core are a set of business processes, designed to combine its state-of-the-art R&D capabilities with a ruthlessly low-cost manufacturing strategy.[1] The company outsources virtually 100 per cent of its shoe production, for example, retaining in-house manufacturing of a few key components of its patented Nike Air

System. Nike's basketball shoe, for example, is designed in Oregon and Tennessee and developed jointly by Asian and US technicians in Oregon, Taiwan and South Korea. The shoes themselves are manufactured in South Korea (men's sizes) and in Indonesia (boys' sizes), from 72 components supplied by companies in Japan, South Korea, Taiwan, Indonesia and the United States. Moreover, the complexity of the product means that each pair of shoes passes through more than 120 pairs of hands during the production process.[2] It also means that there is a danger of extended lead times.

Tying the whole Nike enterprise together are information systems that co-ordinate each step of these far-flung activities, and a logistics infrastructure capable of bringing the components together at precisely the right time, as well as managing the supply of finished goods into the global marketplace. Significantly, both are flexible enough to cope with the constant product, materials and process innovation, allowing the company to bring more than 300 new shoe designs to market each year. However, this punishing rate of innovation brings with it high levels of finished inventory if sales forecasts are not achieved.

In the United States and Europe, primary distribution of Nike products is increasingly outsourced to specialist third parties,[3] who are linked into the company's global sales and customer service support systems. These links allow the contractors to prioritize shipments and manage order fulfilment as cost effectively as possible, while ensuring that product availability information is readily accessible to all decision makers throughout Nike's virtual enterprise. Importantly too, these organizational capabilities should also hold Nike in good stead should fashionable youth turn away from designer sports shoes, forcing the company to rely more heavily on sales of its widening portfolio of sports equipment, clothing, watches and eyewear. When the supply chains are global and the products are fashion oriented the management of logistics becomes a key determinant of business success or failure.

References
1. Seth, Andrew, 'Just Doing It', *Marketing Business*, February 1998.
2. Business Wire, 'Nike Equipment Signs up Manlo Logistics to Manage Distribution Centres in North America, Europe', *Business Wire/Reuter Textline*, 5 February 1998.
3. *Far Eastern Economic Review*, 'The Post National Economy: Goodbye Widget, Hello Nike', 29 August 1996, p. 5.

In developing a global logistics strategy a number of issues arise which may require careful consideration. In particular, what degree of centralization is appropriate in terms of management, manufacturing and distribution, and how can the needs of local markets be met at the same time as the achievement of economies of scale through standardization?

Three of the ways in which businesses have sought to implement their global logistics strategies have been through focused factories, centralized inventories and postponement.

1 Focused factories

The idea behind the focused factory is simple: by limiting the range and mix of products manufactured in a single location the company can achieve considerable economies of scale. Typically the nationally oriented business will have 'local-for-local' production, meaning that each country's factory will produce the full range of products for sale in that country. On the other hand the global business will treat the world market as one market and will rationalize its production so that the remaining factories produce fewer products in volumes capable of satisfying perhaps the entire market.

One company that has moved in this direction is Mars. Their policy has been to simultaneously rationalize production capacity by seeking to manage demand as a whole on at least a regional level and to concentrate production by category, factory by factory. Hence their M&Ms for sale in Moscow are likely to have been produced in the United States. In a similar fashion, Heinz produce tomato ketchup for all of Europe from just three plants and will switch production depending upon how local costs and demand conditions vary against exchange rate fluctuations. A further example is provided by Procter & Gamble who manufacture their successful product Pringles in just two plants to meet worldwide demand.

Such strategies can be expected to become widespread as 'global thinking' becomes dominant.

However, a number of crucial logistics trade-offs may be overlooked in what might possibly be a too-hasty search for low-cost producer status through greater economies of scale. The most obvious trade-off is the effect on transport costs and delivery lead times. The costs of shipping products, often of relatively low value, across greater distances may erode some or all of the production cost saving. Similarly the longer lead times involved may need to be countered by local stock holding, again possibly offsetting the production cost advantage.

Further problems of focused production may be encountered where the need for local packs exist, e.g. with labelling in different languages or even different brand names and packages for the same product. This problem might be overcome by 'postponing' the final packaging until closer to the point of sale.

Another issue is that created by customers ordering a variety of products from the same company on a single order but which are now produced in a number of focused factories in different locations. The solution here may be some type of transhipment or cross-dock operation where flows of goods from diverse localities and origins are merged for onward delivery to the customer.

Finally, what will be the impact on production flexibility of the trend towards focused factories where volume and economies of scale rule the day? Whilst these goals are not necessarily mutually incompatible it may be that organizations that put low-cost production at the top of their list of priorities may be at risk in markets where responsiveness and the ability to provide 'variety' are key success factors.

In response to these issues a number of companies are questioning decisions that previously were thought sound. For example, Sony used to manufacture their digital cameras and camcorders in China, attracted by the lower labour costs. However, they came to recognize that because life cycles were so short for these products, it was better to bring the assembly back to Japan where the product design took place and, indeed, where most of the components originated. Other high-tech companies are also looking again at their offshore production and sourcing strategies for this same reason. Typically less than 10 per cent of a high-tech company's costs are direct labour. Hence the decision to source offshore, simply to save on labour costs, makes little sense if penalties are incurred elsewhere in the supply chain.

All in all it would appear that the total logistics impact of focused production will be complex and significant. To ensure that decisions are taken which are not sub-optimal it will become even more important to undertake detailed analysis based upon total system modelling and simulation prior to making commitments that may later be regretted.

■ **Centralized logistics at Lever Europe** ■

Lever, part of the global corporation Unilever, manufacture and market a wide range of soaps, detergents and cleaners. As part of a drive to implement a European strategy for manufacturing and the supply chain they created a centralized manufacturing and supply chain management structure – Lever Europe. A key part of this strategy involved a rationalization of other production facilities from a total of 16 across western Europe to 11. The remaining facilities became 'focused factories', each one concentrating on certain product families. So, for example, most bar soaps for Europe are now made at Port Sunlight in England; Mannheim in Germany makes all the Dove soap products, not just for Europe but for much of the rest of the world; France focuses on machine dishwasher products and so on.

Because national markets are now supplied from many different European sources they have retained distribution facilities in each country to act as a local consolidation centre for final delivery to customers.

Whilst some significant production cost savings have been achieved, a certain amount of flexibility has been lost. There is still a high level of variation in requirement by individual market. Many countries sell the same product but under different brand names; the languages are different hence the need for local packs; sometimes too the formulations differ.

A further problem is that as retailers become more demanding in the delivery service they require and as the trend towards just-in-time delivery continues, the loss of flexibility becomes a problem. Even though manufacturing economies of scale are welcome, it has to be recognized that the achievement of these cost benefits may be more than offset by the loss of flexibility and responsiveness in the supply chain as a whole.

2 Centralization of inventories

In the same way that the advent of globalization has encouraged companies to rationalize production into fewer locations, so too has it led to a trend towards the centralization of inventories. Making use of the well-known statistical fact that consolidating inventory into fewer locations can substantially reduce total inventory requirement, organizations have been steadily closing national warehouses and amalgamating them into regional distribution centres (RDCs) serving a much wider geographical area.

For example, Philips has reduced its consumer electronics products warehouses in western Europe from 22 to just four. Likewise Apple Computers replaced their 13 national warehouses with two European RDCs. Similar examples can be found in just about every industry.

Whilst the logic of centralization is sound, it is becoming increasingly recognized that there may be even greater gains to be had by not physically centralizing the inventory but rather by locating it strategically near the customer or the point of production but managing and controlling it centrally. This is the idea of 'virtual' or 'electronic' inventory. The idea is that by the use of information the organization can achieve the same stock reduction that it would achieve through centralization whilst retaining a greater flexibility by localizing inventory. At the same time the penalties of centralizing physical stock holding are reduced, i.e. double handling, higher transport charges and possibly longer total pipelines.

One of the arguments for centralized inventory is that advantage can be taken of the 'square root rule'.[4] Whilst an approximation, this rule of thumb provides an indication of the opportunity for inventory reduction that is possible through holding inventory in fewer locations. The rule states that the reduction in total systems inventory that can be expected is proportional to the square root of the number of stock locations before and after rationalization. Thus if previously there were 25 stock locations and now there are only four then the overall reduction in inventory would be in the ratio of $\sqrt{25}$ to $\sqrt{4}$ or 5:2, i.e. a 60 per cent reduction.

Many organizations are now recognizing the advantage of managing worldwide inventories on a centralized basis. To do so successfully, however, requires an information system that can provide complete visibility of demand from one end of the pipeline to another in as close to real time as possible. Equally such centralized systems will typically lead to higher transport costs in that products inevitably have to move greater distances and often high-cost air express will be necessary to ensure short lead times for delivery to the customer.

Xerox, in its management of its European spares business, has demonstrated how great benefits can be derived by centralizing the control of inventory and by using information systems and, in so doing, enabling a much higher service to its engineers to be provided but with only half the total inventory. SKF is another company that for 20 years or more has been driving down its European inventory of bearings whilst still improving service to its customers. Again, the means to this remarkable achievement has been through a centralized information system.

3 Postponement and localization

Although the trend to global brands and products continues, it should be recognized that there are still significant local differences in customer and consumer requirements. Even within a relatively compact market like western Europe there are major differences in consumer tastes and, of course, languages. Hence there are a large number of markets where standard, global products would not be successful. Take, for example, the differences in preference for domestic appliances such as refrigerators and washing machines. Northern Europeans prefer larger refrigerators because they shop once a week rather than daily, whilst southern Europeans, shopping more frequently, prefer smaller ones. Similarly, Britons consume more frozen foods than most other European countries and thus require more freezer space.

> Although the trend to global brands and products continues, it should be recognized that there are still significant local differences in customer and consumer requirements.

In the case of washing machines, there are differences in preference for top-loading versus front-loading machines – in the UK almost all the machines purchased are front loaders whilst in France the reverse is true.

How is it possible to reconcile the need to meet local requirements whilst seeking to organize logistics on a global basis? Ideally organizations would like to achieve the benefits of standardization in terms of cost reduction whilst maximizing their marketing success through localization.

One strategy that is increasingly being adopted is the idea of *postponement*. Postponement, or delayed configuration, is based on the principle of seeking to design products using common platforms, components or modules but where the final assembly or customization does not take place until the final market destination and/or customer requirement is known.

The advantages of the strategy of postponement are several. Firstly, inventory can be held at a generic level so that there will be fewer stock keeping variants and hence less inventory in total. Secondly, because the inventory is generic, its flexibility is greater, meaning that the same components, modules or platforms can be embodied in a variety of end products. Thirdly, forecasting is easier at the generic level than at the level of the finished item. This last point is particularly relevant in global markets where local forecasts will be less accurate than a forecast for worldwide volume. Furthermore the ability to customize products locally means that a higher level of variety may be offered at lower total cost – this is the principle of 'mass customization'.

To take full advantage of the possibilities offered by postponement often requires a 'design for localization' philosophy. Products and processes must be designed and engineered in such a way that semi-finished product can be assembled, configured and finished to provide the highest level of variety to customers based upon the smallest number of standard modules or components. In many cases the final finishing will take place in the local market, perhaps at a distribution centre, and, increasingly, the physical activity outsourced to a third-party logistics service provider.

Gaining visibility in the global pipeline

One of the features of global pipelines is that there is often a higher level of *uncertainty* about the status of a shipment whilst in transit. This uncertainty is made worse by the many stages in a typical global pipeline as a product flows from factory to port, from the port to its country of destination, through customs clearance and so on until it finally reaches the point where it is required. Not surprisingly there is a high degree of *variation* in these extended pipelines.

Shipping, consolidation and customs clearance all contribute to delays and variability in the end-to-end lead time of global supply chains. This is highlighted in the example shown in Table 7.1 below. This can be a major issue for companies as they increasingly go global. It has the consequence that local managers tend to compensate for this unreliability by over-ordering and by building inventory buffers.

Table 7.1 End-to-end lead-time variability (days)

	From point of origin to port	Freight forwarding/ consolidation	Arrive in country of destination	Customs clearance	Transit to point of use	Total elapsed time
Maximum	5	7	15	5	5	37
Average	4	3	14	2	4	32
Minimum	1	1	12	1	2	17

One emerging tool that could greatly improve the visibility across complex global supply chains is supply chain event management.

Supply chain event management (SCEM) is the term given to the process of monitoring the planned sequence of activities along a supply chain and the subsequent reporting of any divergence from that plan. Ideally SCEM will also enable a proactive, even automatic, response to deviations from the plan.

'The SCEM system should act like an intensive care monitor in a hospital. To use an intensive care monitor, the doctor places probes at strategic points on the patient's body; each measures a discrete and different function – temperature, respiration rate, blood pressure. The monitor is programmed with separate upper and lower control limits for each probe and for each patient. If any of the watched bodily functions go above or below the defined tolerance, the monitor sets off an alarm to the doctor for immediate follow-up and corrective action. The SCEM application should act in the same manner.

'The company determines its unique measurement points along its supply chain and installs probes. The company then programmes the SCEM application to monitor the plan-to-actual supply chain progress, and establishes upper and lower control limits. If any of the control limits are exceeded, or if anomalies occur, the application publishes alerts or alarms so that the functional manager can take appropriate corrective action.'

Source: Styles, Peter, 'Determining Supply Chain Event Management', in *Achieving Supply Chain Excellence Through Technology*, Montgomery Research, San Francisco, 2002.

The Internet can provide the means whereby SCEM reporting systems can link together even widely dispersed partners in global supply chains. The use of XML communications across the web means that even organizations with different information systems can be linked together. The key requirement though is not technological, it is the willingness of the different entities in a supply chain to work in a collaborative mode and to agree to share information.

Supply chain event management enables organizations to gain visibility upstream and downstream of their own operations and to assume an *active* rather than a *passive* approach to supply chain risk. Figure 7.3

shows the progression from the traditional, limited scope of supply chain visibility to the intended goal of an 'intelligent' supply chain information system.

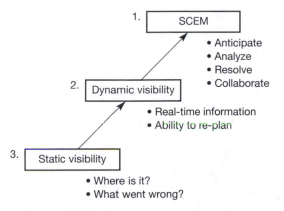

Fig. 7.3 The progression to supply chain event management

Event management software is now becoming available from a number of providers. The principles underpinning event management are that 'intelligent agents' are created within the software that are instructed to respond within pre-determined decision rules, e.g. upper and lower limits for inventory levels at different stages in a supply chain. These agents monitor the critical stage in a process and issue alerts when deviations from required performance occurs. The agents can also be instructed to take corrective action where necessary, and they can identify trends and anomalies and report back to supply chain managers on emerging situations that might require pre-emptive attention.

Whilst event management is primarily a tool for managing processes, its advantage is that it can look across networks, thus enabling connected processes to be monitored and, if necessary, modified.

Clearly the complexity of most supply networks is such that in reality event management needs to be restricted to the critical paths in that network. Critical paths might be typified by such features as: long lead times to react to unplanned events, reliance on single-source suppliers, bottlenecks, etc.

Event management is rooted in the concept of workflow and milestones, and Figure 7.4 uses nodes and links to illustrate the idea of workflow across the supply chain. Once a chain has been described in terms of the nodes that are in place and the links that have been established, the controls that have been defined respond to events across the chain. An event is a conversion of material at a node in the chain or a movement of material between nodes in the chain. Events should only happen as a result of an instruction (control). Therefore on the time horizon over which instructions are issued, events are capable of being monitored for the timeliness and completeness with which they are executed against the original instruction.

So, for example, a simple data string will be attached to the following events at the time the instruction is issued:

- Node point
- Process (conversion or link)
- Date of instruction
- Product code
- Quantity
- Date for commencement of task
- Date due for completion
- Consignment/order number
- Next node in the chain

The data string can be very lengthy depending on the product and industry and the level of data capture that the firm is trying to achieve.

Event management systems rely on being connected to the systems of the players in the extended chain (both internal to the firm and with its suppliers and customers) so that their obligation to comply to the controls that have been set and their actual performance is recorded through a data feed to the event management system, when the event happens.

When an event does not occur on time and/or in full, the system will automatically raise alerts and alarms through an escalation sequence to the people controlling the chain requiring them to take action. Currently, event management systems typically do not determine the actions that are most appropriate or provide optimization capabilities; however, future generations of supply chain event management systems will probably have this capability.

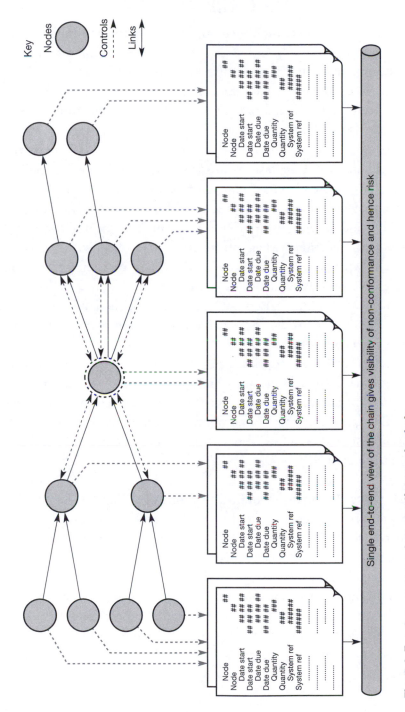

Fig. 7.4 Event management across the supply chain

Source: Cranfield School of Management, *Creating Resilient Supply Chains*, Report on behalf of the Department for Transport, 2002.

Organizing for global logistics

As companies have extended their supply chains internationally they have been forced to confront the issue of how to structure their global logistics organization. In their different ways these companies have moved towards the same conclusion: effectiveness in global logistics can only be achieved through a greater element of centralization. This in many respects runs counter to much of the conventional wisdom, which tends to argue that decision-making responsibility should be devolved and decentralized at least to the strategic business unit level. This philosophy has manifested itself in many companies in the form of strong local management, often with autonomous decision making at the country level. Good though this may be for encouraging local initiatives, it tends to be dysfunctional when integrated global strategies are required.

Clearly there will still be many areas where local decision making will be preferable – for example, sales strategy and, possibly, promotional and marketing communications strategy. Likewise the implementation of global strategy can still be adjusted to take account of national differences and requirements.

How then can the appropriate balance of global versus local decision making be achieved in formulating and implementing logistics strategy?

Because specific market environments and industry characteristics will differ from company to company it is dangerous to offer all-embracing solutions. However, a number of general principles are beginning to emerge:

● The strategic structuring and overall control of logistics flows must be centralized to achieve worldwide optimization of costs.
● The control and management of customer service must be localized against the requirements of specific markets to ensure competitive advantage is gained and maintained.
● As the trend towards outsourcing everything except core competencies increases then so does the need for global co-ordination.
● A global logistics information system is the prerequisite for enabling the achievement of local service needs whilst seeking global cost optimization.

1 Structure and control

If the potential trade-offs in rationalizing sourcing, production and distribution across national boundaries are to be achieved then it is essential that a central decision-making structure for logistics is established. Many companies that are active on an international basis find that they are constrained in their search for global optimization by strongly entrenched local systems and structures. Only through centralized planning and co-ordination of logistics can the organization hope to achieve the twin goals of cost minimization and service maximization.

> if the potential trade-offs in rationalizing sourcing, production and distribution across national boundaries are to be achieved then it is essential that a central decision-making structure for logistics is established.

For example, location decisions are a basic determinant of profitability in international logistics. The decision on where to manufacture, to assemble, to store, to transship and to consolidate can make the difference between profit and loss. Because of international differences in basic factor costs and because of exchange rate movements, location decisions are fundamental. Also these decisions tend to involve investment in fixed assets in the form of facilities and equipment. Decisions taken today can therefore have a continuing impact over time on the company's financial and competitive position.

As the trend towards global manufacturing continues, organizations will increasingly need to look at location decisions through total cost analysis. The requirement there is for improved access to activity-related costs such as manufacturing, transportation and handling. Accurate information on inventory holding costs and the cost/benefit of postponement also becomes a key variable in location decisions.

The opportunities for reducing costs and improving throughput efficiency by a reappraisal of the global logistics network, and in particular manufacturing and inventory locations, can be substantial. By their very nature, decisions on location in a global network can only be taken centrally.

2 Customer service management

Because local markets have their own specific characteristics and needs there is considerable advantage to be achieved by shaping marketing strategies locally – albeit within overall global guidelines. This is particularly true of customer service management where the opportunities for tailoring service against individual customer requirements are great. The management of customer service involves the monitoring of service needs as well as performance and extends to the management of the entire order fulfilment process – from order through to delivery. Whilst order fulfilment systems are increasingly global and centrally managed there will always remain the need to have strong local customer service management.

3 Outsourcing and partnerships

As we have previously noted, one of the greatest changes in the global business today is the trend towards outsourcing. Not just outsourcing the procurement of materials and components but also outsourcing of services that traditionally have been provided in-house. The logic of this trend is that the organization will increasingly focus on those activities in the value chain where it has a distinctive advantage – the core competencies of the business – and everything else it will outsource. This movement has been particularly evident in logistics where the provision of transport, warehousing and inventory control is increasingly subcontracted to specialists or logistics partners.

To manage and control this network of partners and suppliers requires a blend of both central and local involvement. The argument once again is that the strategic decisions need to be taken centrally, with the monitoring and control of supplier performance and day-to-day liaison with logistics partners being best managed at a local level.

4 Logistics information

The management of global logistics is in reality the management of information flows. The information system is the mechanism whereby the complex flows of materials, parts, subassemblies and finished products can be co-ordinated to achieve cost-effective service. Any organization with aspirations to global leadership is dependent upon the visibility it can gain of materials flows, inventories and demand throughout the pipeline. Without the ability to see down the pipeline into end-user markets, to read actual demand and subsequently to manage replenishment in virtual real time, the system is doomed to depend upon inventory. To 'substitute information for inventory' has become something of a cliché but it should be a prime objective nevertheless. Time lapses in information flows are directly translated into inventory. The great advances that are being made in introducing 'quick response' logistics systems are all based upon information flow from the point of actual demand directly into the supplier's logistics and replenishment systems. On a global scale we typically find that the presence of intervening inventories between the plant and the marketplace obscure the view of real demand. Hence the need for information systems that can read demand at every level in the pipeline and provide the driving power for a centrally controlled logistics system.

Thinking global, acting local

The implementation of global pipeline control is highly dependent upon the ability of the organization to find the correct balance between central control and local management. It is unwise to be too prescriptive but the experience that global organizations are gaining every day suggests that certain tasks and functions lend themselves to central control and others to local management. Table 7.2 summarizes some of the possibilities.

Table 7.2 Global co-ordination and local management

Global	Local
● Network structuring for production and transportation optimization	● Customer service management
● Information systems development and control	● Gathering market intelligence
● Inventory positioning	● Warehouse management and local delivery
● Sourcing decisions	● Customer profitability analyses
● International transport mode and sourcing decisions	● Liaison with local sales and marketing management
● Trade-off analyses and supply chain cost control	● Human resource management

Much has been learned in the last 20 years or so about the opportunities for cost and service enhancement through better management of logistics at a national level. Now organizations are faced with applying those lessons on a much broader stage. As international competition becomes more intense and as national barriers to trade gradually reduce, the era of the global business has arrived. Increasingly the difference between success and failure in the global marketplace will be determined not by the sophistication of product technology or even of marketing communications, but rather by the way in which we manage and control the global logistics pipeline. The case of Marks & Spencer, the UK retailer, dramatically underlines this point of view.

The impact of global sourcing

Marks & Spencer (M&S), a major British retailer, had long been a textbook example of a successful extended enterprise. For decades it had been an industry leader in collaborative working with its network of dedicated local suppliers. The formula worked well for more than 100 years, until 1998 when M&S hit trouble. Commentators were quick to highlight M&S's failure to respond to the changing requirements of the company's famously loyal customer base.

M&S's strength had been its ability to satisfy the British middle classes with good quality, fairly conservative apparel at reasonable prices. At the time it was becoming apparent that the mass-market middle ground was being squeezed by discount stores, such as Matalan, at one end and by niche players catering for specific age or lifestyle groups, such as Zara and Gap, at the other. Whatever the changes in the nature of the market, one element that has had a severe impact on the sector as a whole has been the continuing downward pressure on prices. In order to survive, retailers have had to focus on cost reduction. Paradoxically this need for more competitive pricing was accompanied by a demand from consumers for enhanced quality, more fashionable styling and a heightened shopping experience. In short, customers wanted varied and distinctive styles at lower prices, available on demand.

M&S's response to this was to seek to reduce its cost base by insisting that its suppliers source more of their products from locations where labour costs are low. It abandoned its longstanding UK sourcing strategy, first by requiring its established suppliers to relocate production overseas to low-cost manufacturing centres, then by adopting more open sourcing policies. The potential for cost reduction from global sourcing was dramatic, at least on paper. According to the

British Apparel and Textile Confederation, the average hourly labour cost for clothing manufacturers in the UK in 2000 was $9.50 compared to $1.20 an hour in Morocco and less than 50 cents an hour in China, Pakistan and Indonesia. However, as M&S soon discovered, this simplistic calculation failed to take into account the hidden costs of overseas sourcing, particularly the risks relating to significantly extended replenishment lead times. It overlooked the need to secure transport capacity and textile import quotas ahead of season, discovering too late that it lacked the essential logistics know-how needed to support its new sourcing strategy.

Whereas M&S's dedicated domestic suppliers had been able to re-supply relatively rapidly, with overseas sourcing orders typically had to be placed many months ahead of requirement. Inevitably, reliance on forecasts increased. Thus buyers had to predict styles, colours and volumes well ahead of the season. If these forecasts were wrong – and they often were – then the result was either over-stocking or a stock-out. Either way, this had a negative impact on profitability. Indeed one of the major causes of the M&S profit slump in the late 1990s was the lack of interest shown by consumers in the M&S clothing range where the buyers had seriously misjudged fashion trends.

Part of the problem for M&S was that its definition of cost was too narrow, i.e. the purchase cost rather than the total cost of ownership. In the event, what was intended to be a low-cost supply chain solution turned out to be high cost, not least because it had adopted a 'one size fits all' supply chain strategy for its clothing products. It could be argued that the strategy M&S adopted would have been, and indeed is, appropriate for high volume 'standard' items, such as men's shirts and socks. It was nevertheless totally inappropriate for the more 'innovative' or 'special' ranges such as M&S's exclusive designer-led Autograph range, one of several new introductions that had latterly been added to bring spice and variety to the core product mix. These low volume, short life cycle and high value ranges demanded an altogether more responsive supply chain.

In time it was recognized amongst the top management team at M&S that a much more differentiated procurement strategy for garments was essential. A revised strategy was subsequently outlined in M&S's Interim Report of September 2002 when its Chairman and Chief Executive wrote:

▶

▶

> Lack of flexibility has been the major weakness within our supply chain. In the past, we bought stock to cover 100% of budgeted sales well in advance of the season. We have now discontinued this practice. For Spring 2001, while 50% of merchandise is core and therefore bought with long lead times, we will commit to approximately 40% of merchandise much closer to the season, and a further 10% will be bought in the season itself in response to emerging fashion trends.

Likely predictability of demand and the length of the season are now factored in to M&S's purchasing decisions. These issues increasingly determine where products should be sourced, how they should be transported and whether it is a one-off buy or a continuing supply. In spring 2004, 80 per cent of clothing sourced by M&S was manufactured overseas, though it retains close relationships with its leading suppliers, with its top 15 suppliers accounting for 92 per cent of its clothing business. Many of these are UK-owned companies operating overseas, in up and coming Asian countries such as Cambodia as well as some of the newer EU states. 'Journey time' has become a principal deciding factor in product sourcing decisions. The emphasis is on quick response for lines where demand is difficult to predict. These items are manufactured in locations with a journey time of less than four days. Standard items, for which demand is expected to be predictable and continuous, continue to be sourced from low-cost centres around the globe.

Summary

For the last decade or so the continued trend towards the globalization of business has been evident. Markets have become global in the sense that the same brands and products are increasingly offered for sale around the world. Equally apparent has been the move towards global sourcing and manufacturing as companies concentrate their operations so that often just one or two factories serve the whole world.

Paradoxically the trend to globalization has increased the complexity of logistics. Often pipelines are longer with greater reliance on outsourced supply chain partners. Furthermore local differences in requirements still exist so that the needs of local markets must be balanced against the economic advantage of standardized products. Thus the challenge to global logistics management is to structure a supply chain that is agile and flexible enough to cope with differences in customer requirements and yet can enable the benefits of focused manufacturing to be realized.

References

1. 'The Hollow Corporation', *Business Week*, 3 March 1986.
2. Levitt, T., 'The Globalization of Markets', *Harvard Business Review*, Vol. 61, May–June 1983.
3. Roberts, J., 'Formulating and Implementing a Global Logistics Strategy', *International Journal of Logistics Management*, Vol. 1, No. 2, 1990.
4. Sussams, J.E., 'Buffer Stocks and the Square Root Law', *Focus*, Institute of Logistics, UK, Vol. 5, No. 5, 1986.

Managing risk in the supply chain

This chapter:

Identifies the major sources of supply chain vulnerability.

●

Suggests ways in which the supply chain risk profile can be monitored.

●

Proposes a seven-point action plan to manage and mitigate supply chain risk.

●

Highlights the opportunity for using Six Sigma methodologies to reduce variation in key processes.

●

Indicates ways in which supply chain resilience can be improved.

Today's marketplace is characterized by turbulence and uncertainty. Market turbulence has tended to increase in recent years for a number of reasons. Demand in almost every industrial sector seems to be more volatile than was the case in the past. Product and technology life cycles have shortened significantly and competitive product introductions make life-cycle demand difficult to predict. Considerable 'chaos' exists in our supply chains through the effects of such actions as sales promotions, quarterly sales incentives or decision rules such as re-order quantities.

At the same time the vulnerability of supply chains to disturbance or disruption has increased. It is not only the effect of external events such as natural disasters, strikes or terrorist attacks but also the impact of changes in business strategy. Many companies have experienced a change in their supply chain risk profile as a result of changes in their business models. For example, the adoption of 'lean' practices, the move to outsourcing and a general tendency to reduce the size of the supplier base potentially increase supply chain vulnerability.

As a result of this heightened risk, organizations will need to develop appropriate programmes to mitigate and manage that risk.

The impact of unplanned and unforeseen events in supply chains can have severe financial effects across the network as a whole. Research in North America[1] suggests that when companies experience disruptions to their supply chains the impact on their share price once the problem becomes public knowledge can be significant. The research suggests that companies experiencing these sorts of problems saw their average operating income drop 107 per cent, return on sales fall 114 per cent and return on assets decrease by 93 per cent. Figure 8.1 shows the impact on shareholder value of supply chain disruption.

In 2003 the Gartner Group, a US-based research and consultancy company, predicted that one in five businesses would be impacted by some form of supply chain disruption and that of those companies 60 per cent would go out of business as a result.

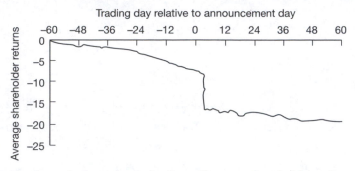

Fig. 8.1 The impact of supply chain disruptions on shareholder value
Source: Singhal and Hendricks[2]

A year earlier Land Rover, part of the Ford Motor Company, announced that it might have to halt production of its Discovery four-wheel drive vehicle because its sole supplier of chassis – UPF-Thompson – had gone into liquidation. It was estimated that it could take up to six months for an alternative source of supply to be brought onstream. At some significant cost, Land Rover had no alternative but to finance the supplier to enable the production of chassis to continue.

A survey by *The Economist*[3] of chief executives stated that a majority of respondents reported a greater dependency on external suppliers and that there was a fear that this could lead to a loss of control and hence greater supply chain vulnerability.

Clearly, there are risks that are *external* to the supply chain and those that are *internal*. External risks may arise from natural disasters, wars, terrorism and epidemics, or from government imposed legal restrictions. Internal risks will be described in more detail later in this chapter but essentially they refer to the risks that arise as a result of how the supply chain is structured and managed. Whilst external risk cannot be influenced by managerial actions, internal risk can.

Why are supply chains more vulnerable?

A study conducted by Cranfield University[4] for the UK government defines supply chain vulnerability as:

an exposure to serious disturbance, arising from risks within the supply chain as well as risks external to the supply chain.

The same study identified a number of reasons why modern supply chains have become more vulnerable.

These factors are considered below in more depth.

A focus on efficiency rather than effectiveness

The prevailing business model of the closing decades of the twentieth century was very much based upon the search for greater levels of efficiency in the supply chain. Experience highlighted that there was an opportunity in many sectors of industry to take out significant cost by focusing on inventory reduction. Just-in-time (JIT) practices were widely adopted and organizations became increasingly dependent upon suppliers. This model, whilst undoubtedly of merit in stable market conditions, may become less viable as volatility of demand increases. The challenge in today's business environment is how best to combine 'lean' practices with an 'agile' response.

The globalization of supply chains

There has been a dramatic shift away from the predominantly 'local for local' manufacturing and marketing strategy of the past. Now, through offshore sourcing, manufacturing and assembly, supply chains extend from one side of the globe to the other. For example, components may be sourced in Taiwan, subassembled in Singapore with final assembly in the US for sale in world markets.

Usually the motivation for offshore sourcing and manufacturing is cost reduction. However, that definition of cost is typically limited to the cost of purchase or manufacture. Only rarely are total supply chain costs considered. The result of these cost-based decisions is often higher levels of risk as a result of extended lead times, greater buffer stocks and potentially higher levels of obsolescence – particularly in short life-cycle markets. A further impetus to the globalization of supply chains has come from the increase in cross-border mergers and acquisitions that we have witnessed over the last decade or so.

Focused factories and centralized distribution

One of the impacts of the implementation of the Single Market within the European Union and the consequent reduction in the barriers to the flow of products across borders has been the centralization of production and distribution facilities. Significant scale economies can be achieved in manufacturing if greater volumes are produced on fewer sites. In some cases companies have chosen to 'focus' their factories – instead of producing the full range of products at each site, they produce fewer products exclusively at a single site. As a result, production costs may be lower but the product has to travel greater distances, often across many borders. Incidentally, at the same time, flexibility may be lost because these focused factories tend to be designed to produce in very large batches to achieve maximum scale economies.

Simultaneously with this move to fewer production sites is the tendency to centralize distribution. Many fast moving consumer goods manufacturers aim to serve the whole of the western European market through a few distribution centres, for example, one in north-west Europe and one in the south.

The trend to outsourcing

One widespread trend, observable over many years, has been the tendency to outsource activities that were previously conducted within the organization. No part of the value chain has been immune from this phenomenon; companies have outsourced distribution, manufacturing, accounting and information systems, for example. In some cases these companies might accurately be described as 'virtual' companies. There is a strong logic behind this based upon the view that organizations are more likely to succeed if they focus on the activities in which they have a differential advantage over competitors. This is leading to the creation of 'network organizations', whereby confederations of firms are linked together – usually through shared information and aligned processes – to achieve greater overall competitiveness. However, outsourcing also brings with it a number of risks, not least being the potential loss of control. Disruptions in supply can often be attributed to the failure of one of the links and nodes in the chain and, by definition, the more complex the supply network the more links there are and hence the greater the risk of failure.

Reduction of the supplier base

A further prevailing trend over the last decade or so has been a dramatic reduction in the number of suppliers from whom an organization typically will procure materials, components, services, etc. In some cases this

236

has been extended to 'single sourcing', whereby one supplier is responsible for the sole supply of an item. Several well-documented cases exist where major supply chain disruptions have been caused because of a failure at a single source. Even though there are many benefits to supplier base reduction it has to be recognized that it brings with it increased risk.

Sometimes a consolidation of the supply base happens through merger and acquisition. Since the rate of merger and acquisition has increased so dramatically over recent years, it follows that the supply base reduction will have accelerated for this reason alone.

Understanding the supply chain risk profile

Many organizations today are addressing the issues of what has come to be termed 'business continuity'. In practice, however, there tends to be a limited focus for much of business continuity management. There is a strong focus on IT and internal process management but often the wider supply risk dimension is not considered. This is paradoxical since it can be argued that the biggest risk to business continuity may be in the wider network of which the individual business is just a part.

To widen the focus on supply chain vulnerability it is suggested that a supply risk profile be established for the business. The purpose of the risk profile is to establish where the greatest vulnerabilities lie and what the probability of disruption is. In a sense this approach takes the view that:

Supply chain risk = Probability of disruption × Impact

Thus the risk profile attempts to seek out the 'critical paths' through a network where management attention should be especially focused. A weakness of this definition of risk is that it may lead to a failure to recognize that supply chains may be at their most vulnerable where the probability of occurrence is small but the potential impact could be catastrophic. For example, in May 2003 a tornado struck Jackson, Tennessee in the US severely damaging Procter & Gamble's sole factory in North America for the manufacture of Pringles. Production of this $1 billion a year sales revenue product was severely curtailed since P&G's only other manufacturing facility for Pringles is in Belgium.

To help identify the risk profile of a business it is helpful to undertake an audit of the main sources of risk across the network. This audit should examine potential risk to business disruptions arising from five sources:

237

1. *Supply risk*

   How vulnerable is the business to disruptions in supply? Risk may be higher due to global sourcing, reliance on key suppliers, poor supply management, etc.

2. *Demand risk*

   How volatile is demand? Does the 'bullwhip' effect cause demand amplification? Are there parallel interactions where the demand for another product affects the demand for ours?

3. *Process risk*

   How resilient are our processes? Do we understand the sources of variability in those processe, e.g. manufacturing? Where are the bottlenecks? How much additional capacity is available if required?

4. *Control risk*

   How likely are disturbances and distortions to be caused by our own internal control systems? For example, order opportunities, batch sizes and safety stock policies can distant real demand. Our own decision rules and policies can cause 'chaos' type effects.

5. *Environmental risk*

   Where across the supply chain as a whole are we vulnerable to external forces? Whilst the type and timings of extreme external events may not be forecastable, their impact needs to be assessed.

Figure 8.2 below summarizes the connections between the five sources of risk.

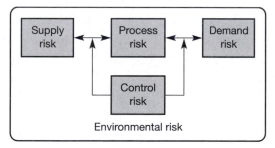

Fig. 8.2 Sources of risk in the supply chain
Source: Adapted from Mason-Jones, R. and Towill, D.R., 'Shrinking the Supply Chain Uncertainty Cycle', *Control*, September 1998, pp. 17–22.

It is important for senior management to understand that the risk profile is directly and indirectly impacted by the strategic decisions that they take. Thus the decision, for instance, to transfer production from a western European factory to one in China should be examined in terms of how it may affect vulnerability from the five risk sources described above.

For multi-product, multi-market businesses the priority should be to identify the major profit streams and to concentrate on creating deep insights into how supply chain risk could impact those profit streams.

■ Mapping your risk profile ■

Rather than cataloguing all the possible risks a company might face, the first stage in strategic risk management is to understand the company's internal processes in order to isolate the most relevant and critical threats. Once a company understands its own internal vulnerabilities, it can monitor the external environment for relevant danger signs and begin to develop mitigation and contingency strategies accordingly. Although companies may not be able to prevent disruptions, they can reduce their impact by understanding how their operations may be affected and by preparing for the possibilities. The goal is to develop operational resilience, foster the ability to recover quickly and plot alternative courses to work around the disruption.

Although global corporations are vulnerable to many of the same risks, each company has a unique risk profile.

There are six steps in developing this profile and appropriate management strategies.

1. *Prioritize earnings drivers*
   Identify and map the company's earnings drivers, which provide operational support for the overall business strategy. These are the factors that would have the biggest impact on earnings if disrupted and a shock to any one could endanger the business. For example, in process industries, manufacturing is the major force behind earnings: wholesalers and retailers must prioritize inventory and logistics operations.
2. *Identify critical infrastructure*
   Identify the infrastructure – including processes, relationships, people, regulations, plan and equipment – that supports the firm's ability to generate earnings. Brand reputation, for example, might depend on product quality control processes, supplier labour practices and key spokespeople within the firm. Research development might depend on specific laboratory locations, critical personnel and patent protection. Again, every company is unique and even companies in the same industry will prioritize their drivers differently. The goal is to identify the essential components required for the earnings driver. One way to do this is by

---

asking 'What are the processes which, if they failed, would seriously affect my earnings?' Put another way, these are the factors that could end up in a footnote in an annual report explaining the rationale behind a charge against earnings.

3. *Locate vulnerabilities*

What are the weakest links, the elements on which all others depend? It could be a single supplier for a critical component, a border that 80 per cent of your products must cross to get to your key markets, a single employee who knows how to restore data if the IT system fails, or a regulation that makes it possible for you to stay in business. Vulnerabilities are characterized by:

- An element on which many others depend – a bottleneck
- A high degree of concentration – suppliers, manufacturing locations, material or information flows
- Limited alternatives
- Association with high-risk geographic areas, industries and products (such as war or flood zones, or economically troubled industries, such as airlines)
- Insecure access points to important infrastructure

Notice that the focus is still on the internal processes rather than potential external events. In many ways the impact of a disruption does not depend on the precise manner in which these elements fail. Whether your key supplier fails because of a fire in a plant, an earthquake, a terrorist attack or an economic crisis, you may have the same response plan.

4. *Model scenarios*

Best-practice organizations continuously assess their strengths and weaknesses by creating scenarios based on the full spectrum of crises highlighted earlier. In a recent *Harvard Business Review* article,[1] Ian Mitroff discussed his approach of spinning a 'Wheel of Crises' to challenge executives to think creatively and randomly. Using supply chain modelling tools to simulate the impact of crises is also useful in gauging risk levels for your trading partners.

5. *Develop responses*

After executives assess the impact of alternative crisis scenarios on the supply chain, they will have detailed knowledge of their operational vulnerabilities and how these soft spots relate to performance goals and earnings. Understanding these weak areas at the enterprise level will clarify critical decisions.

Completing a risk profile will also bring to light opportunities to reduce risk and indicate the value to be gained. Risk-mitigation plans can be put into two broad categories: redundancy and flexibility. Traditional risk-management approaches have focused heavily on redundant solutions, such as increasing inventory, preparing backup IT and telecommunications systems, and fostering long-term supplier contracts. While generally effective in protecting against potential risk, such approaches come with a higher cost – sometimes explicitly and sometimes hidden – that can potentially put organizations at a competitive disadvantage.

Flexible responses, however, utilize supply chain capabilities that not only manage risk but simultaneously increase an organization's competitive capability. Examples include:

- Product design for agility – common components and delayed product differentiation
- Common, flexible and readily transferable manufacturing practices
- Lead-time reduction – duration and variability
- Dynamic inventory planning
- Supply chain visibility
- Cross-training of employees

Just as supply chain modelling tools and techniques can help assess the impact of crisis scenarios, they can also be used to evaluate the costs and benefits of alternative responses.

6. *Monitor the risk environment*

Each vulnerability will suggest a number of potential responses. The challenge is to ensure that the chosen response is proportional to the risk, in terms of both magnitude and likelihood. A company's risk profile is constantly changing: economic and market conditions change, consumer tastes change, the regulatory environment changes, as will products and processes. It is essential to redraw the company's risk map in tandem. Part of the mapping process includes identifying leading indicators based on the key supply chain vulnerabilities. Such an early warning system helps ensure that contingency plans are activated as soon as possible. Although a detailed assessment of a company's excellence in risk management is quite involved, a simple self-assessment can quickly identify the largest gaps.

References

1. 'Preparing for Evil', *Harvard Business Review*, April 2003, pp. 109–115.

Managing supply chain risk

Figure 8.3 below suggests a seven-stage approach to the management of supply chain risk. Each of the seven stages is described in more detail in the following sections.

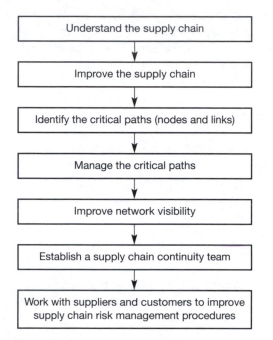

Fig. 8.3 The supply chain risk management process

1 Understand the supply chain

There is in many companies an amazing lack of awareness of the wider supply/demand network of which the organization is a part. Whilst there is often a good understanding of the downstream routes to market, the same is not always true of what lies upstream of first tier suppliers. First tier suppliers are often dependent themselves on second and even third tier suppliers for their continuity.

An example of this is provided by Chrysler who were reviewing the upstream supply chain for the Jeep Grand Cherokee's V8 engine.[5] The company mapped all the hundreds of component flows and found that one of these components – a roller lift valve manufactured by Eaton Corp. – was made from castings sourced from a local foundry. When the Chrysler team visited that foundry they discovered that the clay that was used to produce the castings came from a sole supplier who was losing money and thinking of exiting the business.

It is this detailed level of supply chain understanding that is necessary if risk is to be mitigated and managed. For complex supply chains or where complete mapping of the entire network is not practical it would be appropriate only to look in detail at the 'critical paths' – how these are identified is dealt with later.

2 Improve the supply chain

'Improving' the supply chain is all about simplification, improving process reliability, reducing process variability and reducing complexity. For more long-established businesses it is probably true to say that rarely have their supply chains been planned or designed in a holistic way. Rather they have developed organically in response to the needs and opportunities of the time. Suppliers have been chosen because of their ability to meet the demands for lower price rather than because of the reliability of their supply chains for example.

Variability and *complexity* add to supply chain risk in a number of ways. Variation implies unstable processes with outcomes that are not always predictable. The use of *Six Sigma* methodology can be a powerful way to reduce variability in supply chain processes (see box).

■ Reducing process variability through Six Sigma methodology ■

Conventional approaches to quality management were typically based upon 'inspection'. In other words, a sample of the output of a process would be taken on a periodic basis and if non-standard outputs were detected then remedial action would be taken. Not surprisingly, inspection-based quality management has proved to be less than satisfactory. Often non-conforming items would 'slip through the net' and, in any case, inspection is 'after the event'. Today, our thinking on quality management has changed. Now the recognition is that if we seek consistency in the quality of the output then the only way to achieve this is to ensure that the process that produces those outputs is under control.

Thus *process control* becomes the means by which *variation* in output is identified. Variation in any process is the problem. If everything in life or in business was totally constant or even predictable, then there would be few

▶

243

problems. The challenges arise because of variations. Hence it follows that if variation can be reduced then the consistency (and, by definition, the reliability) of the output can almost be guaranteed.

The Six Sigma way

The Six Sigma route to quality control emerged in the 1980s as Motorola searched for a robust quantitative approach that would drive variability out of their manufacturing processes and thus guarantee the reliability of their products. The term 'Six Sigma' is largely symbolic, referring to a methodology and a culture for continuous quality improvement, as well as referring to the statistical goal, six sigma. The term 'sigma' (σ) is used in statistics to measure variation from the mean; in a business context the higher the value of sigma the more capable the process of delivering an output within customer specifications. The diagram below illustrates the difference between two processes: one with a low capability and the other with six sigma capability.

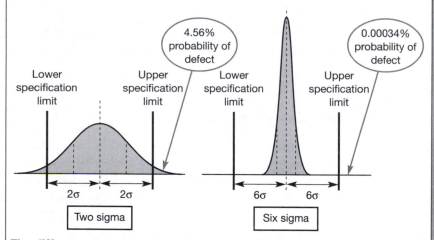

The difference between a two sigma and a six sigma process

The *Six Sigma goal* (which in many cases is an aspirational one) is to squeeze out process variability until the process produces just 3.4 defects per million activities or 'opportunities'; this reduces waste and hence saves money whilst improving customer satisfaction. Whilst Six Sigma performance may be unattainable in many cases, it is used as a target.

Six Sigma is a data-driven continuous improvement methodology that seeks to bring processes under control and to improve process capability. The methodology itself follows the five-stage DMAIC cycle:

Define: What is it we are seeking to improve?

Measure: What is the current capability of the process? What averages, what variability in process output is evident?

Analyze: Map the process, use cause and effect analysis (Ishikawa) and prioritize for action.

Improve: Re-engineer the process, simplify.

Control: Improve visibility of the process. Use statistical process control and monitor performance.

Six Sigma tools and techniques enable the proper execution of the DMAIC cycle and ensure that decisions are based on hard quantitative evidence.

Source: Christopher, M. and Rutherford, C., 'Creating Supply Chain Resilience through Agile Six Sigma', *Critical Eye*, June/August 2004.

Complexity in supply chains has a number of sources: the number of products and variants offered; and the number of components and/or sub-assemblies; and the number of suppliers and customers and their location.

At Motorola, competitive pressure caused the company to extend its range of mobile telephones. However, often there was little commonality of parts across the range. For a single product there could be over 100 possible configurations, i.e. four different colours and 30 software choices. Furthermore, these product variations were made ahead of demand to a forecast that was only accurate 3 per cent of the time![6] To address this problem, Motorola devised a 'Complexity Index' for each product, which included the number of components, the degree of commonality, lead time of supply and so on. Ideas for new products with high scores on the Complexity Index tend not to be proceeded with. As a result of this focus on complexity reduction, Motorola was able to significantly reduce its costs and improve its responsiveness.

3 Identify the critical paths

Supply networks are in effect a complex web of interconnected 'nodes' and 'links'. The nodes represent the entities or facilities such as suppliers, distributors, factories and warehouses. The links are the means by which the nodes are connected – these links may be physical flows, information flows or financial flows. The vulnerability of a supply network is determined by the risk of failure of these nodes and links.

As there will be potentially thousands of nodes and links the challenge to supply chain risk management is to identify which of them are 'mission critical'. In other words, how severe would the effect of failure be on the performance of the supply chain? Companies need to be able to identify the critical paths that must be managed and monitored to ensure continuity.

Critical paths are likely to have a number of characteristics:

● Long lead time, e.g. the time taken to replenish components from order to delivery.
● A single source of supply with no short-term alternative.
● Dependence on specific infrastructure, e.g. ports, transport modes or information systems.
● A high degree of concentration amongst suppliers and customers.
● Bottlenecks or 'pinch points' through which material or product must flow.
● High levels of identifiable risk (i.e. supply, demand, process, control and environmental risk).

To help in identifying where the priority should be placed in supply chain risk management a useful tool is Failure Mode and Effect Analysis (FMEA). The purpose of FMEA is to provide a systematic approach to identifying where in a complex system attention should be focused to reduce the risk of failure. It is a tool more frequently associated with total quality management (TQM) but it is especially applicable to supply chain risk management. FMEA begins by looking at each node and link and asking three questions:

● What could go wrong?
● What effect would this failure have?
● What are the key causes of this failure?

The next step is to assess any possible failure opportunity against the following criteria:

● What is the severity of the effect of failure?
● How likely is this failure to occur?
● How likely is the failure to be detected?

A rating system such as the one shown below is then used to create a combined priority score by multiplying the three scores together.

■ Risk analysis scoring system ■

S = Severity
1. No direct effect on operating service level
2. Minor deterioration in operating service level
3. Definite reduction in operating service level
4. Serious deterioration in operating service level
5. Operating service level approaches zero

O = Likelihood of occurrence
1. Probability of once in many years
2. Probability of once in many operating months
3. Probability of once in some operating weeks
4. Probability of weekly occurrence
5. Probability of daily occurrence

D = Likelihood of detection
1. Detectability is very high
2. Considerable warning of failure before occurrence
3. Some warning of failure before occurrence
4. Little warning of failure before occurrence
5. Detectability is effectively zero

---

4 Manage the critical paths

Once the critical nodes and links have been identified the first question is how can the risk be mitigated or removed? At its simplest this stage should involve the development of contingency plans for actions to be taken in the event of failure. At the other extreme, re-engineering of the supply chain may be necessary. Where possible Statistical Process Control should be used to monitor the critical stages along the pipeline.

'Cause and effect' analysis is another tool that can be used to identify the causes of problems with a view to removing or avoiding the causes. It seeks to separate symptoms from causes by a process of progressive questioning – sometimes known as 'Asking *why* five times' (see box).

■ Asking 'why?' – five times ■

1. Q. *Why* did the machine stop?
   A. There was an overload and the fuse blew.

2. Q. *Why* was there an overload?
   A. The bearing was not sufficiently lubricated.

3. Q. *Why* was it not sufficiently lubricated?
   A. The lubrication pump was not pumping sufficiently.

4. Q. *Why* was it not pumping sufficiently?
   A. The shaft of the pump was worn and rattling.

5. Q. *Why* was the shaft worn?
   A. There was no strainer and metal scrap got in.

Repeating *why* five times like this can help uncover the root problem and correct it. If this procedure were not carried through, one might simply replace the fuse or the pump shaft. In that case the problem would reoccur in a few months.

Source: Taiichi Ohno, *Toyota Production System*, Productivity Press, 1988.

If bottlenecks are the cause of the problem then decisions will have to be made about the options. Can the bottlenecks be removed? Can they be reduced by adding capacity or by holding inventory? Sometimes the bottleneck may be a key supplier who is capacity constrained. If alternative sources are not available at short notice then it will be necessary to manage the bottleneck by carrying strategic inventory to enable the flow through the downstream nodes to be maintained.

Whilst the drive for commonality of components and standardization of platforms in a manufacturing context helps reduce complexity, as was noted earlier, it can also add to risk if the component or platform comes from a single source. The case of Aisin Seiki and Toyota described below highlights the potential danger.

Don't lean too far

On Monday, 3 February 1997, Japan's largest motor manufacturer, Toyota, announced that all of its Japanese assembly lines had been brought to a halt following a devastating fire at the premises of one of its affiliated suppliers, Aisin Seiki. The company supplied brake master cylinders for several Toyota models and was its only supplier of brake-fluid proportioning valves. The fire had shown up one of the weaknesses of Toyota's famous lean manufacturing system, which runs on minimum stock levels using components delivered on a just-in-time basis from a small number of linked-ownership suppliers. The fire left Toyota holding only half a day's stock of the vital components. The motor manufacturer's production lines ground to a halt soon afterwards, as did the lines of all other Toyota suppliers. This was not the first time that a catastrophic event had shut down production throughout the Toyota kieretsu. The company had suffered similar problems in 1995 when the Hanshin earthquake severed its supply lines to component manufacturers in and around the city of Kobe.

Toyota's rival Honda has long worked a policy of dual sourcing, partly because its does not have such a tightly bound network of suppliers and partly to hedge against the loss of a key supplier. Honda maintains that there are advantages in retaining a degree of competitive rivalry among suppliers, believing that this pushes forward quality and cost improvements.

5 Improve network visibility

Many supply chains suffer from limited visibility. What this means is that a particular entity in the network is not aware of the status of upstream and downstream operations of the levels and flow of inventory as it progresses through the chain.

In such a situation it can often be weeks or months before problems become visible, by which time it may be too late to take effective action. The case study of Nokia and Ericsson featured below demonstrates the advantage that supply chain visibility can confer.

Nokia and Ericsson

Nokia obviously has better supply chain management than its competitors, and that definitely helps margins by allowing them to get components when others can't – and at lower prices ... While Nokia does get priority because they're a large customer, they've been a much better customer by ordering sufficient quantities in advance, not cancelling orders, and sharing their projections with customers.[1]

Just how good Nokia's supply chain management is was demonstrated in March 2000. Worldwide demand for mobile telephones was booming and shortages of critical components regularly represented a threat to growth. Two of the international market leaders were Finnish electronics company Nokia and its Swedish rival Ericsson. This is the tale of how a thunderstorm over central New Mexico would trigger a series of events that would eventually severely disadvantage one of the players.

On 17 March 2000, a lightening bolt hit a power line, which caused a fluctuation in the power supply. With no power to keep fans running, a fire broke out in a furnace in a semiconductor plant owned by Dutch firm Phillips Electronics NV. The fire was brought under control in minutes, but eight trays containing enough silicon wafers for thousands of mobile phones were destroyed in the furnace.[2] The damage to the factory from smoke and water was much more extensive than the fire itself, contaminating the entire stock of millions of chips.

Phillips immediately prioritized its customers, according to the value of their business. Between them, Nokia and Ericsson accounted for 40 per cent of the plant's output of the vital radio frequency chips, so these companies were put at the top of the supplier's list. They would be notified of the fire in due course.

Over in Finland Nokia's supply chain managers had almost immediately detected that there was a problem. Within two days of the fire Nokia's event management systems indicated that something was badly amiss. Even then orders were not coming through as predicted. A components purchasing manager telephoned the supplier, who informed him that there had been a fire in the plant, which was likely to disrupt production for around a week. As a matter of routine, Nokia's staff immediately placed the five components produced at the Phillips plant on 'special monitor' list. From then onwards Nokia increased monitoring of incoming supplies from weekly to daily checks.

It soon became clear to both Nokia and Phillips that the problem was so serious that supplies could be disrupted for months. Pressure was brought to bear at the highest levels between Nokia and its supplier to ensure that all other Phillips plants were commissioned to use any additional capacity to meet Nokia's requirements. In addition, Nokia immediately sent representatives out to its other suppliers in the US and Japan to secure priority status for all available supplies of chips and to persuade them to ramp up production as quickly as possible. Because Nokia was such an important customer, they obliged with a lead time of less than one week. Nokia also set about reconfiguring its products to take slightly different chips from other sources.

Ericsson had remained oblivious to the fire or its effects on the phone maker's incoming orders until three days after the event, when a technician from Phillips called a counterpart in Ericsson to notify him of the fire. Accepting the initial assurances from the supplier that the fire was only a minor event, Ericsson did not recognize the need to act until early April. By then Nokia had already moved to secure its supplies, and unlike the quick-acting Finns, Ericsson had no alternative sources of supply. It had taken the decision some years earlier to single source key components in a bid to simplify its supply chains as a cost-reduction measure.

Ericsson lost an estimated $400m in new product sales as a result of the fire. An insurance claim would later offset some of the losses, but nevertheless Ericsson was forced to cease manufacturing mobile phones. In contrast, the vigilant Nokia was able to maintain production levels throughout, enabling it to cement its position as European market leader.

References

1. Gregory Teets, Analyst, in: Gain, B. and Dunn, D., 'Nokia Stays Firmly on Path While its Competitors Stumble', *Electronic Buyers' News*, 30 October, No. 1235, 2000, p. 4.
2. Latour, A. 'Was Sisu the Difference?', *Wall Street Journal*, 29 January 2001.

We referred in Chapter 7 to the potential of supply chain event management (SCEM) to enable better identification of the occurence of unplanned events (or the non-occural of planned events). Tools such as these can significantly reduce supply chain uncertainty and thus reduce the need for additional inventory buffers. Another emerging technology that is enabling dramatic improvements in visibility is Radio Frequency Identification (RFID).

RFID tags enable a supply chain 'track and trace' capability to be created. Tags are either 'active' or 'passive'. Active tags transmit information to receiving stations and passive tags are read by scanners as they move through the chain. As the cost of these tags falls, and as more and more organizations require their suppliers to use them, then the adoption of this technology will accelerate. The impact, for example, of the decisions by Wal-Mart and the US Defense Department to utilize RFID has already had an impact on the rate of adoption.

A parallel technological development that will greatly assist the global management of assets in the supply chain is satellite tracking. Containers and trucks can be fitted with devices that enable the geographical position of the asset to be monitored by satellite, including information on variables such as temperature.

The challenge, as ever, is not technological but is the need to engender a greater willingness amongst supply chain entities to share information with each other, even if that information may not always be good news.

6 Establish a supply chain continuity team

All the foregoing stages in the supply chain risk management process require resources to undertake them. One way to do this is to create a permanent supply chain continuity team.

Many companies already have business continuity teams in place but, as was suggested earlier, often their focus is more limited and largely IT/IS focused. Other companies look at risk mainly from a financial perspective. All of these activities are necessary and essential but the argument here is that these teams should be expanded in their scope to take account of the fact that the biggest risk to business continuity lies in the wider supply chain.

Ideally these teams will be cross-functional and will have access to all the skills necessary to undertake the detailed analysis and implementation involved in the supply chain risk management process. The team should maintain a 'risk register', which identifies the possible points of vulnerability along with the actions that are to be taken to mitigate that vulnerability.

To ensure that high priority is given to supply chain risk management, the team should report to a board-level executive – ideally the Supply Chain Director or Vice-President if that person is on the board.

7 Work with suppliers and customers

Given the complexity of most supply networks, how can risk be better managed upstream and downstream of the focal firm? Ideally, if each entity in a network took responsibility for implementing risk management procedures of the type advocated here with their immediate first tier suppliers and customers then a far more resilient supply chain would emerge.

There are some good examples of collaborative working with both suppliers and customers to develop a greater understanding of the potential vulnerabilities in specific industries. At BAe systems – a major aerospace company – they have a strategic supplier management process with about 200 key suppliers based upon an industry initiative 'Supply Chain Relationships in Action' (SCRIA). BAe put small teams into these key suppliers to find ways of aligning supply chain processes and improving visibility. With their biggest suppliers such as Rolls-Royce there is ongoing contact right up to board level.

This approach is akin to the idea of *supplier development*, which has been quite widely adopted in the automotive sector. Going beyond this there is an opportunity to draw from the experience of companies who have insisted that their suppliers meet rigorous quality standards in terms of the products that they supply. The same practice could be applied in supply chain risk management by requiring suppliers to monitor and manage their supply chain vulnerabilities. In this way a 'snowball effect' might be achieved, with each supplier working with their first tier suppliers to implement supply chain risk management procedures.

Target Stores, the North American retailer, requires its suppliers to sign an agreement that they will comply with Target's requirements on supply chain security and risk management. Pfizer, the pharmaceutical company, also has clearly established performance standards for its suppliers in terms of supply chain management which are audited continuously.

Achieving supply chain resilience

Because even the best managed supply chains will hit unexpected turbulence or be impacted by events that are impossible to forecast, it is critical that *resilience* be built into them. Resilience implies the ability of a system to return to its original or desired state after being disturbed.[7] Resilient processes are flexible and agile and are able to change quickly. In this latter respect it is important to realize that velocity alone is not enough – it is acceleration or the ability to ramp up or down quickly that matters so far as resilience is concerned. Supply chain resilience also requires 'slack' at those critical points that constitute the limiting factors to changes in the rate of flow.

Access to information as rapidly as possible is also a prerequisite for resilience as we observed in the Nokia/Ericsson case study. Through collaborative working this information can be converted into supply chain *intelligence*. Because networks have become more complex they will rapidly descent into chaos unless they can be connected through shared information and knowledge. The aim is to create a supply chain community whereby there is a greater visibility of upstream and downstream risk profiles (and change in those profiles) and a shared commitment to mitigate and manage those risks.

Finally, supply chain resilience requires a recognition that when strategic decisions are taken, such as relocating facilities or changing sources of supply, then the impact of those decisions on the supply chain risk profile must be fully understood. Based upon that analysis it may be necessary to re-engineer the supply chain, or parts of it, to ensure the mitigation or removal of that risk. Figure 8.4 attempts to summarize the different requirements that need to be in place if supply chain resilience is to be improved.

A report by A. T. Kearney[8] suggested a number of stages to supply chain risk management excellence (see Table 8.1). Stage 1 companies have a very limited definition of risk, largely confined to financial, property and IT issues. At the other extreme, stage 5 companies have a supply chain wide perspective and have active programmes for risk mitigation.

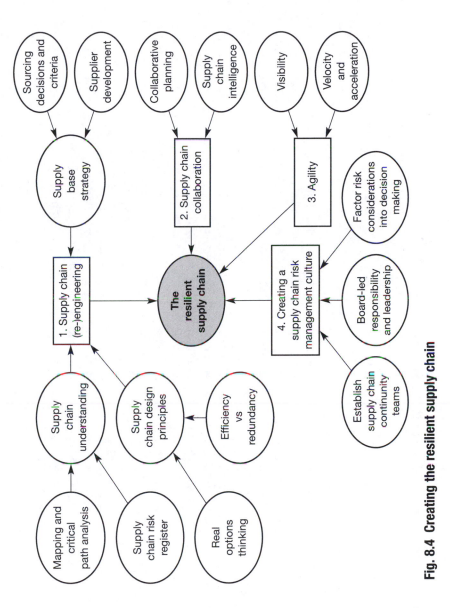

Fig. 8.4 Creating the resilient supply chain

Table 8.1 Stages of excellence in supply chain risk management

Dimension	Stage 1	Stage 2	Stage 3	Stage 4
Responsibility level	● Functional or departmental skills	● Business unit	● Corporate (chief risk officer)	● Extended enterprise (board level)
Scope of risk	● Market risks (foreign exchange credit, commodity) ● Property or safety risks ● IT security	● Market risk ● Property or safety risk ● Operational risk ● IT disruption ● Easily quantified risks	● All enterprise risks ● Business continuity ● Country risk ● Key business processes ● Day-to-day risks	● Strategic risks ● Operational resilience ● Global business environment ● Organizational or cultural component of risk management
Risk-mitigation tools	● Financial derivatives, property insurance	● Incident data and trend analysis ● Supplier contract reviews ● Self-assessment	● Contingency planning ● Scenario analysis ● New business and new venture reviews ● Independent audits ● Risk adjusted performance measures	● Advance warning systems ● Back-up of processes as well as data ● Quarterly drills that include key partners
Motivation	● Follow regulations, reduce financial exposure	● Avoid operational disruptions, avoid costs of accidents	● Protect brand image, maintain earnings stability	● Create competitive advantage, generate shareholder value

Table 8.1 Continued

Dimension	Stage 1	Stage 2	Stage 3	Stage 4
Updates to risk plan	• Never	• After major incidents	• Annually	• Quarterly
Supply chain	• Buffer inventories • Excess capacity	• Alternative suppliers • Recovery plans – select scenarios	• Co-ordinated forecasts throughout supply chain • 'What if' modelling • Agility: products and processes	• Supply chain transparency • 'War gaming' • Dynamic reserves of critical components
Collaboration	• Focus internally	• Communicate policies to suppliers	• Collaborate with suppliers, industry associations	• Lead industry initiatives, collaborate with government

Summary

All the evidence indicates that as markets become more volatile and the business environment more turbulent, so supply chains become more vulnerable to disruption. Not all of the risk to supply chain continuity is external. Significant risk can be created as a result of management decisions that are taken on supply chain design and strategy.

It is imperative that organizations manage supply chain risk in a systematic way. The risk profile of supply chains must be identified and continuously monitored, critical paths through the network assessed and, if necessary, safeguards built in.

Because the financial risk to the business of supply chain disruption can be so great, it is essential that these issues receive top management attention on an ongoing basis. In today's complex and interconnected world supply chain risk management will need to be placed much higher on the boardroom agenda.

References

1. Singhal, V.R. and Hendricks, K., *Supply Chain Management Review*, January/February 2002.
2. *Ibid.*
3. The Economist, *The Extended Enterprise 2002: CEO Agenda*, Economist White Paper Series, 2002.
4. Cranfield School of Management, *Supply Chain Vulnerability*, report on behalf of DTLR, DTI and Home Office, 2002.
5. Houghton, T., Markham, B., and Tevelson, B. 'Thinking Strategically About Supply Chain Management', in *Supply Chain Management Review*, Sept–Oct. 2002.
6. Whyte, C., 'Motorola's Battle with Supply and Demand Chain Complexity', *Supply and Demand Chain Executive*, 12 August 2004.
7. Cranfield School of Management, *Creating Resilient Supply Chains: A Practical Guide*, report on behalf of the Department for Transport, 2003.
8. A.T. Kearney, *Supply Chains in a Vulnerable, Volatile World*, 2003.

Overcoming the barriers to supply chain integration

This chapter:

Considers some of the organizational impediments to implementation of integrated supply chain strategies, highlighting the problems with conventional, functionally focused management systems.

●

Identifies logistics as a planning and co-ordination activity, a force for organizational change and one of several core processes within a horizontally organized, market-facing business.

●

Stresses the need to extend logistics integration upstream to suppliers and downstream to distributors and customers, outlining a series of measures which facilitate the development of integrated end-to-end supply chain processes.

●

Highlights the importance of process benchmarking to identify best practice.

●

Suggests appropriate Key Performance Indicators to support a more responsive, customer-facing organization.

The transition to the twenty-first century seems to have been accompanied by ever higher levels of change in the business environment. Companies that were market leaders a decade ago have in many cases encountered severe reversals of fortune. Mergers and takeovers have changed the shape of many markets and the advent of regional and global competition have changed for all time the rules of the game. On top of all this, as we have noted, has been a growing demand from the marketplace for ever higher levels of service and quality. These pressures have combined to produce a new imperative for the organization: the need to be responsive.

The responsive organization not only seeks to put the customer at the centre of the business, but it also designs all its systems and procedures with the prime objective of improving the speed of response and the reliability of that response. Traditional organizations have grown heavy with layer upon layer of management and bureaucracy. Such companies have little chance of remaining competitive in the new marketplace. Neither is it sufficient to rely upon

> **Traditional organizations have grown heavy with layer upon layer of management and bureaucracy.**

restructuring the organization through removing layers of management, i.e. 'flattening' the organizational chart – as many companies are now seeking to do – if such 'de-layering' is not accompanied by equivalent change to the networks and systems that deliver service to the customer.

Creating the logistics vision

Making service happen is the ultimate challenge. Whilst it is by no means easy to develop strategies for service that will lead to improved competitive performance, the hardest task is to put that strategy into action. How do we develop an organization that is capable of delivering high quality service on a consistent, ongoing basis?

These days most companies are familiar with the idea of 'mission statements' as an articulation of the vision of the business. The mission statement seeks to define the purpose of the business, its boundaries and its aspirations. It is now by no means uncommon for organizations to have such statements for the business as a whole and for key constituent components. What some companies have found is that there can be significant benefits to defining the logistics vision of the firm.

The purpose of the logistics vision statement is to give a clear indication of the basis on which the business intends to build a position of advantage through closer customer relationships. Such statements are never easy to construct. There is always the danger that they will descend into vague 'motherhood' statements that give everyone a warm feeling but provide no guidelines for action.

Ideally the logistics vision should be built around the simple issue of 'How do we intend to use logistics and supply chain management to create value for our customers?' To operationalize this idea will necessitate a detailed understanding of how customer value is (or could be) created and delivered in the markets in which the business competes. Value chain analysis will be a fundamental element in this investigation, as will the definition of the core competencies and capabilities of the organization. Asking the questions 'What activities do we excel in?' and 'What is it that differentiates us from our competitors?' is the starting point for creating the logistics vision statement.

The four elements of logistics-derived customer value highlighted previously are 'Better, Faster, Cheaper, Closer' and the criterion for a good logistics vision statement is that it should provide the roadmap for how these four goals are to be achieved.

The problems with conventional organizations

Amongst experienced observers and commentators of the logistics management process there is general agreement that the major barrier to the implementation of the logistics concept is organizational. In other words, a major impediment to change in this crucial managerial area is the entrenched and rigid organizational structure that most established companies are burdened with.

There is a great danger that those companies that do not recognize the need for organizational change, or that lack the will to make it happen, will never achieve the improvements in competitive advantage that integrated logistics management can bring. The argument advanced here is that the demands of the marketplace for enhanced service provision combined with dramatically heightened competition call for a paradigm shift in the way in which we think about our organizations.

The concept of integrated supply chain management, whereby flows of information and material between source and user are co-ordinated and managed as a system, is now widely understood, if not widely implemented. The logic of linking each step of the process as materials and products move towards the customer is based upon the principles of optimization. In other words, the goal is to maximize customer service whilst simultaneously minimizing costs and reducing assets locked up in the logistics pipeline.

However, in the conventional organization this poses an immediate problem. Most companies are organized on a functional basis. In other words, they have created a division of responsibility by function, so we might find a purchasing function, a production function, a sales function and so on. Typically the organization chart would look like that in Figure 9.1.

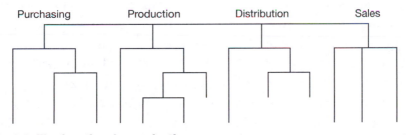

Fig. 9.1 The functional organization

Each of the 'vertical' functions in the conventional organization is normally headed by senior managers who come to regard their functional area as their 'territory'. Indeed in many companies these functional heads are 'barons' who wield considerable power and who jealously guard those territories from what they perceive as unwarranted incursions from other functional barons.

Further reinforcing the functional or vertical orientation in the conventional organization is the budgeting system. Typically, each function will be driven by a budget that seeks to control the resources consumed by those functions. It is almost as if the company is working on the assumption that the prime purpose of any enterprise is to control the consumption of resources. In fact, the leading-edge companies have long since realized that the sole purpose of the business is to create profitable outputs and that outputs, not inputs, should form the basis both for the way we organize and for the way we plan and control.

We will look in detail later at the alternative models for organization and for planning and control, but first let us highlight some of the real problems that the conventional organization creates that hamper the successful implementation of integrated logistics management.

Inventory builds up at functional boundaries

If individual functions are encouraged to 'optimize' their own costs – because of the budgeting system – then this will often be at the expense of substantially increased inventory across the system as a whole. What happens if, say, production seeks to minimize the unit costs of production by maintaining long production runs with large batch quantities is the creation of more inventory than is normally required for immediate requirements. Likewise, if purchasing management seeks low material costs through bulk purchases then again the inventory of raw materials ahead of production will often be excessive. Similar buffers of inventory will exist right across the supply chain at boundaries within organizations and, indeed, at boundaries between organizations.

Not only is this increased inventory a financial burden and a further strain on working capital, it also obscures our 'visibility' of final demand. Thus upstream activities may not have any clear view of what the real demand is downstream, as all they see is a reorder-point-generated order hitting them at short notice (or more often than not, no notice at all). Figure 9.2 illustrates this point.

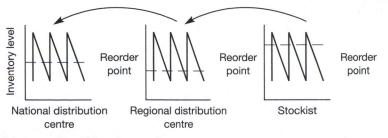

Fig. 9.2 Inventory hides demand

Pipeline costs are not transparent

Closely related to the preceding issue is the problem of cost 'transparency'. What this means is that costs relating to the flows of material across functional areas are not easy to measure. Hence the real costs to serve different customers with different product mixes are rarely revealed.

Once again the problem is that the conventional organization will normally only identify costs on a functional basis, and even then at a fairly high level of aggregation. Hence we may well know our transport costs in total but not necessarily how they vary by customer category or by delivery characteristics, e.g. central delivery to a regional distribution centre or local delivery to a supermarket. Where attempts to estimate the costs of outputs are made they usually require, out of necessity, crude allocation procedures. As we noted in Chapter 3, there has recently been much interest in 'throughput accounting' and 'activity-based costing', both of which are attempts to pin down costs as they occur and hence to make the total pipeline costs easier to identify. The problem need not exist, it is only a problem because the costing systems we have are designed to monitor functional or input costs rather than flow or output costs. Figure 9.3 makes this point.

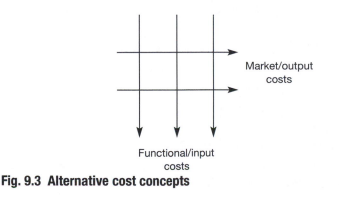

Fig. 9.3 Alternative cost concepts

Functional boundaries impede process management

The process of satisfying customer demand begins with in-bound supply and continues through manufacturing or assembly operations and onwards by way of distribution to the customer. Logically the ideal way to manage this process is as a complete system, not by fragmenting it into watertight sections. Yet that is more or less what happens in the conventional business as we have seen. Not only is this inefficient, it actually leads to a loss of effectiveness in competitive terms.

Many of the variations in the order-to-delivery cycle, for example, are caused by the variability that inevitably arises in the inefficient procedures that have to be created to manage the interfaces between functions. The time taken to process orders, for instance, is often extended purely because of the paperwork, checking and re-checking, that conventional systems generate. Because organizations grow organically they tend to add to existing processes in a patchwork manner rather than taking a 'clean piece of paper' approach. As a result the systems in use tend to owe more to history than to any concept of holistic management. This phenomenon is further compounded by the inability of managers to detach themselves from their familiar surroundings and to see the 'big picture'. Instead there is a natural tendency to focus on piecemeal improvements within their own narrow functional area.

To achieve a smooth-flowing logistics pipeline requires an orientation that facilitates end-to-end process management. The principle can be compared to the management of an industrial process, say an oil refinery, where to ensure the achievement of optimum efficiency the entire process is managed and controlled as a system, not as a series of adjacent, independent activities.

The cost to an organization, and indeed to the economy as a whole, of these fragmented processes can only be guessed at, but it must be huge.

Conventional organizations present many faces to the customer

Perhaps the most damning criticism of the traditional organization is that it does not present a 'single face' to the customer. Rather than the customer having to do business with just one organization, in effect they deal with many.

This criticism goes beyond the obvious problems that arise when a customer, seeking, say, information on an order, is passed from one section of the company to another – although that is a common enough

266

occurrence. The real problem is that no one person or department is empowered to manage a customer from enquiry through to order delivery – in other words, to service the customer.

Consider for a moment how the conventional organization processes orders. Typically there will be a sequence of activities beginning with order entry. The point of entry may be within the sales or commercial function but then it goes to credit control, from where it may pass to production planning or, in a make-to-stock environment, to the warehouse. Once the order has been manufactured or assembled it will become the responsibility of distribution and transport planning. At the same time there is a separate process involving the generation of documents such as bills of lading, delivery notes, invoices and so on. The problem is that these activities are sequential, performed in series rather than in parallel. Each function performs its task and then passes the order on to the next function; at each step it is as if the order is 'thrown over the wall'. Figure 9.4 depicts this classic process.

Traditional sequential order processing system

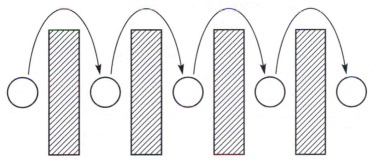

Fig. 9.4 Managing the order

Developing the logistics organization

Some commentators have suggested that the solution to the problems outlined above lies in creating a higher level of authority in the form of a logistics function that links together the purchasing, production and distribution tasks. Appealing as this may appear at first sight, it will not solve the underlying conflicts that the traditional organization creates. It merely adds another layer of management. At a time when the trend is towards 'flattening' organizations, this solution is unlikely to gain ground.

Instead radical solutions must be sought which may require a restructuring of the conventional 'vertical' organization and lead to the creation of a 'horizontal', or market-facing, business. Figures 9.5 and 9.6 contrast the 'vertical' with the 'horizontal' organization.

The horizontal organization has a number of distinguishing characteristics. It is:

● Organized around processes
● Flat and de-layered
● Built upon multi-functional teams
● Guided by performance metrics that are market-based

It is the focus on processes rather than functions that is the key to the horizontal organization. The basic precept of process management is that it is through processes that customer value is created. Hence the logic of seeking to manage processes on an integrated basis.

Traditional, functional organization

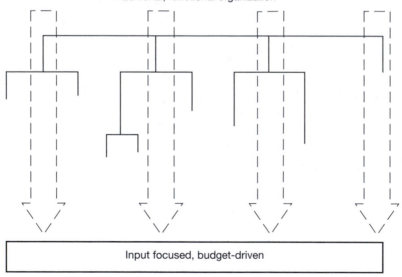

Input focused, budget-driven

Fig. 9.5 Vertical organizational focus

Market-facing organization

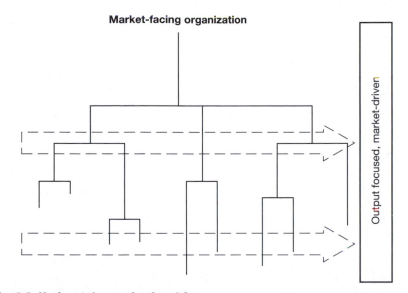

Output focused, market-driven

Fig. 9.6 Horizontal organizational focus

In most organizations there will only be a limited number of core processes and the following are likely to be central to most businesses:

- Innovation (including new product development)
- Consumer development (primarily focused on building loyalty with end users)
- Customer management (creating relationships with intermediaries)
- Supplier development (strengthening upstream and alliance relationships)
- Supply chain management (the cash-to-cash process)

Typically, companies that focus upon process management have recognized that they are best managed by cross-functional teams. These teams will comprise specialists drawn from the functional areas (which now become 'centres of excellence') and will be led by 'integrators' whose job it is to focus the process team around the achievement of market-based goals. In such organizations a different type of skills profile is clearly required for managers at all levels. Equally the reward systems need to change as the horizontal organization by definition is flatter and hence the traditional upward promotion opportunities are fewer.

Making the change from the 'vertical' to the 'horizontal' poses many challenges and yet it is critical to the implementation of a market-driven logistics strategy.

The achievement of this transformation might begin by the recognition that logistics is essentially a planning orientation – in other words the logistics management process entails the linking of production plans with materials requirements plans in one direction and distribution requirements plans in the other. The aim of any organization should be to ensure that production produces only what the marketplace requires whilst purchasing supplies production with what it needs to meet its immediate requirements. How can this fairly obvious idea be converted into reality?

Developing process management skills at Unipart

Unipart Group of Companies (UGC) was formed in 1987, when the group's Chief Executive John Neill led a buy-out of a disparate collection of functional parts of the failing nationalized Rover Group. Within the privatized UGC the autonomous functional groups – automotive parts manufacturing, warehousing and distribution, sales, marketing, information systems and communications – became divisions of UGC.[1] Most prominent was the large and successful automotive parts manufacturing division, Unipart Industries, which had found itself in the happy position of being able to acquire leading-edge lean manufacturing and process management know-how from two of its Japanese customers, Honda and Toyota.

UGC's divisions, though operating as independent business units, were to some extent interdependent, and the company's senior management were quick to recognize that the less efficient and agile parts of the business would, in time, impede the development of the others. To lift the competitiveness of the whole enterprise, each division was charged with identifying best practice in its field, tailoring it to Unipart's needs and then – as a centre of excellence within the business – passing this learning on to other departments. Unipart's now famous training establishment 'Unipart University' was devised as a means of transcending divisional barriers and speeding up the dissemination of know-how throughout the business. In practice this meant that all employees, from shop floor to directors, became involved in continuous learning programmes and team-based problem-solving exercises. Unipart was in fact amongst the first British companies to introduce truly cross-functional team working. The move highlighted the need for employees to acquire a working knowledge of each other's roles and to extend their own skills beyond those required to perform their functional tasks. Unipart University is therefore equipped to help and encourage all employees to acquire voluntarily a much wider range of skills and qualifications, offering everything from remedial adult literacy programmes to the chance to study for an MBA.[2]

The development of process management skills throughout the business has been amongst the most significant breakthroughs in organizational learning at UGC. Unipart Industries had been working to strengthen its relationships with key suppliers through a mutually agreed continuous improvement process known as 'Tend-to-Zero'. Tend-to-Zero provides a framework for identifying the ten most critical factors in the business relationship – quality, cost, delivery times, product range, environmental issues, etc. – and assessing the shortcomings of each on a scale of zero to ten. A score of ten means that something is unacceptable, so both sides work together towards a world-class zero, with scores continually reassessed as the relationship and business performance improves.

The transfer of this process expertise from Unipart Industries to the former warehouse and distribution division, Unipart Demand Chain Management (DCM), became an early priority within the group. The aim was to get DCM to co-operate more closely with Unipart Industries and its major suppliers so that together they could work more effectively to fill orders on time. DCM went on to place an increasing focus on teaching employees how to improve both internal and supplier processes to eliminate waste from the supply chain.[3]

References

1. Womack, James P. and Jones, Daniel T., 'From Lean Production to the Lean Enterprise', *Harvard Business Review*, March–April 1994, pp. 93–102.
2. Bassett, Philip, *The Times*, 28 May 1997.
3. Unipart Group of Companies, *Annual Review*, 1995, pp. 9, 21.

The key lies in the recognition that the order and its associated information flows should be at the heart of the business. It may be a truism but the only rationale for any commercial organization is to generate orders and to fulfil those orders. Everything the company does should be directly linked to facilitating this process, and the process must itself be reflected in the organizational design and in its planning and control systems.

All of this leads to the conclusion that the order fulfilment process should be designed as an integrated activity across the company with the conventional functions of the business supporting that process. To assist this transition the development of a customer order management system is a vital prerequisite.

A customer order management system is a planning framework that links the information system with the physical flow of materials required to fulfil demand. To achieve this requires the central management of forecasts, requirements plans, material and production control, and purchasing.

At the heart of the customer order management system is a requirements plan that is market-driven. The inputs to this plan include data and information relating to enquiries and orders, price changes, promotional activity and product availability. This information provides the basis for the forecast that then drives the requirements plan. Alongside this is a process for the fulfilment of current orders. They are not separated but closely integrated through the information system.

Order fulfilment groups

Given that the process of managing orders can be refined along the lines described above, what scope exists for improving the 'process architecture'?

Several companies have experimented with the idea of a cross-functional, cross-departmental team to take responsibility for the management of orders. This team may be termed the order fulfilment group. The idea behind such a group is that rather than having an organizational structure for order management where every activity is separated with responsibility for each activity fragmented around the organization, instead these activities should be grouped together both organizationally and physically. In other words, instead of seeing each step in the process as a discrete activity we cluster them together and bring the people involved together as well – ideally in a single open-plan office. Thus the order fulfilment group might comprise commercial or sales office people, credit control and accounts, the production scheduler and transport scheduler – indeed anyone involved in the crucial business processes of *converting an order into cash*.

It is likely that in a large business serving many different customers a number of these teams may be required. Indeed for the biggest, most important accounts it is probable that a single dedicated team will be required to manage the relationship.

The effect that such groups can have is often dramatic. Because all the key people in the order fulfilment process are brought together and linked around a common entity – the order – they are better able to sort out problems and eliminate bottlenecks. Order cycle times can be dramatically reduced as teamwork prevails over inter-departmental rivalry. New ways of dealing with problems emerge, more non-value-added activities are eliminated and customer service problems – when they arise – can quickly be resolved, since all the key people are in close connection with each other.

Schonberger[1] gives a number of examples of how the concept of a manufacturing 'cell' – where linked actions are performed in parallel by multi-functional teams – can work just as effectively in order processing. One of the cases he quotes, Ahlstrom, a Finnish company, has reduced lead times in order processing from one week to one day, and variation in total lead time has dropped from up to six weeks to one week. Another case was that of Nashua Corporation in North America, where order entry lead time has been reduced from eight days to one hour, with a 40 per cent reduction in space and a 70 per cent reduction in customer claims.

This approach has been likened to a game of rugby rather than a relay race! What this means is that a team of closely integrated colleagues run up the field together passing the ball as they run. In a relay race no one can run until they receive the baton from the preceding person in the chain. The end result is that this vital part of the service process can be speeded up whilst simultaneously improving the quality of the output, hence a major competitive advantage is achieved.

In a manufacturing context the customer order management system must be closely linked to production planning and the materials requirements plan. Ideally all the planning and scheduling activities in the organization relating to the order and its satisfaction should be brought together organizationally.

Logistics as the vehicle for change

As markets, technologies and competitive forces change at ever increasing rates the imperative for organizational change becomes more pressing. The paradox is that because organizational structures are rigid, even ossified, they do not have the ability to change at anything like the same rate as the environment in which they exist.

> As markets, technologies and competitive forces change at ever increasing rates the imperative for organizational change becomes more pressing.

The trend towards globalization of industry, involving as it does the co-ordination of complex flows of materials and information from a multitude of offshore sources and manufacturing plants to a diversity of markets, has sharply highlighted the inappropriateness of existing structures. What we are discovering is that the driving force for organizational change is logistics.

To compete and survive in these global markets requires a logistics-oriented organization. There has to be nothing less than a shift from a functional focus to a process focus. Such a radical change entails a re-grouping within the organization so that the key tasks become the management of cross-functional work flows. Hewlett Packard is an example of a company that has restructured its organization around market-facing processes, rather than functions. Order fulfilment has been recognized as a core process and so, on a global scale, there is one order management system architecture that links order entry, order management and factory order/shipment processing. This core process is supported by a common information system that provides 'end-to-end' visibility of the logistics pipeline from order through to delivery.

In fact it is through such breakthroughs in information technology that the type of organizational change we are describing has been made possible. The information network now defines the organization structure. In other words, the information that flows from the marketplace at one end of the pipeline to supply points at the other will increasingly shape the organization – not the other way round.

274

Such a change will be accelerated by the trend, commented upon earlier in this book, for companies to focus on what might be termed 'core competencies' and to outsource everything else. In other words, the business of tomorrow will most likely only perform those activities in the value chain where they believe they have a differential advantage, and all other activities will be performed by partners, co-makers and logistics service providers. In cases such as this the need for co-ordination of information and materials flows between entities in the supply chain becomes a key priority, further highlighting the central role of logistics as a process-oriented management task.

In this brief review of the challenges facing the organization in a changed environment we have emphasized the need to break down the 'walls' that traditionally have fragmented the organization and impeded the cost-effective achievement of customer service requirements. Clearly there is a need for 'pattern breaking' on a major scale. The only way such significant change will be achieved is through leadership from the very top of the organization. It is no coincidence that the handful of companies who have achieved excellence in logistics have been through a process of change that was driven from the top. Companies like Xerox, Hewlett Packard, Nokia and Philips have experienced, and are still experiencing, often painful change as they transform themselves from functionally based businesses to market-facing businesses. Whilst the impetus for change differs from company to company, the engine of change has been the same – the search for superior performance through logistics management.

Benchmarking

The intense level of competitive activity encountered in most markets has led to a new emphasis on measuring performance not just in absolute terms, but rather in terms relative to the competition, and beyond that to 'best practice'.

In the past it was usually deemed to be sufficient simply to measure internal performance. In other words, the focus was on things such as productivity, utilization, cost per activity and so on. Whilst it is clearly important that such things continue to be measured and controlled it also has to be recognized that such measures only have meaning when they are compared against a relevant 'metric' or benchmark. What should be the metric that is used in assessing logistics and supply chain performance?

There are in fact several dimensions to the measurement problem. The first key point to make is that the ultimate measuring rod is the customer, hence it is customers' perceptions of performance that must be paramount. Secondly, it is not sufficient just to compare performance to that of immediate competitors. We must also compare ourselves to the 'best in the class'. Thirdly, it is not just outputs that should be measured and compared but also the processes that produce that output. These three ideas lie at the heart of what today is termed competitive benchmarking.

Competitive benchmarking might simply be defined as the continuous measurement of the company's products, services, processes and practices against the standards of best competitors and other companies who are recognized as leaders. The measures that are chosen for the comparison must directly or indirectly impact upon customers' evaluation of the company's performance.

One of the earliest firms to adopt benchmarking was the Xerox Corporation who used it as a major tool in gaining competitive advantage. Xerox first started benchmarking in their manufacturing activity with a focus on product quality and feature improvements. Following success in the manufacturing area, Xerox's top management directed that benchmarking be performed by all cost centres and business units, and by 1981 it was adopted company-wide.

Initially there was some difficulty in performing benchmarking in departments such as repair, service, maintenance, invoicing and collection and distribution, until it was recognized that their 'product' was, in fact, a process. It was this process that needed to be articulated and compared with that used in other organizations. By looking at competitors' processes step-by-step and operation-by-operation, Xerox were able to identify best methods and practices in use by their competitors.

Initially benchmarking activities were concentrated solely on competitors until it became clear that Xerox's objective in achieving superior performance in each business function was not being obtained by looking only at competitors' practices.

The objective of creating competitive advantage involves outperforming rather than matching the efforts of competitors. This, together with the obvious difficulties in gaining all the information required on competitors and their internal systems and processes, led to a broader perspective on benchmarking being adopted. Thus benchmarking was expanded from a focus solely on competitors to a wider, but selective, focus on the processes of top performing companies regardless of their industry sector.

Xerox have successfully used this broader perspective on benchmarking as a major element in increasing both quality and productivity. Collaborative co-operation between firms in non-competing industries offers significant opportunity in this regard. For example, in the Xerox logistics and distribution unit, annual productivity has doubled as a result of benefits obtained from non-competitive collaborative benchmarking.

Camp[2] has identified a number of benefits that a company derives from benchmarking. These include the following:

● It enables the best practices from any industry to be creatively incorporated into the processes of the benchmarked function.
● It can provide stimulation and motivation to the professionals whose creativity is required to perform and implement benchmark findings.
● Benchmarking breaks down ingrained reluctance of operations to change. It has been found that people are more receptive to new ideas and their creative adoption when those ideas did not necessarily originate in their own industry.
● Benchmarking may also identify a technological breakthrough that would not have been recognized, and thus not applied, in one's own industry for some time to come.

What to benchmark?

One useful framework for benchmarking is that devised by a cross-industry association – The Supply Chain Council.[3] Their model, known as SCOR (Supply Chain Operations Reference), is built around five major processes – Plan–Source–Make–Deliver–Return – and covers the key supply chain activities from identifying customer demand through to delivering the product and collecting the cash. The aim of SCOR is to provide a standard way to measure supply chain performance and to use common metrics to benchmark against other organizations.

Identifying logistics performance indicators

One benefit of a rigorous approach to logistics and supply chain bench-marking is that it soon becomes apparent that there are a number of critical measures of performance that need to be continuously monitored. The idea of 'Key Performance Indicators' (KPIs) is simple. It suggests that, whilst there are many measures of performance that can be deployed in an organization, there are a relatively small number of critical dimensions that contribute more than proportionately to success or failure in the marketplace.

Much interest has been shown in recent years in the concept of the 'Balanced Scorecard'.[4] The idea behind the balanced scorecard is that there are a number of key performance indicators – most of them probably non-financial measures – that will provide management with a better means of meeting strategic goals than the more traditional financially oriented measures. These KPIs derive from the strategic goals themselves. Thus the intention is that the balanced scorecard will provide ongoing guidance on those critical areas where action may be needed to ensure the achievement of those goals.

These ideas transfer readily into the management of logistics and supply chain strategy. If suitable performance measures can be identified that link with the achievement of these strategic goals they can become the basis for a more appropriate scorecard than might traditionally be the case.

A logical four-step process is suggested for constructing such a scorecard:

Step 1: Articulate logistics and supply chain strategy
How do we see our logistics and supply chain strategy contributing to the overall achievement of corporate and marketing goals?

Step 2: What are the measurable outcomes of success?
Typically, these might be summarized as 'Better, Faster, Cheaper, Closer'. In other words, superior service quality, achieved in shorter time-frames at less cost to the supply chain as a whole, built on strong relationships with supply chain partners.

Step 3: What are the processes that impact these outcomes?
In the case of 'Better, Faster, Cheaper, Closer', the processes that lead to 'perfect order achievement', shorter pipeline times, reduced cost-to-serve and stronger relationships need to be identified.

Step 4: What are the drivers of performance within these processes?

These activities are the basis for the derivation of the key performance indicators. Cause and effect analysis can aid in their identification.

In this framework the four key outcomes of success are suggested to be: Better, Faster, Cheaper, Closer. This quartet of interconnected goals are almost universal in their desirability. They are significant because they combine customer-based measures of performance in terms of total quality with internal measures of resource and asset utilization.

The idea behind the logistics scorecard is to produce a number of measures against each of the four broad aims. There should be no more than 20 measures in total since the aim is to focus on the major drivers of excellence in each area. Like any dashboard or cockpit, there is a need for simplicity and to focus on the 'mission critical' measures. Figure 9.7 summarizes this idea.

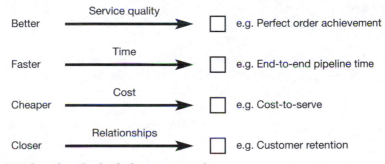

Fig. 9.7 Creating the logistics scorecard

As the old cliché reminds us: 'What gets measured, gets managed.' Hence it is important to ensure that the logistics scorecard is designed to encourage the actions and behaviour that will lead to the fulfilment of the 'logistics vision' that we earlier described. Indeed it can be argued that if organizational change is necessary, the place to begin that change process is with a review of the performance measures currently in use. Many companies seek to be responsive and market-facing and yet they still use performance metrics that relate to internal efficiencies. As a result they are unlikely ever to change.

Summary

Responsive supply chains are by definition highly integrated. They are internally integrated across functions and they are externally integrated with upstream suppliers and downstream customers. Many companies are impeded in their attempts to become more agile and responsive because of an entrenched functional structure. They manage functions rather than processes and hence have a fragmented approach to the marketplace. It is also difficult for such firms to contemplate external integration when they lack internal integration.

Making the transition from a 'vertical' to a 'horizontal' structure requires a commitment to organizational change. To assist in this change process it will be helpful if best practice can be defined through a benchmarking programme. Equally important is the identification of appropriate Key Performance Indicators (KPIs) to ensure that everyone within the organization is focused upon the things that will enable a more responsive supply chain.

References

1. Schonberger, R.J., *Building a Chain of Customers*, The Free Press, 1990.
2. Camp, Robert, *Benchmarking: The Search For Industry Best Practices That Lead to Superior Performance*, ASQC Quality Press, 1989.
3. For further details of the SCOR model, visit www.supply-chain.org.
4. Kaplan, R.S. and Norton, D.P., *The Balanced Scorecard*, Harvard Business School Press, 1996.

Chapter 10

Entering the era of network competition

This chapter:

Suggests that a new business model is required to cope with the radically changing nature of the business environment.

●

Describes the emergence of the 'network organization' and explores the implications for supply chain management.

●

Highlights seven major business transformations that must be undertaken for competitive success in tomorrow's marketplace.

●

Underlines the importance of developing the wider profile of skills that will be needed to manage the supply chain of the future.

●

Discusses the need for supply chain orchestration and proposes ways in which complex networks might be better co-ordinated.

Throughout this book the emphasis has been upon the achievement of competitive advantage through logistics excellence. Many of the ideas presented are relatively untried and still, for some companies, the area of logistics and supply chain management is unexplored territory.

However, an increasing number of organizations can be identified in which logistics is quite clearly recognized as a major strategic variable. Companies like Xerox, Dell, Nokia, Benetton and 3M have invested significantly in developing responsive logistics systems. Whilst their success in the marketplace is due to many things there can be no doubting the role that logistics has played in achieving that success.

A study carried out in North America for the Council of Logistics Management sought to identify the characteristics of companies that were at the leading edge in logistics and the essential features of these organizations seemed to be that they:

● Exhibit an overriding commitment to customers
● Encompass a significant span of cross-functional control
● Commit to external alliances with service suppliers
● Have a highly formalized logistical process
● Place a premium on operational flexibility
● Employ comprehensive performance measurement
● Invest in state-of-the-art information technology

The new organizational paradigm

It will be apparent that to achieve success in all of these areas will require significant change within the company. It requires a transformation that goes beyond re-drawing the organization chart and entails a cultural change that must be driven from the top. In fact the basic principles that have traditionally guided the company must be challenged and what is required is a shift in the basic paradigms that have underpinned industrial organizations for so long.

The need for new business models

Most of us work in organizations that are hierarchical, vertical and functionally defined. The organization chart for the typical company resembles a pyramid and provides a

> Most of us work in organizations that are hierarchical, vertical and functionally defined.

clear view of where everyone fits in relation to each other and will also normally reflect reporting relationships. In essence, the conventional organization structure is little changed since the armies of the Roman Empire developed the precursor of the pyramid organization.

Whilst there can be no doubting that this organizational model has served us well in the past, there are now serious questions about its appropriateness for the changed conditions that confront us today. Of the many changes that have taken place in the marketing environment, perhaps the biggest is the focus upon 'speed'. Because of shortening product life cycles, time-to-market becomes ever more critical. Similarly, the dramatic growth of just-in-time (JIT) practices in manufacturing means that those companies wishing to supply into that environment have to develop systems capable of responding rapidly and flexibly to customers' delivery requirements, Indeed, the same is true in almost every market today as organizations seek to reduce their inventories, and hence a critical requirement of a supplier is that they are capable of rapid response.

The challenge to every business is to become a responsive organization in every sense of the word. The organization must respond to changes in the market with products and services that provide innovative solutions to customers' problems; it must respond to volatile demand and it must be able to provide high levels of flexibility in delivery.

Perhaps one of the most significant breakthroughs in management thinking in recent years has been the realization that individual businesses no longer compete as stand-alone entities, but rather as supply chains. We are now entering the era of 'network competition', where the prizes will go to those organizations who can better structure, co-ordinate and manage the relationships with their partners in a network committed to delivering superior value in the final marketplace.

The emergence of the 'network organization' is a recent phenomenon that has given rise to much comment and analysis. These 'virtual' organizations are characterized by a confederation of specialist skills and capabilities provided by the network members. It is argued that such collaborative arrangements provide a more effective means of satisfying customer needs at a profit than does the single firm undertaking multiple value-creating activities. The implications of the network organization for management are considerable and, in particular, the challenges to logistics management are profound.

To make networks more effective in satisfying end-user requirements demands a high level of co-operation between organizations in the network, along with the recognition of the need to make inter-firm relationships mutually beneficial. Underpinning the successful network organization is the value-added exchange of information between partners, meaning that information on downstream demand or usage is made visible to all the upstream members of the supply chain. Creating 'visibility' along the pipeline ensures that the manufacture and delivery of product can be driven by real demand rather than by a forecast and hence enables all parties in the chain to operate more effectively.

Supply chain management is concerned with achieving a more cost-effective satisfaction of end customer requirements through buyer/supplier process integration. This integration is typically achieved through a greater transparency of customer requirements via the sharing of information, assisted by the establishment of 'seamless' processes that link the identification of physical replenishment needs with a 'just-in-time' response.

In the past it was more often the case that organizations were structured and managed on the basis of optimizing their own operations with little regard for the way in which they interfaced with suppliers or, indeed, customers. The business model was essentially 'transactional', meaning that products and services were bought and sold on an arm's-length basis and that there was little enthusiasm for the concept of longer-term, mutually dependent relationships. The end result was often a high-cost, low quality solution for the final customer in the chain.

This emerging competitive paradigm is in stark contrast to the conventional model. It suggests that in today's challenging global markets, the route to sustainable advantage lies in managing the complex web of relationships that link highly focused providers of specific elements of the final offer in a cost-effective, value-adding chain.

The key to success in this new competitive framework, it can be argued, is the way in which this network of alliances and suppliers are welded together in partnership to achieve mutually beneficial goals.

Managing the supply chain as a network

The new competitive paradigm that we have described places the firm at the centre of an interdependent network – a confederation of mutually complementary competencies and capabilities – which competes as an integrated supply chain against other supply chains.

To manage in such a radically revised competitive structure clearly requires different skills and priorities to those employed in the traditional model. To achieve market leadership in the world of network competition necessitates a focus on network management as well as upon internal processes. Of the many issues and challenges facing organizations as they make the transition to this new competitive environment, the following are perhaps most significant.

1 Collective strategy development

Traditionally, members of a supply chain have never considered themselves to be part of a marketing network and so have not shared with each other their strategic thinking. For network competition to be truly effective a significantly higher level of joint strategy development is required. This means that network members must collectively agree strategic goals for the network and the means of attaining them.

2 Win-win thinking

Perhaps one of the biggest challenges to the successful establishment of marketing networks is the need to break free from the often adversarial nature of buyer/supplier relationships that existed in the past. There is now a growing realization that co-operation between network partners usually leads to improved performance generally. The issue then becomes one of determining how the results of that improved performance can be shared amongst the various players. 'Win-win' need not mean 50/50, but at a minimum all partners should benefit and be better off as a result of co-operation.

3 Open communication

One of the most powerful drivers of change in marketing networks has been the advent of information technology, making the exchange of information between supply chain partners so easy and so advantageous. Electronic Data Interchange (EDI) was an early precursor of the information highway that now exists in some industries enabling end-to-end pipeline visibility to become a reality. With all parties 'singing from the same hymn sheet' a much more rapid response to marketplace changes is achieved with less inventory and lower risks of obsolescence. For network marketing to work to its fullest potential, visibility and transparency of relevant information throughout the supply chain is essential. Open-book accounting is another manifestation of this move towards transparency by which cost data is shared upstream and downstream and hence each partner's profit is visible to the others.

The supply chain of the future

Clearly, markets and supply chains are always in a constant state of dynamic change and adaptation. However, the evidence is that the rate of change has accelerated to the point where the business models that have served us well in the past may no longer work today and will, almost certainly, not work at all tomorrow.

Figure 10.1 highlights the challenge. We have moved from a business environment where the supplier held the power – often through their ownership of resources, technology and brands – to a situation where the customer, or even the consumer, is now in the driving seat. Where once it was a 'seller's market', today it is a 'buyer's market'. Simultaneously, the prevailing marketing philosophy has moved from the idea of mass markets serviced by mass production to the idea of 'markets-of-one' serviced by mass customization.

Even though this fundamental shift has been observable for some time, it has not been reflected in a similar shift in thinking about supply chain design.

The traditional supply chain business model was based around maximizing efficiencies, particularly through the exploitation of the 'economies of scale'. So our factories were designed to produce things in large volumes and to maximize the use of capacity. This business model worked well in the conditions for which it was designed, e.g. the production of standard products designed for mass markets.

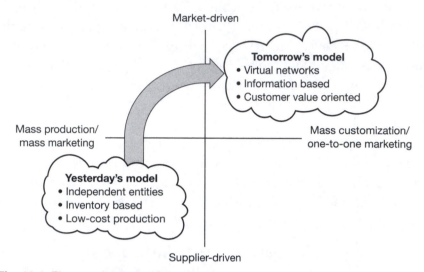

Fig. 10.1 The supply chain of the future

The problem now is that the context has changed. We have seen a move from the lower left quadrant in Figure 10.1 to the upper right quadrant, and yet many companies have not recognized the implications of this shift for supply chain design. What is now required are supply chains that are far more agile and better able to cope with rapid change and higher levels of variety and even customization. Our systems today need to be able to cope with small numbers and to react in ever shorter lead times.

Accompanying this change in the marketing environment are a number of other critical business transformations, all with significant implications for supply chain management.

Seven major business transformations

1 From supplier-centric to customer-centric

Traditionally supply chains have been designed from the 'factory outwards' rather than from the 'customer backwards'. The emphasis in the past was on how to ensure that a batch-oriented production process could most efficiently distribute its output. Thus the goal in supply chain design was often cost minimization. In today's highly competitive marketplace the goal must change to the attainment of higher levels of customer responsiveness. Thus agility rather than cost becomes the key driver.

2 From push to pull

Closely linked to the first transformation is the idea of moving from a 'production push' mentality which seeks to optimize operations through level scheduling and long planning horizons to a 'demand pull' philosophy in which, ideally, nothing is made, sourced or moved until there is a demand for it. This in essence is the Japanese 'Kanban' principle, with the modification that the quantities triggered by the Kanban should be variable depending on demand. Clearly the success of such a system requires the highest level of flexibility of all the supply chain's resources, including people.

3 From inventory to information

Logistics and supply chain management have conventionally been forecast-driven rather than demand-driven. In other words, the focus has been to look ahead over a planning horizon and to predict demand at a point in time and then to build inventory against that forecast. As markets become more volatile and turbulent so too have they become harder to predict. The risk of over- or under-stocking increases. The challenge today is to enable supply chains to become demand-driven as a result of better visibility of real demand. Real demand occurs at the end of the supply chain and if that information can be captured and shared upstream then the dependency on inventory reduces.

4 From transactions to relationships

There is a growing recognition that the route to sustained profitability is through building long-term relationships with selected customers. The focus in the past was on volume and market share and the company was transactional in its orientation. Today, customer retention is a key measure of success in the world of relationship marketing. One of the drivers of improved customer retention is the delivery of superior customer service. Hence there is a very clear connection between logistics and customer retention. Managing customer relationships has become a critical business process as organizations seek to improve the quality of their earnings.

5 From 'trucks and sheds' to 'end-to-end' pipeline management

Over the last two decades there has been a dramatic broadening of the scope of logistics and supply chain management in many organizations. Previously logistics – or, more properly, distribution management – was seen as being primarily a concern with transportation and warehousing. As such, the focus of managerial effort tended to be on cost minimization and the 'optimization' of networks and resources. Whilst the need for efficient distribution is still as strong now as in the past, there is a widely held view that the real task of supply chain management is to co-ordinate the wider end-to-end pipeline. In-bound logistics is just as critical as the distribution of final product under this paradigm and the emphasis is now on time compression from one end of the supply chain to the other.

6 From functions to processes

Only recently have companies come to challenge the primacy of functions in the organizational structure. Traditionally the business has been organized around functions and those functions have provided a convenient mechanism for the allocation of resources and for the promotion of personnel. The classic business organization could be described as 'vertical' with a multi-layered hierarchical decision-making structure. However, in today's turbulent business environment questions are increasingly being asked about the ability of such organizations to respond rapidly to the fast-changing needs of the market. It is now suggested that the emphasis in organizations should be upon the key business processes that create value for customers. These processes, by definition, are cross-functional and market-facing. They are, more than likely, team-based and they draw their members from the functions whose roles are now transformed to 'centres of excellence'.

7 From stand-alone competition to network rivalry

The conventional business model has always been that companies succeed or fail on the basis of their own resources and competencies. However, as the trend to outsourcing has increased, there has come a realization that the competitive vehicle is no longer the individual firm but rather the supply chain of which that firm is a member. Whereas once a single firm might encompass almost the whole supply chain, today that is no longer the case. Instead, today the company finds itself a member of an 'extended enterprise'. This extended enterprise is in reality a complex network of specialist providers of resources and competencies. The companies that will be the most successful in this era of network competition will be those that are best able to utilize the resources and competencies of other partners across the network.

The implications for tomorrow's logistics managers

Transformations of the type outlined above have significant implications for the type of skills profile that will characterize successful logistics and supply chain managers.

Table 10.1 suggests some of the elements of the necessary skills profile that flow from the seven business transformations.

Table 10.1 The key business transformations and the implications for management skills

Business transformation	Leading to	Skills required
From supplier-centric to customer-centric	The design of customer-driven supply chains	Market understanding; customer insight
From push to pull	Higher levels of agility and flexibility	Management of complexity and change
From inventory to information	Capturing and sharing information on real demand	Information systems and information technology expertise
From transactions to relationships	Focus on service and responsiveness as the basis for customer retention	Ability to define, measure and manage service requirements by market segment
From 'trucks and sheds' to 'end-to-end' pipeline management	A wider definition of supply chain cost	Understanding of the 'cost-to-serve' and time-based performance indicators
From functions to processes	The creation of cross-functional teams focused on value creation	Specific functional excellence with cross-functional understanding; team working capabilities
From stand-alone competition to network rivalry	More collaborative working with supply chain partners	Relationship management and 'win-win' orientation

This is only indicative, but what it does suggest is that there is a real need for formal education and training in areas as diverse as information systems and change management. The skills that are indicated cannot be acquired solely through osmosis and experience; the foundation for mastery of these skills must be gained through appropriate management education programmes.

This is the challenge for today's logistics educators: how to establish programmes that have the breadth as well as the depth to create 'T-shaped' managers.

'T-shaped' managers are so called because of their skills profile. Even though they have a specific specialism (the down-bar of the T) with in-depth knowledge and capability, they also have a significant understanding of the other key business processes (see Figure 10.2). This breadth of understanding is critical for the supply chain manager of the future, given the need to think and manage 'horizontally', i.e. across functions and between businesses.

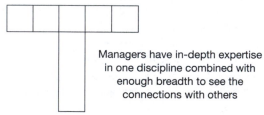

Effective process management requires significant cross-functional skills

Creating the 'T-shaped' skills profile

Managers have in-depth expertise in one discipline combined with enough breadth to see the connections with others

Fig. 10.2 Creating a T-shaped skills profile

Supply chain orchestration

With the emergence of the virtual organization and the extended enterprise comes a heightened requirement for some way of managing the complexity that is inevitably created. Consider for a moment the difference between the supply chain at Ford during the time of Henry Ford with Ford's supply chain today. Henry Ford had an integrated supply chain because in effect he owned most of it. As well as manufacturing the vast majority of all the components that went into the vehicle, the company also owned steel mills, rubber plantations and mahogany forests! Today's Ford could not be more different. Most of the component manufacturing business was floated off as a separate company, Visteon, and the steel mills have long since gone. Instead Ford is at the centre of a network of specialist service providers, first tier suppliers and collaborative alliances. The task of managing, co-ordinating and focusing this value-creating network might usefully be termed *supply chain orchestration*.

The idea of orchestration is that there has to be a common agreed agenda driving the achievement of the supply chain goals. This itself implies that there must be a supply chain strategy that is subscribed to by the entities in the chain. By the very nature of things, the orchestrator will probably be the most powerful member of the network, i.e. a Wal-Mart or a Dell, but not necessarily. Innovative organizations can utilize their superior supply chain capabilities to act as orchestrators, as the Li & Fung case study below demonstrates.

Li and Fung: supply chain orchestrator

Li and Fung (L&F) is a long established Hong Kong-based trading company, orchestrating one of the largest and most successful of all outsourced manufacturing networks. It supplies apparel, accessories, sporting equipment, household goods and toys to retail chains located mostly in North America and Europe. Valued at around $5.5bn[1] with a return on equity of more than 30 per cent per annum for much of the last decade, it is the envy of almost every other company in its sector.[2]

L&F does not manufacture anything in-house, but as network co-ordinator it oversees the manufacturing and delivery processes end-to-end. Its *modus operandi* is, however, in sharp contrast to automotive industry-style supplier management programmes. L&F does not micro manage or monitor each and every process of a handful of first tier suppliers. Nor does it control its network through intricately worded contracts or sophisticated IT capabilities. The secret of L&F's success is that it has learned how to manage outsourced operations through hands-off relationships with over 7500 trusted and very specialized manufacturing organizations, working with up to 2500 at any time. L&F's suppliers are located in around 40 countries, stretching across South East Asia, into China, the Indian subcontinent, the Mediterranean, Africa and across to the Americas. Together the suppliers represent a highly flexible

293

and highly skilled resource pool, able to meet the requirements of almost any customer. L&F ensures their loyalty by pre-booking between 30 and 70 per cent of the selected suppliers' capacity each season and rewarding high performers with more business.

When an order is received, L&F is able to draw on this vast array of talent, selecting yarn from one country, to be woven and dyed in another, cut in a third and assembled in a forth, before being shipped to retailers elsewhere. For each stage of manufacture and distribution it carefully picks the organization best able to undertake that particular value-adding activity, but then leaves the company to determine exactly how that should be achieved. For each value-adding step, L&F will provide specifications for the work – relating to what must be achieved – but not how – and the deadline by which the supplier must have shipped the work to its next destination. In doing so L&F gets the benefits of control without stifling innovation. It gets the product or service it requires, but leaves it to the supplier to determine the most efficient way of achieving it. If a quality problem or some logistical difficulty arises, then the network is flexible enough for production to be transferred very quickly to an alternative source or location.

L&F is constantly searching for new companies to add to the network, as well as new product opportunities. Over 90 years of experience has provided the company with a deep knowledge of its business and the ability to identify those organizations that have the right capabilities to enhance and sustain the growth and diversity of the network. Co-ordination costs are high, but L&F have demonstrated that these are more than offset by the advantages of flexibility offered by its loosely coupled network. The company does use technological advances where they offer opportunities to enhance efficiency or its trading relationships, such as the provision of dedicated extranet sites for its largest customers in the United States, home to around 75 per cent of its customer base. Elsewhere it uses Internet-based and e-mail-based communications with suppliers if local conditions permit. However, in many less developed countries much of its trade continues to be conducted by telephone, fax and even old-fashioned personal visits.

References
1. Felgner, B., 'Li & Fung "look to the source"', *Home Textiles Today*, 19 April, Vol. 25, No. 32, 2004, p. 19.
2. Bown, J., Durchslag, S. and Hagel, J., 'Loosening up: How Process Networks Unlock the Power of Specialization', *The McKinsey Quarterly*, 2002.

Another model for the co-ordination of complex networks that has been proposed is the idea of a 4PL™ or a Lead Logistics Service Provider.

From 3PL to 4PL™

Third-party logistics service providers are companies who provide a range of logistics activities for their clients. They might operate distribution centres, manage the delivery of the product through their transport fleets or undertake value-adding services such as re-packing.

The idea of the fourth-party logistics service provider was originated by the consulting company Accenture (previously Andersen Consulting). The underpinning principle was that because modern supply networks are increasingly global and certainly more complex, the capabilities to manage the network probably do not exist in any one organization. In such situations, there is a need for an organization – possibly coming together with the focal firm through a joint venture – who can use its knowledge of supply chains and specialist third-party service providers to manage and integrate the complete end-to-end supply chain.

The 4PL™ would assemble a coalition of the 'best of breed' service providers and – using its own information systems capability – ensure a cost-effective and sustainable supply chain solution. Figure 10.3 summarizes the principle behind the 4PL™ concept.

In this particular business model a joint venture (JV) has been formed between the client and the partner. As well as putting in equity the client will also transfer its existing logistics assets (e.g. distribution centres) to the JV. Probably too, the staff who manage and run the existing logistics system will move to this new company. The partner's contribution might include, as well as start-up equity, its information systems capability, its strategy development skills and its process re-engineering skills.

The JV will then identify those specialist providers of logistics services who between them will execute the different activities in the supply chain. Using its information systems the JV now becomes the supply chain orchestrator and delivers to the client, against agreed service and cost goals, a complete network management capability.

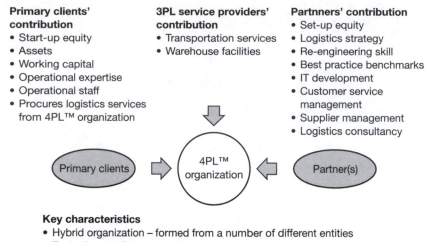

Primary clients' contribution
- Start-up equity
- Assets
- Working capital
- Operational expertise
- Operational staff
- Procures logistics services from 4PL™ organization

3PL service providers' contribution
- Transportation services
- Warehouse facilities

Partnners' contribution
- Set-up equity
- Logistics strategy
- Re-engineering skill
- Best practice benchmarks
- IT development
- Customer service management
- Supplier management
- Logistics consultancy

Primary clients → 4PL™ organization ← Partner(s)

Key characteristics
- Hybrid organization – formed from a number of different entities
- Typically established as a JV or long-term contract
- Alignment of goals of partners and clients through profit sharing
- Responsible for management and operation of entire supply chain
- Continual flow of information between partners and 4PL™ organization
- Potential for revenue generation

Fig. 10.3 The 4PL™ concept
Source: Accenture.

Whether the 4PL™ be a joint venture or some other model there are four key components that must be in place. These are:

- Systems architecture and integration skills
- A supply chain 'control room'
- Ability to capture and utilize information and knowledge across the network
- Access to 'best of breed' asset providers

Figure 10.4 summarizes these key requirements.

One such joint venture that has delivered significant cost and service advantages is that created by General Motors and Menlo Logistics. The two companies jointly invested $6 billion of start-up equity, General Motors having the majority share, to create Vector SCM.

Vector became responsible for managing all of GM's in-bound and out-bound logistics and for co-ordinating all the individual transportation, warehousing and other logistics service companies. Underpinning the whole operation is a state-of-the-art logistics information system, 'Vector Vision', which enables much higher levels of synchronization across the whole of General Motors' supply and demand network.

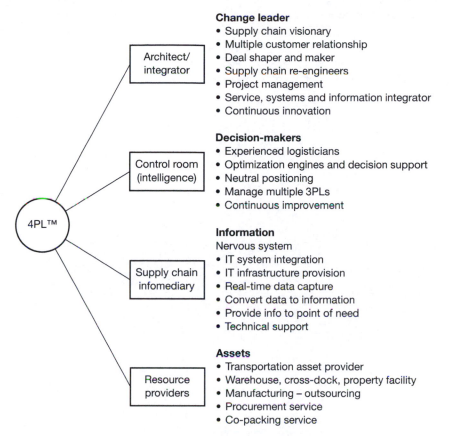

Change leader
- Supply chain visionary
- Multiple customer relationship
- Deal shaper and maker
- Supply chain re-engineers
- Project management
- Service, systems and information integrator
- Continuous innovation

Decision-makers
- Experienced logisticians
- Optimization engines and decision support
- Neutral positioning
- Manage multiple 3PLs
- Continuous improvement

Information
Nervous system
- IT system integration
- IT infrastructure provision
- Real-time data capture
- Convert data to information
- Provide info to point of need
- Technical support

Assets
- Transportation asset provider
- Warehouse, cross-dock, property facility
- Manufacturing – outsourcing
- Procurement service
- Co-packing service

Fig. 10.4 Four key components a 4PL™ must assemble
Source: Accenture.

The last word

We are seemingly entering an era where the rules of competition will be significantly different from those that prevailed in the past. A new paradigm of competition is emerging in which the supply chain network increasingly will provide a source of sustainable advantage through enhanced customer value.

If such an advantage is to be achieved, then it is critical for the organization to review the way in which it currently delivers value to its customers and to consider whether the time has come to reconfigure the chain to utilize the strengths of other players in the supply chain. One thing is for certain, companies that believe that they can continue to conduct 'business as usual' will find that their prospects for success in tomorrow's marketplace will decline rapidly.

> It is not the strongest of the species that survive nor the most intelligent, but the one most responsive to change.

Charles Darwin

Index